THE SUN-EYED CHILDREN

I saw them cross the twilight of an age,
The sun-eyed children of a marvellous dawn,
The great creators with wide brows of calm,
The massive barrier-breakers of the world
And wrestlers with destiny in her lists of will,
The labourers in the quarries of the gods,
The messengers of the Incommunicable,
The architects of immortality.

Sri Aurobindo, Savitri, Book III, Canto 4

THE SUN-EYED CHILDREN

A SAGA OF SPIRITUAL ADVENTURE
ACROSS SPACE AND TIME

VOLUME 1
EARTH

JOEL KOECHLIN

Leadstart

ISBN: 978-93-5438-013-6

Cover design: Aurrimā Maréchal, The Goliath Studio
Layouts: Kshitij Dhawale, Leadstart
Editing contribution: Miriam John
Printing: Thomson Press

Published in India 2022 by
Leadstart
A Division of One Point Six Technologies Pvt Ltd
119-123, Building J2, Shram Seva Premises
Wadala (East), Mumbai 400 022, Maharashtra, INDIA
T + 91 96 99933000 **E** info@leadstartcorp.com
W www.leadstartcorp.com

Quoted poetry is excerpted from Sri Aurobindo's epic poem, Savitri, unless otherwise stated.

This book is dedicated to the hundreds of
anonymous Matrimandir Workers
who have consecrated months, years or decades
of their life to this monumental realisation.

ABOUT THE AUTHOR

JOEL KOECHLIN, born in France, has lived his entire adult life in India. Ever eager to embrace every aspect of life in a perpetual quest for personal development and progress, he is an engineer, a pilot, a motorcycle enthusiast, a mountain lover, and a freelance author.

An accomplished photographer, he has fostered an unwavering passion for the craft over several decades, encompassing a wide canvas of subjects, from architectural and corporate work, to travel and adventure. Writing articles for travel magazines has been part of the journey.

His co-authored book (for the photography) *Beyond Asanas,* is published by Penguin Random House. He has translated into French, Sri Aurobindo's epic work *Savitri,* published on Amazon Kindle. *The Sun-Eyed Children* is his first novel.

Author web page: https://lum-ind.com/blog/

CONTENTS

GENESIS OF A BOOK

A Special Acknowledgement by the Author

If it had not been for my friend Edzard Loesing*, this book would not exist. Though a work of fiction, the narrative has been woven using threads of personal experience, intertwined with bold extrapolations. My friend and I would occasionally have afternoon tea at my home, accompanied by those delicious cookies he always brought along. Among the motley topics of conversation, we often shared tales of the event-filled adventures that had brought us from our respective European countries to far-off South India. That was decades ago, back in the early seventies.

One day, he declared: "You know, it's about time someone wrote a book about these remarkable moments!"

"You can't be serious! There's no material here that would interest anyone but us," was my dismissive reply.

A week later, my persistent friend brought up the subject again. My reaction was the same. This went on for months.

At long last, having changed tack, he proposed: "May I at least ask a few questions about your tribulations and audio-record your replies?"

It sounded like some weird kind of interview but simply out of weariness, I agreed. The next day, Edzard arrived at five in the afternoon, carrying his customary cookies, and most unusually, a microphone to plug into his smart phone. Though unconvinced about the value of something that appeared to me to be a waste of time, I nevertheless complied and answered his queries. Edzard was delighted, and with great care, recorded the conversation.

And so began the story-telling.

Tropical summer was at its peak in the reclaimed rainforest where we lived in South India. Taking place well after the searing heat had subsided, these late afternoon tea-meetings turned into welcome breaks. Over time, we went through a sizable number of recording sessions, and then one day, suddenly, Edzard was gone! A week later, I got news he was in Norway, on a retreat, and I soon forgot about the whole thing.

Several months passed, autumn set in, and a cool breeze swept gently through the forest next to the house. It was tea time. I heard a gentle knock on the door. It was Edzard, returned from the countries of the cold. He had a wide grin across his face, and carried his usual cookies. I welcomed him warmly. He came in and proceeded to pull out of his battered backpack, a bundle of loose sheaves of paper, which he handed to me. I sat down and began to shuffle through the pages while he busied himself in the kitchen, preparing tea.

Great was my surprise when I realised I was holding the transcript of our recorded conversations! Yes, he had done it; labouring to put down my words on paper during two months spent in an isolated house overlooking a beautiful Norwegian fjord, as he explained. And while I read these lines in an impersonal, detached manner, it dawned on me at last, that yes, there *was* material here! Edzard had created the backbone on which one could build. But there was a downside: I was the one who would have to write the book. I quickly realised that anyone who had not *lived through these experiences* could not possibly translate them into words without losing a significant chunk of their gist. The tree had many visible branches, but more essential were the roots, hidden deep, accessible only to me.

And so it came about, challenging the call of destiny, I sat down at my keyboard, and mused...

[* Edzard Loesing, author of: *The Reluctant Clairvoyant; Or The Indigo Blue Dream,* available on Amazon.]

FOREWORD

I was reluctant to write a Foreword for this book because when I read *The Sun-Eyed Children,* I couldn't help but see my father in every sentence – his shortcomings and his strengths. And I couldn't help but recall my childhood, filled with his wonderful storytelling and his impossible temperament. And I thought, well the reader doesn't know him the way I do, so it's not the same book for them.

But I decided to do so because I believe the duality of this book, part fact, part fiction, part real, part imagination, needs to be revealed to you, the reader. This is a book about my father; about the journey of his mind. A mind full of games, strange dreams, irritable obsessions, inexplicable fears, intense creativity, and most of all, tenacious endurance.

I've always been captured by the mind, partly because it is so limitless and that's exciting as an actor, but mostly because it is the lifejacket to sanity in a sea of emotions that sometimes overwhelms life's experiences. The mind is wired through evolution to protect us from danger, to keep us alive, but simultaneously it catapults us into an unknown future where reality and the virtual meet, where imagination can be as tangible as the physical. It is very much this duality, of being trapped by the very same engine that propels one to earth, defying flight, that I see in this book.

There is a theory that when Christopher Columbus approached the shores of America, the native people could not see the ships coming in because the idea of a ship was inconceivable to them, so the brain did not register the message; it had no pre-written code for 'ship'. The rest is history, as they say. But what if one had been able to consciously plug in the knowledge of ships to the Indians, from a future-America? Would the fate of the North American continent have been different? Can both be possibilities, and our brains simply do not have the code to decipher it?

From the moment we are born, we register things around us, but nature has constructed walls that expand only as our experience of the world does. A newborn baby, for instance, has blurred vision for the first few months of its development, because if we were to see everything in fine detail from the moment of birth, it would be too much for the brain to handle at once. Instead, by seeing only the 'big picture' for a while, such as the faces of our parents or caregivers, we are able to build better emotional ties.

So what is this idea that the brain only takes in what it's ready for? And does that mean we are constantly missing out on details of the world we are not yet ready for? *The mind is both a prison and the key to escaping our material and physical circumstances.*

In this light, I urge you to read this book as a piece of fiction that has already happened in someone's mind and is therefore conceivable in the empirical world. Allow yourselves to be transported through the time machine of the mind. Who knows what you will stumble upon – chaos, freedom, adventure, the past, the future, facts you might not be ready for, and imaginary worlds that can propel you into new ways of seeing reality.

KALKI KOECHLIN
July 2020

THE TIMELINE

Year	Event	Location
539	Beyond Hadrian's Wall	Island of Britain
1429 - 1431	The Maid of Orléans	Kingdom of France
1944	D-Day, The Longest Day	France - Normandy
1948	Birth	France - Lorraine
1967	The Dam	Netherlands - Amsterdam
1970	Migration Begins	Middle East - India
1971	Quest Begins	India - Himalayas
1972	Ambush	France - The Alps
1973	The Last Pillar	India - City of Dawn
1998	Saving Private Ryan	India - Bangalore
2005	Pileup at Anantnag	India - Kashmir
2068 (Darian 243)	Storm at Jezero Crater	Mars - Syrtis Major

In recent times, advances in the fields of physics, mathematics and cosmology have been such that theories postulating that we live in a multi-dimensional Universe, where time itself is a fourth dimension, have come to be widely accepted.

However, while we embrace the concept of time as another dimension, without giving it a second thought, we perhaps fail to realise that we should be able to navigate at will in that dimension too, just as we navigate in our day-to-day physical three-dimensional world: left-right, front-back, up-down.

Once we accept this assumption, we understand that, as a corollary, any moment in time which has ever been or will ever be, exists forever, and can theoretically be reached or connected with, irrespective of it being present, past, or future. We should be able to sail through this fourth dimension – TIME – with the same effortlessness as in the other three.

Unfortunately, matter itself throws a spanner in this beautiful logic. If a china cup falls off the edge of a table, it shatters into multiple pieces when it hits the ground. Why has no one observed the reverse, except perhaps on film? The law of entropy, the same that governs the amount of disorder in our material Universe, is the most fundamental observation of the flow of time, and it is a one-way street.

This is a disturbing conundrum: on the one hand we have Albert Einstein's legacy of the concept of Space-Time as a multi-dimensional Universe, and on the other, a fixed-pointed arrow of time at the heart of matter. Could there be unexplored concepts of time? Or is time but an illusion?

If we assume that it is indeed possible to escape the confinement of matter and sail free across the sea of time, a troubling dual-question remains: why are we incapable of doing so? And how does one access the modus operandi?

Let's try and imagine boldly this universe where we can journey, not only forward and back, left and right, up and down, but also across yesterday and tomorrow. And perhaps, in this endeavour, we shall discover an unforeseen fifth dimension that overlays everything, discreet and unassuming, until it reveals itself in its full, overpowering light-force.

PROLOGUE

Part 1

FIRE AND DARKNESS

1972, FRANCE, SOUTHERN ALPS, COL DE LA PUCELLE

On that hot day in June, a small column of twelve commando Alpine Troops, known to the French as *Chasseurs Alpins,* slowly trudged up a rocky path towards a far-off ridge. Each chasseur was heavily armed and carried a bulky survival backpack. The whole group was sweating profusely under the fierce summer sun. It has been a while since they had cleared the treeline at an elevation of about 1,800 metres and left the relatively cool shade of the forest behind. It was just past mid-day, and there was not a single cloud in sight to give hope of a recess in the crushing heat.

The thick silence was broken only by the shrill song of the cicadae, residents of the scattered, scrawny bushes, the sharp sound of rocks rolling down the slope when kicked off by a soldier, and the occasional cussing, spat out through parched lips.

A tall, lanky trooper, going by the name of Pottier, dragged his feet, huffing and puffing, some ten metres behind the rest of the pack. His face crimson, he looked as if he might faint under his *tarte,* pulled askew in the most comical way. The Alpine Troops were renowned for wearing this strange, over-sized black beret that resembled a pancake. Strangely, Pottier had the habit of lagging behind and complaining while moving at the same pace as the rest.

A trooper in his early twenties, Lionel Kalmer, closed the march, nudging Pottier none too gently to ensure the group stayed compact.

"Hey guys, come on! Let's stop for a minute. I've got to drink water!" called Pottier.

Sergeant Grandjean, up ahead, threw him an irritated look but realised that after two hours of non-stop hiking, it made sense to comply with Pottier's request. There was nothing noteworthy as far as he could see on the deserted slope, except for a group of thorny bushes scattered along the trail a hundred metres ahead; nothing remotely susceptible to hiding the enemy.

The group halted and everyone sat down on the nearest rock, dropping backpacks and weapons. Lionel grabbed his water canteen for a few sips and absent-mindedly rubbed his shoulders, sore from the straps of the backpack loaded with the heaviest weapon of the group. Pottier was too hopelessly tired to share the burden of carrying the AA-52 light machine gun nicknamed *la Nana,* the 'Chick'.

After a five-minute pause, Sergeant Grandjean stood up. "Break's over; time to go!" he declared.

Everyone got up reluctantly, piled the packs onto their backs again, and moved along the path. Beyond the scanty bushes ahead, the path wound up in a series of hairpin bends, leading to the top of the barren Col de la Pucelle, a pass culminating at about 2,000 metres. They all welcomed the hairpins as impending relief, aware that on the northern side of the mountain, the way down to the valley of La Chevreuse, would be less exposed to the afternoon sun, with the cool forest not far away. They all cheered up and braced themselves for the final effort to the pass. Soon enough, the group reached the first hairpin on the path.

Abruptly, the deafening thunder of machine guns erupted in an explosion of *TACATACATA! TACATACATA! TACATACATA!* The bushes, now less than ten metres away, had come alive with a sweeping horizontal rain of fire and metal that shredded and tore apart everything in its way. Torn flesh and blood spattered and flew, mixed with the fire from Hell. The small column of petrified, helpless men were methodically decimated, mowed down by the swivelling barrage of two-inch long bullets and tracers, delivered almost point blank. The screams of the wounded and the dying were drowned in the clamour of the guns.

Sergeant Grandjean looked on in horror as his own severed arm bounced and fell onto a nearby rock, leaving a crimson trail. Pottier grabbed with both hands his open throat, from which a stream of blood gushed. Taken by complete surprise by the seemingly impossible attack, Lionel, like the rest of his group, was unable to fight back. He numbly registered the rounds penetrating his chest, not even feeling the pain, till the world slowly tumbled away. Then, with a last gaze fixed on the lonely sun hanging high in the sky, his world gradually turned cold and black.

The thunderous staccato ceased as abruptly as it had broken out, and an eerie silence settled on the mountain. A single minute of Hell had annihilated the entire group. All that remained were twelve grotesque corpses sprawled amid scattered backpacks, and the sickening smell of blood and gunpowder.

On that day, Alpine Trooper Lionel Kalmer, 159th Alpine Infantry Regiment, 2nd Company, 2nd Section, learned one of the most important rules of warfare: the perfect ambush is the one that lies in plain sight. But it was a purely theoretical piece of knowledge he would perhaps carry into another life. When the mastermind of the ambush calmly emerged from his almost invisible hideout, made of a single flimsy bush and a few rocks and dust, he walked slowly among the dead till he came to the last body lying across the path. Lionel's pale face bore a faint smile.

An eternal instant passed. Through closed eyelids, Lionel felt a shadow approach and obscure the sun. He opened his eyes and saw a tall silhouette towering over him, with a hand outstretched to help him get to his feet.

PROLOGUE

Part 2

THE COLD DEATH

There are Secrets locked in our Past,
We cannot begin to fathom.

1998, SOUTH INDIA, BANGALORE

India was boldly marching into a new era.

The combination of isolationism and socialism that may have been an aid for the country's development from Independence to the eighties, had gradually turned into a hinderance. In the mid-nineties came the strong realisation that a change of policy was necessary to develop a self-sustained economy capable of competing with the leading powers of the world. As a result, one witnessed a radical reform in government policies related to trade with Western countries. Product imports were submitted to fewer restrictions than in the past, while exports were encouraged with de-taxation incentives, to attract a much-needed in-flow of foreign exchange.

Meanwhile, the West was taking notice of the huge economic potential of this immense nation, at the time about one-billion strong, suddenly opening its borders. The reform gave birth to a social phenomenon entirely new in India: the advent and growth of an empowered middle class; at first concentrated in the metropolitan cities, and later spreading to the large towns. This new segment of society was well educated, neither cast nor religion oriented, spoke

English, and aspired to show itself as the modern face of India. Obvious reflections of the new trend would appear in the average citizen's day-to-day life, such as in the cinema industry – the prime source of entertainment for the masses. It now released English movies in real time with the rest of the world, in vivid contrast to the past, when the Indian public had to wait a year or two to at last get a chance to see the latest James Bond film in theatres.

Owning a private car became common place. The backlash of this economic expansion appeared in the form of increasingly dense vehicular traffic within the fast-expanding Indian metros, mostly incapable of developing the adequate infrastructure at the same pace as the exponential growth of the sea of vehicles. Bangalore, one of the largest cities in South India, and the hub of a fast-growing Information Technology industry, known as the Silicon Valley of India, suffered this modern-day disease.

A dark blue Tata Sierra SUV was struggling on Mahatma Gandhi Road, the commercial and entertainment heart of the city, manoevering to extract itself from the chaotic snarl and find a parking spot at a reasonable walking distance from the Plaza Theatre. At the wheel, Lionel Kalmer was fighting a growing urge to scream unspeakable profanities at some fellow drivers caught in the wild stream of cars, although they too, were suffering the same predicament. But Lionel was a hot-headed Frenchman, and some three decades in the country had done little to calm his volatile nature. The only element in his life that could exert a certain degree of control was his beautiful Indian wife, who had the unique gift of being able to tame his temper, usually with one little word said in a quiet voice, accompanied by a loving smile.

At last, a parking slot became free, a mere hundred metres from the theatre, which under the circumstances was a rare boon that deserved appreciation. Lionel and his wife, Priyadarshini, got out of the Sierra. The shabby-looking but genial attendant standing alongside the car, handed them a parking coupon, the fee to be paid when they returned. It was about six in the evening, the warm light beckoning the dusk was as gorgeous as it can only be in India. Priyadarshini looked smart, slim, and beautiful in tight jeans, high-heeled boots, and a delicate blouse ornate with golden leaves twinkling in the sunset. She was rather petite, and her beautiful features, enhanced by subtle make-up, radiated as always, freshness and intelligence. She was the archetype of the modern Indian woman, combining in perfect harmony the feminine qualities of both Eastern and Western worlds.

A short stroll along the busy pavement, encroached on by street sellers of all kinds, took them to one of the city's oldest cinema theatres. It gave the impression of having been built at the advent of the talkies and showed all the signs of old age and decay. Being an early evening show, the customary queue to an Indian theatre was short and Lionel purchased two tickets at the counter, after which they went up the shabby staircase leading to the balcony. It felt stuffy and smelled of mildew. The lights were dim, with several holders missing bulbs, and the paint-peeling walls lavishly decorated with dried-blood-red *paan* spit marks. The Plaza was one of the rare air-conditioned theatres in the city. Inside the auditorium, the air was freezing in contrast to the humid heat outside, while still retaining its musky odour. They settled into their respective numbered folding seat, made of wood and upholstered in the faded glory of once purple velvet. Fortuitously, their seats were unbroken and functional. They made themselves comfortable, waiting for the movie to begin.

Lionel was unreservedly sold on American film director Stephen Spielberg, who had established himself with several landmarks in cinema. Amongst them was the acclaimed *Schindler's List,* which boldly explored the horrors of the Nazi death camps during the Second World War. Priyadarshini too, was keen to see Spielberg's latest work, which had just released, and was already garnering an array of awards – *Saving Private Ryan.* They had precious little information about the movie except that it referenced events that had occurred during the Second World War. Blissfully unaware that the story of *Private Ryan* revolved around the events of D-Day, the day the Allied Forces had landed on the beaches of Normandy, France, in 1944, and the battle that followed, Lionel was unprepared for the blow that was to hit him with full, unexpected force.

The lights grew dimmer, the *samosa* vendors retreated towards the exit, and the auditorium went dark. Following a few *de rigueur* film trailers and advertisements, everyone rose to stand in respect as the National Anthem played on screen; an unavoidable civic gesture at all Indian theatres.

The movie began. Almost at once, the realistic combination of images and loud sounds bounced off the screen like a multi-dimensional replication of reality. Barges packed with Allied soldiers were tossed on a wild sea, heading towards a strategic beach in Normandy – Omaha Beach – the notorious site of an Allied massacre. As the invading barges closed in, German fire began; streams of bullets ricocheted off the armoured plates of the landing craft; seasick soldiers vomited their guts out and pissed their pants in terror, their hands shaking uncontrollably, yet no one had been hit by a bullet thus far. Fear, uncontrollable fear at its most basic level!

That's when Lionel suddenly realised a slap of fate was about to strike him, even as he was sitting in a comfortable theatre chair in South India, fifty-four years after the event. He was familiar with the feeling, and recognised all the symptoms. D-Day, the Longest Day, was nothing new to him. D-Day was something intimately woven into every fibre of his being. D-Day was a mystery that had haunted him his entire life, as far back as early childhood.

There was an anomaly, though. On D-Day, 6th June 1944, he had not yet been born.

The movie went on.

At the cost of tremendous casualties, the Allied Forces had overpowered the decimating Axis fire at Omaha Beach, and were now progressing inland, earning each kilometre of land against fierce resistance. Lionel bore it all with not so much as a blink, body and face frozen, senses dulled, as if under some kind of anaesthesia.

One may, or may not, appreciate war movies, but in both cases credit should be given to the director who created this masterpiece. True, *Private Ryan* is violent; true, it is rich in explicit war-ridden graphics; and true again, *Private Ryan* is sickening to the core, as a few lame critics have pointed out. More importantly, *Private Ryan* is unparalleled because it's not an entertaining war movie like most in the genre. There is no pleasure, fun, or excitement, to be experienced; there are no parties to side with, no heroes and no villains, only men. This is war. War as it is. War as a rampage of death, suffering, and destruction; war as a melting pot of mankind at its worst and best; a symphony of thunder, screams, and redeeming love. War as a forge where splendid Death savagely pounds and shapes humans into statues of gods.

… And from each window peered an ominous priest
Chanting Te Deums for slaughter's crowning grace,
Cities uprooted, blasted human homes,
Burned writhen bodies, the bombshell's massacre.
'Our enemies are fallen, are fallen,' they sang,
'All who once stayed our will are smitten and dead;
How great we are, how merciful art Thou.'
Thus thought they to reach God's impassive throne
And Him command whom all their acts opposed,
Magnifying their deeds to touch his skies,
And make him an accomplice of their crimes. [II-8]

Saving Private Ryan is a grim reminder of what war, in fact, is; an epic testimony to a piece of history never to be forgotten.

Priyadarshini is pure, she has no past, no karma hanging over her head, she is a princess of old, and she was sailing through this vivid re-enactment of carnage like a swan on a lake in a heavy thunderstorm. Explosions, screams, and blood dripped off her immaculate feathers, leaving her with a strange expression of puzzlement on her beautiful face. How and why on earth would humans engage themselves in such savagery? This whole thing was coming to her as some kind of unfathomable mystery. Thus, after a while, she threw a side glance at her husband, and what the dreadful scenes could not bring to her heart in terms of emotions, she found with shock in Lionel's expression: ashen face drained of blood, lips trembling, fists clenched, breath suspended.

Returning to the cinema screen, in that moment there was a young marine who had been struck by a volley of shrapnel. He was lying on the ground, chest perforated in multiple places, belly torn open, guts flowing onto the grass, forming an indistinguishable mixture of blood and mud. His buddies, his brothers-in-arms, gathered around him. One attempted to soak and curb the endless flow of blood oozing from the innumerable punctures, while another gave him a morphine shot right through the sleeve of his fatigues. He cried... And his last words were, "I am cold, I am so cold, man, so cold…"

He was just a boy.

In this instant, Lionel turned to Priyadarshini and grabbed her hand. "Priya dear, help me please, I have to get out. I am coming out…"

"Out of the theatre?"

"No, out of my body, darling. The cold is taking me out of the body, just help me get to the corridor."

Both rose from their seats, struggling in the dark to reach the side aisle without stepping on too many toes on the way. Once there, Lionel felt so weak in the knees that he had to lean on his wife till they re-entered the damp, gloomy corridor outside, now empty of people, while along the way, his body and self slowly drifted apart. He allowed himself to slide down along the filthy wall, and she gently helped him to stretch out on the dusty floor, keeping his head between her hands, cradled on her lap.

"Keep me here for a while and make sure nobody disturbs," he murmured.

By then Lionel had completely drifted away from his body and was calmly watching the whole scene from above: his immobile body stretched beside the wall, and Priyadarshini sitting crossed-legged at his head like a tranquil, strong sentinel. He knew that, like a female falcon watching over her brood, she would have torn apart any intruders.

Absolutely detached and free, he could at last understand the symbolism of it all. His void husk of a body resting on the floor below, the perforated agonising marine on the prairie, the Alpine trooper lying sprawled across the track below the Col de la Pucelle… It was all linked; all one and the same thing. They all bore a unique, formidable, appalling signature. D-Day, 6th June 1944.

PART I
MIGRATION

1
A PINK HOUSE AMONG OLIVE TREES

1970, GERMANY, MUNICH

It was almost mid-night in the deserted alley of a Munich suburb. In these last days of December, winter was an all pervasive, chilling presence. A soggy sleet had been dripping from the leaden sky for several hours past, and the pavement was dangerously slippery. A few ghostly street lamps struggled to penetrate the thick mist and cast some light; the kind of sodium lamps which radiate an eerie yellowish gloom and give one the feeling of gliding across a frigid version of Hell.

Lionel walked down the lane to the main street ahead and turned left towards the nearest bus stop. His long chestnut hair, flowing from under a Norwegian woollen cap, gathered tiny icicles in the cold. He was wearing a pair of faded jeans, well-trodden hiking shoes and an old-fashioned canvas skiing jacket with a fur-lined hood, which had once belonged to his father when he had been about his age, in his early twenties. His green eyes squinted when flakes landed on his clean-shaven face.

On the other side of the street was a weatherproof glass enclosed bus stop with metallic benches; its awning read *MGV* (acronym for the German Munich Transport Corporation). He crossed the street, entered the shelter and stood there shivering, having dropped his military surplus backpack beside him on the bench. Looking about, he viewed this urban décor from the vantage point of a polar bear that has taken refuge in an aquarium. Not a soul around, not a car on the road. Everything outside this glass box was cold, bleak and oozing hostility. Why on earth was he standing here? What was this madness that had gripped him?

He had just left the apartment of some friends he was staying with in Munich, after a last joint for the road. It was late at night. Shivering and alone at the bus stop in the freezing December night, he waited for the bus to take him to the *München Hauptbahnhof,* the central railway station. There, he would board a train that would take him south towards welcome warmth. Given some twelve hours, he would reach the city of Brindisi, on the south-eastern tip of Italy's boot, the first stage of an ambitious Far-Eastern destination.

Sometimes, one cannot help but wonder about the fragility of life and its thin, brittle guiding threads, or how things hang in such a fine balance. The gloomy atmosphere at this bus stand in Germany was so unwelcoming and ominous that anyone would have felt their firmest resolutions shaken by cold doubt. Waves of fog whirled about, creating bizarre dancing patterns around the sodium street-lights in some strange partnership. Something inside him chipped away at his determination. A small insidious voice whispered within: *This is all bad! What are you doing here, with almost no Deutsche Mark, Francs or Dollars in your pocket, harbouring illusions you are seriously getting somewhere? This reckless project makes little sense! Go back to warmth and comfort now. Your friends are waiting for you.*

That was the faint-hearted mind in him, cringing in that crucial instant, frightened – no, terrified – at the prospect of the Great Unknown. When one looks within with honesty, deep inside, this poltroon mind is always prowling somewhere in the background, although dormant most of the time. At this moment, it had raised its ugly head, intending to take control of its host. But there was a way to trick it too (this part of the mind is not very smart). This could be achieved with just one simple suggestion: *Okay, let's travel to Corfu; it's not that far away. I can spend a pleasant vacation under the blue Greek sky and return any time I feel like.*

He was still young, still learning that the art of living a real life implies ignoring the poltroon's loud speech and paying heed to the gentle voice of vision whispering from a higher source. With the former voice insistently and annoyingly whispering in his ears, he almost turned around.

But fortunately, not a minute too soon, the bright blue bus came gliding out of the fog like a friendly dragon. It stopped, and the doors slid open with a beckoning *whoosh*. With no other thought, Lionel hopped in.

The few friends who should have been here today, with him on this spot, had already back-tracked, and here he had been, a loudmouth, looking to shamefully retreat into their footsteps too. Instead, he had kicked his own ass and with the famous line from Frank Zappa on his mind, *Don't make a fuss, just hop on the bus!*, he drove away from the gloomy, teetering moment, straight to the railway station.

Predating the digital age, the early seventies was a very different time. Those were days when one could find it difficult to leave everything behind and set course towards a vague, far-off Eastern destination, using local transportation, with little money in one's pocket, knowing perfectly well it would dry up on the way and was insufficient for a return journey. The extended global Information Technology revolution occurred well into the 2000s. There was no Internet, no Facebook, no e-mail, and none of the magical objects such as cell phones or personal computers. None of the fancy gadgetry one takes for granted today had yet been invented, or brought to global use. Even wired telephone communications were primitive; a conversation was almost impossible once past Istanbul; certainly not affordable to a budget traveller. In the same vein, having emergency funds wired by friends or family was a tortuous, slow process; rumours circulated about desperate junkies waiting for a money transfer for months, holed up in some dungeon-like dormitory in Kabul, Old Delhi, or the Thamel district of Kathmandu.

Deadly diseases such as cholera, yellow fever, hepatitis, to mention the most common, were still rampant as soon as one had crossed the Bosphorus, that narrow strait separating Europe from Asia (the bridge wasn't built and a multitude of ferries of all shapes and sizes sailed across). Health care was basic at best, and access to modern medicines limited. Heading on such a journey could be seen as a deep chasm in one's life path, one that some would never cross back.

In the long run, it required an unspoken set of prerequisites that only a minority of departing travellers possessed: good health, freedom from loved ones, emotional detachment, courage, physical stamina, and more than anything else, a great faith in one's own destiny. Travelling to the Far-East in this manner demanded a firm commitment, and it felt like plunging into a new life fraught with risk and uncertainties.

From another point of view, this was all part of the thrill of a *real* adventure.

Thus, no wonder that most of the original contenders had chickened out and gone back home to mama, or into the warm bed of some sexy girlfriend. That was okay with Lionel anyway, because he had never been fond of being part of a large group. As for himself, for quite a few years now, he had had this strange perception that some benevolent entity behind the veil, something that in a very naïve way he might have called his guardian angel, was always watching over him and taking care of his safety, even in the worst situations. It was something difficult to define, like an invisible companion. For obvious reasons, he did not share this with anyone, even more so since he was fiercely non-religious. Notwithstanding, he could feel the presence in the background at all times.

As for the poltroon mind, it knew the odds, but subdued, pretended to have forgotten, at least till the next worrying cross-road.

A mysterious pink house among the olive trees on the Greek island of Corfu was to be the next stop after Brindisi, but deep inside, Lionel's unspoken dream destination was nothing less than Kabul, Afghanistan.

2
THE INK BOTTLE

One force shall be your mover and your guide,
One light shall be around you and within;
Hand in strong hand confront Heaven's question, life:
Challenge the ordeal of the immense disguise. [IV-3]

1948, FRANCE, A SMALL TOWN IN LORRAINE

He had come with a bang! When someone would point this out to him, he would laugh and exclaim: "I never asked for this!"

June 6th, 1948, was the day Lionel Kalmer was born. The surname had been carried by a long lineage of Alsace-Lorraine industrialists, a province of France that had been one of the major centres of the textile industry since the Industrial Revolution. The spinning and weaving mills were owned by a few affluent families, and had been for generations, jealously transmitted from fathers to sons.

The owners lived in splendid mansions surrounded by spacious gardens, nested behind the high-walls of protected estates. Men drove at slow speed, shiny black *Citroën Traction* cars, while women sped around in elegant convertibles, a scarf wrapped around the head floating in the wind. In summer, Sundays were marked for hunting game or riding horses in the countryside, while the posh winter weekend occupation was skiing on the snow-covered mountain slopes. In this part of France, influenced by Calvinism, the elite privately referred to themselves as affiliates of an implicit community, the PHS or *Protestant High Society*.

June 6th, a Sunday, was a day the doctors and nurse-midwives on duty at the maternity hospital in the small town of Bellefontaine, in the Vosges mountains, some hundred kilometres from the border with Germany, would not soon forget. Dawn was breaking and Lionel's mother, in her final days of pregnancy, was ready to give birth.

It was common for thunderstorms to occur in these mountains during hot, summer afternoons. However, on this day, Providence chose to disrupt the old, predictable weather pattern. An out-of-the-ordinary, early morning thunderstorm, caused the clouds overhead to break water in a loud staccato, even as Lionel's mother broke hers. The doctor muttered something under his breath about the unusual weather shift, and then concentrated on his task as the baby's head became visible. In a last effort, the labouring mother freed herself of her burden and the rest of the birth proceeded smoothly.

Everything was over; the baby, cleaned and swaddled, rested at peace on his mother's bosom. The doctor washed his hands in a white enamelled basin the nurse had rolled into the room, while speaking comforting words to the new mother. She whispered his name: Lionel.

KABANG!

A single bolt of lightning abruptly surged down from the dark clouds above, shattering the peace of the moment. It hit the granite sill of the window behind which the doctor had just been standing, chipping off a significant piece of ultra-heated granite from the slab. The powerful thunderclap exploded in the same instant, making the doctor and his assisting nurses jump a few centimetres off the ground.

Strangely, the thunderclap would be the first significant sound Lionel would hear in his brand-new life, a queer reminiscence of near-by thundering cannons and mortars.

Meanwhile, the hospital didn't burn; it was not the birth of some little Frankenstein, and there was no cause for alarm. It may just have been Zeitgeist and Destiny having a ball.

A lightning from the heights that think and plan,
Ploughing the air of life with vanishing trails,
Man, sole awake in an unconscious world,
Aspire in vain to change the cosmic dream. [III-4]

The mother was naturally exhausted from her labours, but as soon as possible, she found a quiet moment with the friendly nurse to perform a thorough visual check of the infant. The lightning and thunder (amazingly, the glass of the window had remained intact) had given her a shock and worried her. The nurse, with empathetic intuition, held the newborn, turning him this way and that so the mother could see from all angles. Apart from a faint birthmark on the chest, reminiscent of a lion's head, all seemed normal and well. The young mother heaved a sigh of relief. All was apparently fine.

Perhaps not quite.

Little did the mother know that in that auspicious moment, perhaps because of the lightning, who knows, her infant had had some subtle inner compass implanted, which would reveal itself as he grew up. A compass that would sometimes show him the direction in which he should progress, provided he paid attention. Like a dazzled moth attracted to the light, he would feel compelled to follow an inner *force,* regardless of all obstacles, counter-pressures, the conventions of society, and people's expectations. He would follow the 'sparkling', as he would label it, whenever he saw it. This marvel would appear unexpectedly, irrespective of physical location, or time of day. It would lend its illuminating aura to a racing horse in a spa-resort in Lorraine, or flash and hover on the spires of a cathedral in Paris, turning the scene into an instant vision of total clarity with an awed message: *Oh! This is for me!* A rush of warmth would burn through his heart. Then he would simply surrender to the moving force, and allow it to carry him away.

But what on earth was this force, capable of moving a born system-evader across the globe; a transformative power that would turn him into a migratory bird with the same dynamics as the wind under its wings? A force apparently benevolent, though it could be ruthless and wild in its actions if that was the need of the hour. Through storms and breakdowns, it would carry him on journeys spanning thousands of kilometres across some of the most amazing landscapes on this planet, trying to synergize with the morphogenetic fields of resonance in his path.

And as the day of the child's birth slipped into night, the darkness hid future distress; that he would simultaneously tread an inner abyss, and inevitably crash into an absolute void where all old patterns and habits would dissolve, all meaning, mind and sense disappear into madness, absolute, terrifying and overwhelming.

Yet, there remained within him at every instant, *something* persisting, vague, indestructible – the something that would help him rise like a Phoenix from the ashes of his mind and the wreckage of his body, without pharmaceutical drugs, without shrinks or drinks, without mental asylums.

Nevertheless, there was a heavy price to pay for each of his falls: loss of time on the path, and possibly loss of life.

Time passed and Lionel was soon a school boy. But the advent of education marked the commencement of an unforeseen ordeal for his hapless mother, who, every year, sometimes even mid-term, had to hunt for a new school to enrol him in. Being indisciplined (the terminology used in his school reports), lay at the root of all his troubles. In the army, they would have referred to it as insubordination. In Lionel's life, circumstances tended to be severe and it took him a while to understand that even when the immediate cause was not obvious, he was always the creator of his circumstances, never the victim. All the hardships were for him to progress, without exception.

However, he would realise that they were not so bad, his crimes that is. There were often other boys around him who did things far worse, and got away with it. Then why was he always the one on the docket? Well, because the teachers perceived him as the odd one, the strange one, the one who did not conform, who did not fit in. This was bizarre. He had no physical malformation; nor was he the village idiot. Without false modesty, he believed he was a decent-looking, intelligent boy. But maybe he had been marked since birth as some kind of fiercely individualistic oddity. Thus, for some unfathomable reason, the teachers got upset with whatever message he was trying to convey.

Lionel was six, and it was his first year in school. There were some concepts he found difficult to accept. The religious fantasies in particular: infant Jesus, Mary, Joseph, the donkey and the lambs; all the mythology that went with this biblical theme, in Old and New Testaments alike; the way it was naïvely presented in picture books. It sounded to him like a bedtime story invented for retarded children. Although he himself was just a child, he began to perceive the whole narrative as something fictionalised and considerably distorted in a flagrant attempt to instill devotion in the listener.

This did not mean he did not believe there had been an actual Messiah; on the contrary. But if this figure had indeed had such an impact on history, it would have been someone with more powerful charisma and depth of character than the clichéd picture painted of him. And perhaps, supposing he himself had been born in the time of Christ, surely it was not unreasonable to think he would have enjoyed wandering among Jesus' companions?

However, the tales offered to him, designed to suit a single obtuse religious mindset, were so unsatisfactory that Lionel felt compelled to ask his mother to do something about it. He did not want further exposure to what he perceived to be boring and untrue. Since his mother, a progressive and obstinate woman, complied and had him exempted from religious education (the only student in the entire school to be so excused), he soon fell out of whatever remaining favour he retained with several of the conservative teachers.

Lionel had reached age nine when his class was given the task of building a scaled-down model of the landscape surrounding his little town of Bellefontaine, featuring the village and mountains, forest, rivers, etc. This model was to be built of mud and sand, on a large table flanked by four planks, which stood in the middle of the classroom. The teacher saw it as a major undertaking of practical work, and each student had to contribute towards the project. He asked everyone to bring in materials such as mud, toy trees, houses and more. Now Lionel loved to build things, and the construction of this model suited him well. He had a toy-village kit at home. Out of it, he picked out all the miniature trees, made of wood and painted green. Satisfied it would be an adequate contribution, he brought these little trees to the teacher the next day.

The teacher, a tall, lean, bald fellow named Monsieur Thiebaut, responded in an unpleasant, angry tone: "What is this rubbish you are bringing us here, Kalmer? What is this stuff? I wanted plenty of branches and leaves. This is useless! I want none of this, take it away and leave my sight!"

In silent obedience, the boy took back his trees and without a word, went back to sit in the last row of benches, which was his place, where he belonged. What happened next took time to build up, like when water takes a while to reach boiling point in a kettle, and the whistle blows. In the same way, for ten minutes the pressure of injustice slowly but steadily rose inside the little boy.

Everyone had blissfully forgotten about him and the trees incident, when abruptly, from his place in the last row, he bolted upright like a Jack-in-the-box, and with a violent mixture of indignation and fury, screamed at the teacher.

"You are so unjust! I am giving you the exact objects you asked us to bring, and you react like this! You are a bad, wicked person!"

At that point, from the last row of benches in the class, the boy began to throw all kinds of objects at the teacher – pencils, erasers, notebooks, books, and finally, like the final glorious finale of a symphony, an open ink bottle. The trajectory of the bottle as it flew through the length of the classroom, revolving on itself, transformed it into a masterfully efficient warhead, distributing its dark blue contents over students and teacher alike. It finally bounced off the chalkboard behind the teacher's shoulder, missing his bald head by inches.

The students, hypnotised by these extraordinary events, either sat open-mouthed or dived for cover under their respective benches. Monsieur Thiebaut, pink with rage and stained with dark blue ink, came storming towards him like a hurricane, screaming and spitting with rage. He grabbed Lionel by the arm, and having slapped him a dozen times in front of his goggling classmates, dragged him out of the classroom, and headed towards the Principal's office.

In modern times, a teacher can go to jail for beating a child. But in those days, some physical punishment was considered normal, even good for the soul, and certainly nothing unusual. So, in a wild fury, the man dragged the boy out of class and up to the first floor, where the Principal had his office. The stairway had a banister, sitting atop vertical wrought-iron rods set in decorative baroque patterns. Halfway up the steps, Lionel grabbed one of the vertical rods, first with one hand, then with both, and held on for dear life, with a furious determination unexpected in a child.

From that moment, the little boy sat there, clinging to that bar, refusing to budge. A livid Monsieur Thiebaut, despite his best efforts to prise open the fingers one by one, could not loosen the boy's grip. He did not care to slip deeper into violence, as by now, attracted by the commotion, other students and teachers had arrived on the scene, and were crowding the staircase.

No one could pull Lionel off the stairs, though not for lack of trying with tugging, shouting, and even smooth-talking. Finally, the Principal, alerted by the ruckus, came down to check on the strange sounds of revolution in his normally orderly kingdom. Even then Lionel would not budge. He remained fused to the vertical baroque rod as if born of it.

Ultimately, to break the stalemate, the Principal phoned Mr Kalmer, Lionel's father, who came all the way from his work place. Thirty to forty minutes later, the distressed father reached the school, and to his astonishment, found Kalmer Jr. still on the staircase, still welded to his railing, all alone, since by then everyone else had returned to their respective occupations.

Then and only then did Lionel gracefully surrender. He went off with his father without a fuss, sure now that no one in the school would dare beat him. However, as soon as they were both in the car, out of sight of curious eyes, Lionel's thoroughly upset father slapped him hard for good measure.

The whole episode was rather awful. But in Lionel's mind, the essential message remained engraved: injustice is not acceptable. In such cases, one has to take a stand, no matter how dire the consequences.

It came as a surprise that nine-year-old Lionel was not expelled from the school. After a few days cooling period for both parties, he went back and sat down at his desk in the last row.

Soon, he noticed two things. First, Monsieur Thiebaut was deliberately ignoring his presence, as if he were a mere flowerpot on the windowsill; which suited Lionel fine. Second, the other students were keeping a respectful distance, displaying a mix of alarm and envy. From that day onward, he was never again bullied, by student or teacher, for he had earned a new reputation as the Unpredictable Wacko.

He had won his battle.

3
ANTI-GRAVITY DREAM

1970, GREECE, CORFU

It was late afternoon in the Greek island of Corfu, and Lionel was walking alone among the olive trees towards the setting sun. The landscape was beautiful, and he was immersed in a peculiar peace; of a kind he had never experienced before. It was almost as if behind this peace there was a whole new world brooding, but still hidden.

He had reached the Pink House two days earlier, only to find it unoccupied. Thankfully, the caretaker who lived at a nearby farm, had made no difficulty in handing over the keys. He had been informed in advance, by old-fashioned postal mail – a folded hand-written piece of paper in a sealed envelope, affixed with an Italian post stamp on the top-right corner, and delivered by a Greek uniformed postman on a cycle – that *...a few odd-looking strangers, most of them wearing long hair and worn-out clothes, would arrive soon. Have no fear, they are peace-loving people and they will not cause trouble.*

It had been a long, tiring journey from Munich. A solid fifteen hours in a train moving at its own lazy pace, punctuated by so many stops in Italian cities that he could not remember them all. The heating in the compartment had been erratic – too hot or too cold. The winter scenery outside the windows had been unattractive, either foggy and dull, or depressingly grey, except while crossing the Alps, covered with a bright blanket of fresh, scintillating snow. Travelling on a budget, he did not have the luxury of a berth, and had spent most of his time dozing on the bench with his head resting against the window. And the train was behind schedule by several hours.

Having finally alighted at Brindisi railway station early in the morning, he had asked awkwardly, in his limited Italian, for the nearest health centre, where he could get his cholera vaccination shot. He would need a medical certificate while crossing borders eastwards. Having concluded this unpleasant chore, he had shoved the booklet into his backpack and moved straight to the harbour, where he had boarded the first ferry for Corfu.

In modern times, opportunities to travel by ship have become rare, and following the exhausting and boring train journey, the ten-odd hours of sailing on open seas had Lionel somewhat elated. Despite the bitter cold, he stood most of the time at the bow, leaning on the railing, breathing in the fresh, saline air, sometimes whipped by a splash of ocean spray. It was like a slap of adventure with a capital A hitting his face, and was received with mixed feelings of happiness and apprehension. His life was moving full-steam ahead, towards the Great Unknown. Lionel had enjoyed those moments immensely.

The ferry had reached Corfu harbour late at night. After a simple dinner of bread, butter, cheese and sausage, eaten on a bench in a public park, he wandered about looking for a suitable lodging, a personal palace, in the outskirts of the city, where he could spend a peaceful night. A house under construction in a quiet suburb seemed to fit the bill. He made sure the place was deserted and no neighbours, or a zealous Greek cop, would notice him. Furtively, he climbed to the top floor, picked an empty room devoid of cement and rubble, and spread out his sleeping bag, using his backpack as a pillow. Stretching out fully, his body filled with a pleasant sense of weariness, he fell asleep in an instant.

The next morning, he had boarded a country bus that had taken less than an hour to get him to Pelekas, the village his Italian friend Giovanni, had mentioned to him during his recent visit to Rome, a month before. He had walked leisurely down a narrow, dusty road till he spotted, coming into view from behind a hillock, half-hidden between the olive trees and a fence of creepers, like a haven on the way to heaven, the Pink House.

Now, two days later, Lionel walked the serpentine road past the house, winding its way through an alternate sequence of cypress copses and olive orchards. The contrast was striking between the vertical surge of the straight pyramidal cypresses and the tortured limbs of the age-old olive trees, each seeming to represent some elfin creature. After a short, thirty-minute walk, the road which had by then turned into an unpaved track lined with olive trees, abruptly ended on top of a barren hill, commanding a magnificent vista of a large part of the island, and the turquoise Mediterranean Sea beyond. There, he sat on a flat rock, alone, facing west. Swept by a wave of sweet sadness, he watched a huge vermilion sun slowly setting into the sea, much like the Little Prince of Saint-Exupéry, when he was preparing to leave his lonely planet.

Lionel walked all the way back to his rustic, chosen home, reaching just before the sky turned black. It was his third night in this magical house. He was still alone. That night, he had a remarkable dream which unsettled him somewhat because it bore the vivid mark of a prophecy rather than the simplicity of a casual dream. It was so crystal clear that he perceived it as an experience or revelation of his own future, hitting him with abrupt finality.

A faceless voice whispered: *You have come here now, and with this act you have launched an irreversible process. You have consciously taken this decision, and now there is no question of turning back.*

He stood on a wide expanse of grass, surrounded by a group of friends. The picture in the dream was vivid. He could even recognise a particular face because they had been close in the recent past, having shared an apartment. They had all gathered on this lush hillock, waiting for something to happen, when suddenly, Lionel realised that, out of the centre of this group, he was taking off, literally lifting off vertically, slowly at first, then gaining speed, pulled by an irresistible *force* that cancelled his body's gravity; a force beyond his or anyone's control. He looked down as his friends became smaller and smaller below. A few glanced up at him in astonishment, and he shouted, "I'm sorry, I can't help it! I am being taken away. But don't worry, I will be okay, and I will not forget you."

Among them, only his close friend seemed to grasp the magnitude of what was happening; he smiled and waved at Lionel. The others, not understanding what was happening, lost interest, altogether missing the beauty of this miracle. And then he was moving upwards, higher and faster, reaching outer space and beyond, cruising at an unspeakable speed towards an entirely different universe, carried by an anti-gravity force that nobody or nothing could have resisted.

It soon became clear he had no choice but to surrender unconditionally. In that instant, he understood that something or *someone* had now hijacked his destiny and that he wouldn't have much say in upcoming events. But, unlike at the Munich bus stop, he felt no fear; he knew with absolute certitude that this *someone* was his guardian angel, revealed in an all-powerful form. The new path he was being taken on was the best thing that could ever happen to him.

When Lionel woke, recollecting every detail, he knew for certain that his life had completely changed its course.

This moment in Corfu was an edge in time.

Later, when he had resumed moving eastwards, through Greece and Turkey, he often reflected on this and understood that a particular phase of his life was over. The beat-goes-on life in Switzerland, Paris, Rome and Amsterdam, the acid trips, the drug deals and the rock concerts was a chapter closed, the page turned with irreversible finality. With it came the realisation that he could not have reversed his course, had he tried. As if there was a wormhole in front of him, he had to plunge in and pass through. There was no way around, no way back. The gravitational forces pulling him were too great and resistance would have been futile, or deadly. If there was a way back, it would have to be through another wormhole, from another point in space and time.

It was like he had switched universes.

Soon enough, this took an entirely new dimension: from one incident to the next, he gradually realised that this force which had by then become inseparable from himself, was something to reckon with, because it took its own decisive actions in his so-called real life. If he attempted to disobey, or veer off the predetermined course, he would get a bang on the head. It would start with a mild discomfort in the mind, signalling that something was amiss. If the error persisted uncorrected, it would turn into a painful physical blow through some worldly medium like an incident or accident, or more ostensibly, some angry guy hitting him with a stick.

This realisation caused Lionel a considerable anguish: he was so used to being in control of his life, or so he thought. Then, one step at a time, he learned how to navigate through life avoiding the pain, to dodge it, and thus set his course in the right direction. It took a while and many miles, but in time, it became clear that this force was taking him towards an unexpected, unforeseen destination.

But who that mightiness was he knew not yet.
Impalpable, yet filling all that is,
It made and blotted out a million worlds
And took and lost a thousand shapes and names. [III-1]

At nine o'clock the next morning, Lionel was sitting on a bench at the long wooden table in the back garden of the Pink House, having a cup of tea with a light breakfast. He was still preoccupied, sifting through the data conveyed to his agitated neurones by the strange dream he had had during the night. As usual, this part of the island was very peaceful, with no noises other than those of nature. No cars on the small road, no people. The deep blue winter sky was clear, and the morning air chilly, pervaded by the smells of local herbs. Dew dripped from the olive trees. On the creeper vine that provided shade to the table, a spider had woven a large intricate web that sparkled with dew drops in the morning light.

Suddenly, he could hear voices coming from the road-facing side of the house, and then someone calling his name. He got up, went around the house and was pleasantly surprised to recognise two of his friends, Max and Milien, who had just arrived from Italy.

Happy to be reunited, they hugged and hooted for a while, then sat down at the garden table to chat. Lionel went to the kitchen to prepare more tea, while Max rolled a fat joint to start the day on a healthy note.

Looking back at the events of the past year, it became clear to Lionel that it had all begun in Rome. That was where the seed of this adventure had sprouted.

4
A BOOK AT PIAZZA CAMPO DE' FIORI

1970, ITALY, ROME

Having started from beyond Lake Geneva, Switzerland, Lionel and Milien had arrived in Rome mid-October, at the end of a ghastly motorcycle journey. There had been unusual early snowfalls that year, temperatures were sub-zero most of the way, and the bike was overloaded with pillion rider and luggage. The one-thousand-kilometre trip was ill timed and lacked preparation, with barely enough money for the petrol and a couple of sandwiches. But then, there was the excuse of emergency.

Both of them had left in something of a hurry. They were not close friends and had seldom met. Milien was a rather short and stout guy. Though he was about the same age as Lionel, he showed precocious signs of baldness. For some reason or perhaps no reason at all, he always wore a preoccupied expression on his face, as if torn by the perpetual dilemma: *Should I do this or should I do that?* And no way to decide on a proper course of action. He had a particular affection for military camouflage jackets and was never seen without one. In Lionel's perception, this was a particularly irritating trait, since at the time he had a poor opinion of the military, which he viewed only as a tool of government-sponsored violence.

However, they shared a common predicament which had led to their precipitous departure. A mutual acquaintance had betrayed them to the Swiss authorities. The cowardly act had resulted in their arrest and a stint in a Swiss jail. With investigations digging deeper day by day, they had decided that a change of scene would be appropriate to avoid a second extended period of confinement, likely to be counted in years.

Man! What a journey!

They had crossed the high Alpine passes on a road covered in five centimetres of snow, only to hit the fog when they reached the plains along the river Po, in northern Italy. Never had Lionel encountered such dense fog. Night had fallen and he could barely see a few metres ahead in the headlights; it was like navigating through a yellowish soup in which one could not even see the embankments on either side. Then, to top it all, in one sharp turn in a village, there was something extra slippery mixed with the sleet, and they fell into a long, spinning slide. Fortuitously, they escaped serious injury as the bike had been moving at a slow speed, but man, what a hellish ride! They did not have the money for a hotel room, and had no option but to keep moving ahead, teeth clenched, frozen to the bone.

At long last, at the end of what seemed like an infinite journey, they had reached Rome. The Eternal City had greeted them with a burst of warm sunshine, and their survival rating went up a few notches.

Back in Switzerland, Lionel had met this guy who had told him, "When you get to Rome, meet Giovanni, he will help."

Lionel exited the traffic-busy Via Salaria and entered a narrow street. There, he stopped and parked the motorbike, close to an isolated telephone booth. Both men entered the booth, and from his jacket pocket, Lionel pulled out what drifters called the 'Wire'. Everyone had one of those. It was a simple one metre-long piece of electric wire, with both ends stripped. The Wire was the indispensable tool of free communication. Lionel lifted the phone from the hook and inserted one end of the wire into the perforated plate at the speaking end of the phone, while Milien held the other end to ground it, on the main panel. In most European booths, this trick cancelled the need to insert coins into the slot. One just had to dial the number and talk. And lo! Free telephone conversation. Lionel dialled a few numbers and got in touch with Giovanni soon enough. They arranged to meet in a café.

Giovanni was a handsome young man, in a seductive Italian way. He had long black, straight hair, which he wore shoulder length, and a beautiful face, always thoughtful in a romantic kind of way. He and Lionel struck up an instant friendship. Giovanni regretted not being able to take them into his own little room in his mother's house. Instead, he straddled his red Flandria motorcycle and told them to follow. He led them through the chaotic traffic of Rome, punctuated with countless exclamations of *pezzo di merda!* and *figlio di puttana!* to an unoccupied house in an old picturesque district of Rome.

They reached a beautiful square called Piazza Campo de' Fiori, seat of a lively market in the centre of the old city, featuring several ornate fountains with phantasmagorical bronze creatures spitting water. They parked their bikes on the pavement, against a wall, and following Giovanni's steps, entered a dilapidated multi-storied house standing at one corner of the plaza, slightly in recess. A small party was staying there already, comprising three hippies-beatniks-junkies – take your pick. Huber and Vera, an adorable couple, he Italian, she his German girlfriend, plus a third solitary, untalkative guy from Spain, who spent most of his time in deep introverted fixes.

Huber was tall and lean, with the permanent hint of a mocking expression on his face, as if the entire world and life's proceedings were nothing but an elaborate practical joke. He wore his straight black hair long, and his tight pants made him look even slimmer. His companion, Vera, was a gorgeous girl with waist-long, silky blond hair. One could have dressed her in leathers and bronze, and she would have passed with ease for the perfect incarnation of a Valkyrie of yore. Lionel had met them many times before, in Switzerland, and he was fond of them both. They were always cheerful, radiating love, even in hard times. Together, they formed an enviable, rare kind of couple. They too, had precipitously fled the Swiss cops' ire to Italy.

Giovanni was often hanging around when there was quality stuff to share, or just to be amongst friends. Lionel and Giovanni got along well. Both were soft-spoken and fond of solitude and independence. Giovanni was more introverted though, and spent a considerable amount of time stoned, in a meditative, sometimes sombre mood, sitting in a dark corner of the house. But his smile was always warm and his generosity endless.

When he wasn't stoned, Giovanni worked at odd, part-time jobs, and Lionel helped him repaint and renovate his mother's apartment, among other tasks. A typical Italian matron, she cooked wonderful pasta for them and gave them some money for the work they did. For income, Lionel hand-crafted silver and copper jewellery on the floor of one of the empty rooms of the house. It sold well in the market at Piazza Campo de' Fiori. Even more than jewellery, he loved to create large copper sculptures, which once erected near the fountains, attracted the crowds of tourists visiting the famous square.

All individual incomes were thrown into a community kitty. There was unquestioned trust between them and they just about made ends meet. Their needs were few, and greed didn't consume them. They had nothing to complain about.

Although the house was devoid of furniture and in bad shape, the roof and windows were intact and everyone enjoyed being sheltered from the occasional rain, and the cold. At night, candles provided the only source of light. The house's power supply had been disconnected a long time ago: no one knew when the last bill had been paid.

Doing simple manual work, reading books, getting stoned, loving each other, they didn't need more.

One day, a tall, good-looking Italian guy turned up. He wore decent clothes, had short hair, and spoke with aristocratic elegance. His looks were more those of a normal citizen rather than that of a rebel. He enjoyed the company and stayed. His name was Max. There was so much space in this house that it was not a problem; besides it was nice to have someone contributing generously to the kitty. Max, at least, didn't have cash problems. His family was well off, and he had a close relationship with his mother.

However, he had a difficult crisis to resolve. He had been called to serve in the Italian military a few months before, but as a conscientious objector, he had refused to report. Now, the Italian cops were looking for him. So, he stayed at

Campo de' Fiori, in hiding. Although he appeared collected, he was in fact quite tortured by this dilemma. He loved his mother dearly, and did not want to hurt her. He also had a girlfriend he loved. She visited him sometimes, careful not to be followed. Their *rendez-vous* bore the marks of a cloak-and-dagger conspiracy.

At this stage of escalation, even if he had gone to the authorities and surrendered, Max would have had to serve a harsh jail sentence of several years for desertion, on top of the military service. So he was stuck in a nasty situation, with no solution in view.

As for Lionel and Milien, besides looming Swiss jail time, they had aggravated the situation with their implicit complicity in Max's situation, by harbouring him. This modest assembly had gradually turned into a group of renegades, one small crime at a time.

That was precisely when the idea had grown amongst them, to take off from Europe for good.

One particular evening, they held a spontaneous council. Night had fallen, and everyone was sitting in Giovanni's room. There were a few candles to provide light, and Giovanni rolled a behemoth of a joint out of Afghan hash, which he passed among the group. It was fortunate that acid wasn't available that day, or the planet Mars could have turned up as a whimsical destination, a generation or two ahead of time...

The brainstorming session began. The primary *sine qua non* requirement for this exodus was hassle-free access to high-quality cannabis at the destination. Two main options came up: the first and most popular was Marrakech, Morocco; the second option, more challenging, was Kabul, Afghanistan.

The Beat and Hippie generations had a lot of trouble understanding an obvious contradiction, which was unfortunately ruining their otherwise careless life: what was all the fuss made by the Establishment about cannabis? In their experience, it was a mild drug, if consumed in moderation, just like alcohol, no more, no less. Alcohol consumed in excess could, in fact, be far more destructive than cannabis. The surprising thing was that in some cultures, alcohol was good and cannabis bad. Most European countries had chosen to label it as evil. In some Eastern communities, cannabis was okay and alcohol evil. So, the entire problem was not a question of health or even ethics, just social customs. But because of these traditions, in some countries one would go to jail, while in others, one remained free. Here a crime; there not a crime? Where was the sense in that? This contradiction was an assault against simple logic and common sense, difficult to accept, and they kept cracking jokes about the stupidity and close-mindedness of the Western Establishment. The sad fact was that jail time was inevitable for those who weren't careful. And jail time was no joke.

Giovanni was inclined towards Marrakech, but for him it was like a vacation, devoid of long-term implications, since he hadn't entangled himself with the police yet, though a few of his friends were in jail. He had been lucky.

As for Max and Lionel, Kabul felt right. Morocco was too close to the Italian police for Max to feel comfortable, and in Lionel's opinion, Marrakech was a place for wimps. He needed something more dramatic. Perhaps there was already a timid subconscious voice telling him that east was the right direction, not west; he wanted Kabul. All his past dreams, right from teenage days, were pulling him eastwards. Envisioning proud Afghan warriors on horseback, this destination was infinitely more seductive.

Horse riding across the steppes of Mongolia fell into a similar bracket. As a boy, Lionel had often devoured a novel titled *Land of Swift-Running Horses* by Mabel Waln Smith, a magical book of stories about nomads and semi-wild horses roaming the deserted steppes of Mongolia. Joseph Kessel was likewise a prominent author among his readings. These books had a tremendous impact on his young self and helped nurture a strong desire to leave the parental home as early as possible.

Mongolia had been postponed for years, and now, since the opportunity was at last coming his way, he decided not to waste it. He would make sure he headed east, only east.

As for Milien, unsure of himself as always, he would move in the direction the wind blew the strongest.

Huber and Vera were hesitant, but being less implicated than Lionel in the Swiss affair, wished to return there once the dust had settled. This disappointed Lionel, for he would have loved to travel in their company.

The hard-core Spanish guy didn't give a shit. He was only concerned about his next fix.

Last but not least, in the Rome succession of events, Piazza Campo de' Fiori became the setting for a powerful moment of serendipity.

A few days after having taken up residence in the house that would turn into a long-term squatters' home thereafter,

Lionel, in an idle mood, was roaming the premises, exploring every floor, room and recess. It was so very Italian, built over four floors like a maze. He meandered through the empty rooms connected by crooked staircases and corridors, with the plaster cracking off the walls and ceiling. He was also on the lookout for electric switchboards, hoping against all odds for some way to reconnect the electricity, which would make his work on leather and handicrafts easier. Then he descended to the basement. In the upper rooms, sufficient light entered through the mostly intact windows. But here in the basement, there were only narrow light-wells at street-pavement level, with iron bars across them, allowing a little diffused daylight to filter through.

Halfway down the staircase, Lionel stopped, waiting for his vision to re-adjust to the dim light. With mild curiosity, he allowed his eyes, still tuning-in to the lack of light, wander over a pile of rubble in the middle of the cellar. With his powers of discernment increasing, he could distinguish heaps of plaster of Paris debris, piles of old newspapers and magazines, lying in disarray, a broken sink, and empty bottles. A lone rat disappeared into a crack in the wall with a feeble squeal. The air was thick with the stench of mildew. There was nothing of interest here apparently, and he was about to turn around and leave this damp, repulsive place, when something made him hesitate.

Fancy that: did he really see a diffused beam of light making its way through the narrow opening at the top of a wall and falling onto the rubble? The modest ray of filtered daylight hit the apex of the trash pile directly. There was something there, protruding, that looked like the corner of a book. It seemed to sparkle in the dark, like it was trying to say, *Here I am; come pick me up!* Perhaps some new and free science-fiction? Lionel had not had much opportunity to read since his recent vacation in the Swiss jail.

He walked towards the pile, carefully navigating through the foothills of the formidable mountain of trash, avoiding sharp objects like protruding glass shards. His hand reached for the dusty corner of the book and pulled it out effortlessly: he felt like Arthur extracting Excalibur from the Stone. Cautiously retreating all the way back, he turned to look at his bounty. There wasn't enough light to read the title, so he clambered back up the staircase with its cracked tiles, to the ground floor, where bright sunlight flooded in through the dusty windows.

Wiping off the thick layer of dust on the cover, Lionel was a tad disappointed. This did not look like a science fiction novel. It was a book in French. What was the author's name – Satprem? Odd name; he had never heard of this author. Same thing with the title: *Sri Aurobindo ou l'Aventure de la conscience — Sri Aurobindo or the Adventure of Consciousness*. He had absolutely no idea what all that was about. But Lionel had nothing urgent to do (to be honest, in those days, the word 'urgent' had little meaning for him). So he ventured up to the first floor and entered his humble domicile – a large room empty of furniture, and peeling walls that had once been white. A mat was spread on the wooden floor, with his sleeping bag on it, his rucksack to one side. On the other side was a battered silver chandelier with three branches, each holding a candle. It served as his only source of light to read at night; his royal bedroom... On the window sill, besides a pouch of tobacco and rolling paper, a large ashtray cradled a weathered *chillum,* carved out of a stone resembling obsidian. There were also rolls of copper sheets, metal rods, and various other materials, in a corner. The tools of his trade lay scattered around a small anvil on the floor.

Sitting down crossed-legged on the sleeping bag, he buried his nose into this strange, yet somehow mysteriously attractive book, and began to read.

And in that squatter's house at Piazza Campo de' Fiori, as he dove deeper into the book, for the first time in his life, Lionel discovered something about the mystery of existence which made sense to him, which rang true; something which resonated within the depths of his being; the closest he had come to finding actual answers to the most profound questions about life. Not philosophy, not religion by any means, just a clear vision of where mankind was heading in the next step of evolution. It was something simple, direct and untainted, natural and logical at the same time. It did not compel; it did not preach; it just sang a sweet note of unassuming truth.

It was nothing like the tales they had attempted to force-feed him in school, or those harassing attempts by a stubborn aunt, who thought he should attend the Sunday service at the Protestant church in his hometown or be damned. At last, something spiritual that made sense and did not thrive on bullshit.

Amazingly, this was the original edition. *Extraordinaire!* French was his mother-tongue. In those days, he could only read and speak French and German; not a word of English and just twelve words of Italian learned since he had reached Rome. These languages weren't fashionable in the eastern parts of France and weren't taught in school; people didn't travel like they do today.

Here summarised, was the dazzling marvel: he was a French tramp fleeing the Swiss Police, stranded in Rome, Italy, where he discovered the book that was to change his life, in the original French edition, in the dark basement of an abandoned house, protruding from of a pile of trash; a book that would eventually become a guiding beacon on an epic, radical, life-journey. It also referred to a mysterious geographical location, somewhere in far-away South India, an old French trading post – *La Ville Blanche,* the White Town. And in this town, there was an Ashram of a peculiar kind. That, too, aroused his curiosity.

Come to think of it, how on earth had this book landed here? Who had bought it? Had this person even read it? It looked perfectly new to him, and even appeared to have been published recently. How did it end up in a pile of rubbish? Who threw it in the basement, disregarded? It could as well have been completely buried under all that plaster of Paris, and he would never have found it.

Or was it destiny's hand that had carefully brought it to that specific spot for him, using the crudest means it could, to reach him?

Every time he pondered the impossible chain of coincidence, he couldn't help but be struck with awe. From that moment, the world's ways never ceased to amaze him. And later, much later, he would come to understand that a new consciousness was infiltrating the world, and it was at work in the most material plane.

Down to a pile of trash.

5
MIDNIGHT EXPRESS

1971, TURKEY

On the Road, Part 1

In the picturesque Pink House in Pelekas, Lionel had expected to encounter an exodus of sensitive and intelligent avant-garde youth from several European countries, all looking for a new Promised Land. From their perhaps naïve perspective, such a land would be the ideal place on earth – a real life Shangri-La, where people did not surrender to an endless cycle of consumerism; where there was no conflict or war; where *Make love, not war* was an universal motto; where long hair was not stigmatised, and police forces did not exist. They assumed they would find this Shangri-La somewhere in the Far-East, and that's all they knew. However, it had yet to be discovered. And the scheme that had been clandestinely planned (beyond the intrusive disapproving gaze of the Establishment), was designed to snowball-morph into a mass-movement that engulfed at least half a generation of youth, and would someday conquer the whole planet. And lo! Mankind would be transformed.

The reality check was disappointing. The movement had shrunk to two arrivals – Lionel's not-so-favourite travel companion, Milien, who had by now earned the nickname of Parasite, thanks to his skill for hanging around with no positive personal contribution, and Max, who had at last made a choice and left Italy in an attempt to dodge the mandatory military draft. The man was full of contradictions: he had taken this drastic step, a bold one certainly, yet he never missed a chance, whenever the conversation permitted, to whine and lament with words like, "I shall never see my beloved mother again! When shall I ever walk in our family vineyard?" He got some rather rude comments from Lionel, who told him not to turn the pleasant garden around the Pink House into a 'whine-yard', while thinking to himself, *so very Italian, this tears-loaded drama!*

But these two moaners stuck to Lionel like leeches. On one side an undecided Parasite, and on the other, mad Max, singing blues about the girlfriend he had to leave behind. This didn't feel like freedom and fun at all. So Lionel's decision to move on was hastened. After seven days in Corfu, enjoying the sunsets displayed at his secluded viewpoint, he packed his bag and headed to the harbour. The two leeches, having no better option, trailed along.

It looked like mankind's transformation would have to wait for better days.

From Corfu, they sailed to Greece. The ferry-ride was short but pleasant. After a brief and scenic bus journey through Greece, they arrived in Istanbul, perhaps Lionel's favourite city. This mysterious gateway to Asia, with which he had fallen in love a few years earlier, during a road trip to Lebanon, was still vibrant with the tales of *One Thousand and One Nights*. The energy was captivating, the mix of cultures, the melting pot of West and East enticing, and let's not forget, the *hammam!* One could plunge into mosaic lined pools, under ancient Roman-built domes and cupolas, still heated from below with wooden fires, as in Roman times, soak in the steam, and then have the stress of one's past life and experiences, such as unfair jail-time, massaged out of one's ecstatic body by professional, strong Turkish hands!

However, a queer twist of Fate seemed to consider it necessary to swiftly turn any afterglow of happiness into serious trouble. Here, the master source of an endless array of problems was Parasite.

They were in Istanbul, and in need of a fresh supply of *charas,* as hashish is often referred to in Asia. Parasite took it upon himself to arrange an absurd meeting in the middle of the night, in a rather shady corner of the city, behind an ancient Roman wall, with a dealer who had a limp. The test sample had been fantastic, and so, with an appreciable part of the little money they had, Parasite bought the stuff. Hell and damnation! It turned out to be useless compressed grass, probably picked in some city park and made by expert crooks to look like the real thing.

Though this fact dawned on them rather quickly, it was still not quick enough. As soon as he had collected the money foolishly handed over by Parasite, the limping fellow disappeared at lightning speed, literally vanishing into the maze of antique ruins. This was surprising, considering his slight disability which, seen in retrospect, might have been an act, too. As a professional con artist, he had staged a perfect Houdini escape, having offered the customary test-smoke rolled from top-quality stuff.

Parasite had, cleverly he thought, arranged it all. To balance out his failure, however, he did at last get some decent shit. The three of them then proceeded on the next leg of the journey to mythical Shangri-La, by train this time, to Ankara.

But Parasite's true genius had yet to fully reveal itself.

They were on the Turkish train, pulled by a diesel engine spitting filthy greasy sooth. It could have been re-baptised *Midnight Express,* referencing the classic movie that would hit the screens a few years later, about a young American caught with a serious amount of dope while boarding a flight back to the U.S. of A. In the aftermath of his capture, he finds himself thrown into a Turkish dungeon to rot and live a life of torture for years.

In Turkey and Iran, though smoking charas was commonplace, it was considered a risky affair, more so if you were a foreigner caught in possession, as the poor bastards locked in Turkish prisons could bear witness to. As for the crime of trafficking, it attracted far worse consequences than in Switzerland. Turkey was definitely one of those countries where one ought not to get caught with drugs.

The three travellers were aware of this fact, but used to being victimised by society, the danger of being caught in possession was an integral part of their lives. They had not consciously assessed the severity of the consequences, or perhaps they simply saw it as a way to stand up to what they perceived to be the tyranny of the Establishment; probably something of both. As it transpired, Lionel, Max and Milien would tread close, far too close, to the ugly situation described in *Midnight Express,* coincidentally in the same year the events depicted on screen occured.

Mad Max and Lionel always smoked their charas in the train loo, and kept their environment and behaviour under control. Lionel especially, was self-trained to get stoned to the roots of his long hair, and yet act sober and normal. There was a regular back and forth between the compartment and the bathroom for this purpose.

Enter 'Calamity-Pa', as it was tempting to call him; alias Parasite, alias Milien. He came back from the loo giggling, smoke evaporating from every orifice of his swaying body. He took his seat in the compartment, still unable to wipe the silly grin off his face. Losing control over the movements of his hands, he dropped the fat plastic-wrapped piece of charas into the gap between his seat and the neighbour's, which was still vacant. It got wedged in the gap and stayed there. He noticed none of this, or anything else of importance, he was so stoned. Neither did the others.

The trio's freedom for the next ten years at least was now hanging by a silken thread… a person of sensitivity sitting next to them would have no doubt seen the sword of Damocles hanging over their heads, swinging gently, ever so gently, back and forth.

A well-dressed, friendly Turkish gentleman entered the compartment, enquiring politely if he could sit down on the empty seat next to Parasite. The trio welcomed him cordially. In the course of the ensuing lively conversation, it became soon apparent that the gentleman was in fact a plain-clothes police officer. As he boasted about his 'holy war' against drug smugglers who, according to him, were ruining the values of his country's youth, his fascinated audience, Milien, Max, and Lionel, turned pale. Suddenly, all his senses on professional alert, the man found something wedged into the crevice of the seat between him and Parasite. He gave it a quick look, then, with a victorious grin, pulled it out and brandished the package before their horrified eyes.

Shock-waves ran through the compartment, which suddenly felt too hot. It did not matter how much they were under the inebriated influence of cannabis, they all realised they were trapped in a dreadful situation. Lionel's heart sank into his shoes, and he began to feel nauseous. The prompt reaction of the plain-clothes policeman confirmed that the trap door had snapped close.

While staring and sniffing at his surprise find, he exclaimed, "But this is hashish, my dear little friends! A strictly forbidden substance in my country! Is it yours?"

He stared hard at the shrinking Parasite, from whom he got a high-speed reply. "No Sir, of course not, Sir! Must have been left on the train before we got on, Sir."

Next, when he turned his gaze questioningly on Mad Max and Lionel, with the clear body language of a pro-interrogator, they were so quick to give a synchronised reply with Parasite, that it seemed somewhat suspicious.

However, while the three of them sweated and stewed, the Terminator cop, after a few more deep sniffs, concluded that the specimen was of superior quality, worth intensive investigation off the record. Preferably at home, not in any Government office, or better yet, right then.

"Well..." he said with a crooked smile, "in that case, as it is not yours, I shall keep it with me for further analysis."

The goggling trio almost fainted when he guilelessly opened the package, took a cigarette from a pack in his pocket, emptied the tobacco onto his palm, mixed a generous fifty-fifty proportion for a solid joint, and refilled the cigarette. And so they sat, poor victims expecting infinite jail time, having to watch (and smell, and breathe) the Terminator sucking and puffing on his joint like a chimney, soon transforming the air of the compartment into a thick hashish fog, which intoxicated them even further! All of this with a wide grin and total impunity, since he was a cop and none, train conductor or whoever, would have dared question him.

After a while, the train reached the next station. The man stood up abruptly, and without a word or glance at them, got out of the compartment and walked briskly down the platform. The three friends sat petrified in their seats: surely a patrol of frantic soldiers would storm the train any minute? Unsure of what to do, they waited a long time. The train was not moving. Tension was palpable in the air. Finally, as the engine's whistle blew, the train shaked itself from its inertia and moved slowly in a crescendo of squealing and creaking. The sound of the diesel engine speeding up was sweet music in Lionel's ears. No one had arrested them and they were on their way to Ankara.

This experience came as a first inkling of the daily paradoxes of the East. The Terminator, perhaps too stoned to think with clarity, had probably lost interest in jailing them; he would have had to bury himself in endless and tedious paperwork, and had probably preferred to settle for the more comfortable option of sneaking away with the trio's stash. Regardless of the Turkish cop's goodwill or neglect, nobody will ever know, from that day on, despite his peaceful nature and Shangri-La ideals, Lionel toyed with the idea of murdering Parasite.

As the train reached Ankara station, Max stood up first and conducted a discreet but thorough check of the platform to make sure there were no soldiers or policemen expecting them. On his signal, they alighted and at a brisk pace exited the station. Never more appreciative of a freedom almost lost, they quickly got their visas for Iran, rushed back to the station, and boarded the first train eastwards.

From Ankara, they journeyed in another worn-out country train through the dry and dusty land, to Erzurum. At which point, following a night of poor sleep, spent in some kind of strange, dilapidated and frigid caravanserai, a reminder of the days when horses and camels were the modes of travel, they switched from rail to road. They boarded a decent, modern and comfortable Mercedes bus, to take them across the border to Tabriz, Iran, along an endless, straight, boring road. Mount Ararat loomed in the distance. Lost in thought in the plush reclining seat, bathing in the cosy atmosphere of the well-heated bus, Lionel allowed his mind to drift while admiring the beautiful, arid mountain. It was believed by some to be the resting place of Noah's Ark; a Bible buff had found an old piece of wood lying there on a ridge. But it could as well have been one of those myths mankind excels at perpetrating, in its endless need for religious fodder. Another evangelist explorer could as well have proved it to be the handle of Adam's axe. Who is to say?

In truth, Lionel's weak attempts at taking things lightly were just an effort to avoid the looming thoughts of how close he had come to rotting in a Turkish jail; he could not imagine a worse fate. Thus, while he contemplated the magnificent deserted hills along the Erzurum-Tabriz highway, his mind wandered back to Switzerland.

6
GERANIUMS ON THE WINDOWS

1969-1970, SWITZERLAND

Lionel had been regularly shuttling back and forth between Paris and Switzerland; he had found a rhythm to it and called it 'oscillating' – a term he had borrowed from early aborted engineering studies. He had developed an obsession about becoming financially self-sufficient, not dependent on parental support which inevitably came with strings attached. This was also the reason for getting involved in some shady parallel businesses; independence at any cost! As a result, he had been oscillating between his school of photography in Switzerland, and Paris, where he eventually got a job in the advertising field, hoping to put into practice what he had learned. This advertising agency, the Studio Molinari, had a graphics department. They contracted, among other prestigious assignments, all the ads for the *Club Méditerranée*, a mammoth holidaying organisation. The proprietor of the studio, Mr Molinari, was fair to Lionel and had even given him a small apartment on the top floor of a building on rue Saint-Martin, rent-free.

In the studio, the boss noticed that Lionel's technical skills were better than average. As a result he found himself, more often than he would have wished, put in charge of processing lab work, down in the basement, rather than on actual sites of photo shoots, which was the part he wished to perfect with time and practice. This was prior to the digital revolution, and Lionel spent long hours in the dark room, under that faint yellow glowing light, processing all kinds and sizes of enlargements, enhancements, and retouches. It was disappointing, but still he was doing some honest work.

One day, he was called up to the office to take a phone call. It was a fine, warm day; the birds were chirping, one could still see multitudes of sparrows and swallows flying in the Paris' skies in those days, and this confirmed his impression of it being a lovely day. He ran up the stairs in good shape and high spirits to take the call from his dad. It surprised him when his concerned father told him the local police had landed up at their doorstep looking for him on behalf of the Swiss police. What was it all about? He explained that the police in Switzerland urgently required his presence to ask a few questions. He had been asked to report as soon as possible to avoid further complications.

"Nothing to worry about, son, they were very civil and said it was just a routine matter," concluded his dad.

Obediently, the very next morning, Lionel straddled his Honda CB motorcycle to ride all the way from Paris to Switzerland.

Right upon arrival in the modest town of Vevey, on the shores of Geneva Lake, he headed to the town's police station; it happened to be located on the ground floor of the municipal jail. He parked the motorbike in one of the designated spaces facing the building. Tired from the 500-kilometre-long bike ride, but still in good spirits, he walked inside, noticing the beautiful flowering geraniums decorating the window sills.

"Good afternoon, Officer. My name is Lionel Kalmer, and

I got word you wished to see me for some clarifications?"

Hell! Within seconds, he found himself arrested and locked in a prison cell! So much for the fine day, chirping birds, and all.

"But excuse me Sir, I understood I was wanted for an amicable conversation and a few questions?"

"You were wanted all right, son, as in being on the list of WANTED people!"

What was going on? It seemed he had been called to his execution! He understood that this was linked to his illegal activities during the past couple of years, and his not-so-successful-but-sustainable little business of cannabis and LSD retailing. How deep the investigation had gone, he had no clue.

A priori it wasn't too bad. The Swiss police officers were decent, known to treat his kind with more respect than their French counterparts. Swiss prisons were not particularly dreadful places either. This one in particular, Vevey being a small town, was set in a modest, classic-looking ancient building, almost an archetype of the coveted Swiss chalet everyone dreams of in retirement. Except for the unusually small windows, one would never have guessed it was a prison. Well maintained, flowerbeds in top shape, geraniums flowering at every window... Wow! Almost welcoming. It faced the main plaza of the town, and even the view from the small window (he had to climb on the bed to see, through thick iron bars) was a relaxing one – trees, decorative shrubs and flowers.

One prisoner perched on a ladder in the central hall, humming a song, a cigarette hanging at the corner of his mouth, was whitewashing the walls. Oh my God! Some uninvited pigeons had soiled the wall with brownish-green droppings… With only a dozen inmates, it was certainly not ominous Alcatraz.

Ever the odd one, Lionel was the only guy with long hair, so he attracted some sideways stares. Switzerland is the country of honesty par excellence; thieves and criminals are remarkably rare; usually Turks or French, but perhaps the occasional Italian too. Inside, the cells were ancient; the wooden floor worn by the steps of hundreds of prisoners having paced up and down through possibly a century. There was just a narrow metal bed, bolted to the floor, with a lousy, uncomfortable mattress, but a warm blanket and clean sheets (we were in Switzerland after all), and that was it. No sink, just a Turkish loo in a corner, with a tap and a bucket. For a washbasin, one had to request permission from the warden, who would then kindly escort the inmate to the bathroom. A hot shower was available three times a week. A two-star hotel for sure, or family home-stay, one could decide.

This picturesque prison building was close to the focal point of those times: Vevey and Montreux were forming an elongated twin town along the Geneva lakeshore, and where they joined, one could walk into a nightclub called The Strobe. That was where all the questionable youth, like him, met. It was conveniently close to the Montreux concert hall, at the casino, where all the new rock bands, still in their meteoric rise to stardom, came to play: Led Zeppelin, Santana, Pink Floyd, to name a few.

No one would have guessed that one year later, the same

casino would accidentally burn down to ashes during a concert. In the aftermath of this incident, a legendary piece of music was born: *Smoke on the Water* by Deep Purple. Meanwhile, these icons all came to Montreux, because the town in general, and the town council in particular, were unconventionally open and welcoming to the new wave. One had to give them credit for this at a time when, more often than not, society systematically rejected the Beat and Hippie generations. Walking along the lakeshore, nationality, beliefs, religion, length of hair and dress, didn't matter much.

Vevey-Montreux was one of those rare places of tolerance in Europe. It was the main reason Lionel had enjoyed spending almost two years in the region. To-le-ran-ce – a simple word, yet so powerful. It represents the first requirement on the path towards human unity; so easy to embrace, yet so rare.

In this French-spoken part of Switzerland, a cosy canton nested between the Alps and the Jura, adorned with snow-covered peaks and many lakes, there was this relaxed and broad-minded atmosphere, in stark contrast to most cities in France and Italy. In Switzerland, marginalised youths were generally tolerated and left in peace, while in France, they were hunted down; having long hair was reason enough. And in Italy, it was even worse; one could earn ten years in jail for the unspeakable crime of possessing a few grams of hashish. Lionel had friends who had been locked up for months, for being caught in possession of a joint.

The simple act of casually strolling through Paris' Quartier Latin could land one in the confines of some police station because *he* had long hair, or *she* wore an Afghan jacket, thus standing out from the mass of sheep-like citizens. With no other reason than the convenient pretext of identity verification, the cops would shove them unceremoniously into a police van and take them away to the nearest *Commissariat de Police.* There, they would have to face humiliating interrogations, full body searches, and produce countless fingerprints before being released after a few hours or a night in detention, with blue-inked fingers to make sure they remembered the experience.

This constant harassment took place for no other reason than the fact that they looked different from the average exemplary citizen – the one who returns home in the evening, totally spent after a long day of boring work, and kills his evening watching TV, sunk in his fake-leather sofa, with beer in hand.

This harassment, akin to persecution, was mentally exhausting and instilled a constant feeling of insecurity.

But then, speaking of security and safety, there was Enrique. He was Lionel's self-appointed bodyguard. Not that Lionel felt he needed one, but Enrique seemed to believe so. Enrique was of Spanish origin – short, stocky, broad-shouldered, strong – the son of migrant labourers who had come to Switzerland from Spain to do menial work. His father was a mason. They were humble, hospitable people.

Formidable Enrique just popped up out of nowhere one day, and attached himself to Lionel as his bodyguard. Lionel believed it was more from love than necessity. Enrique had no interest in money or anything else, he was just always there, almost invisible, never imposing himself, always respecting Lionel's vast need for privacy, recognising his need to be alone even before he realised it himself, and withdrawing gracefully in such moments. Enrique was simply amazing.

It was a time when a lot of sharing was taking place amongst the marginal youth communities; they considered it a normal way of life. Whoever had something would share it. If someone had an apartment, friends would come to stay or live there. Thus, for a while, Lionel lived in a huge built-in cupboard in a friend's apartment. It had wide sliding doors and one could step inside and have enough space for truckloads of clothes and storage, or in his case, a mattress and a few belongings, like boots, helmet, some books, and his girlfriend's guitar. It was well lit and ventilated, and Lionel lived in this closet with complete satisfaction for an entire month, at times with his girlfriend. They had their privacy. And just by opening the sliding door, they could be in the middle of a party.

In the same building, on another floor, there was a guy who had bought a comprehensive second-hand sound system from a broadcasting radio station in Geneva, with a huge deck covered with dials, switches and sliders. The contraption occupied half of his living room. It had come with monster speakers and delivered top-quality sound. The whole building listened to the new emerging rock-bands, but none needed to go to him to do so, for he left the door of his flat open and the entire community had free music day *and* night. The walls of the building would shake, but nobody ever complained.

There was a certain atmospheric density.

Inside Lionel, however, something remained unsatisfied; some essential, undefinable element was missing. He felt he would have to leave soon, no matter the grand parties this lifestyle offered. He was not the kind who'd ever save money, but for once in his life, in view of a possible departure, he had saved a small amount, some 20,000 odd Swiss Francs, that he had earned working at restoring boats in the shipyards on Lake Geneva, and doing other menial jobs.

But one day, Lionel found the money had vanished from his cupboard home. It was all gone, evaporated. He told Enrique about it, and Enrique became enraged. Hissing furious! How could anyone dare to steal something from Lionel, whom he protected? He made Lionel think – who would have had the chance to get inside his cupboard-living-quarters unobserved? Lionel began thinking aloud, mumbling the names of a few guys who might have had the opportunity.

When one particular name came up, Enrique exclaimed, "That's it! Has to be him!" He had a natural gift of intuitive divination.

Without losing a moment, he pulled Lionel by the sleeve into the night, towards the place where the suspect lived. It was ten o'clock at night in a small Swiss town, and on top of it all, the guy in question lived with his parents.

Once there, Enrique planted himself in front of the wooden door and banged on it with a firm fist, *POMP! POMP! POMP!* Not unlike some Gestapo SS officer raiding a suspected nest of Resistance fighters. The entire building woke up, and the neighbours started to show up in the corridor. The guy opened the door, but before he could even react, Enrique jumped at him and grabbed him by the collar in some weird police grip. He proceeded to squeeze the air out of him, all the while demanding, "Where is the money? You give it back right now, all of it, and I may let you live!"

The terrified guy melted instantly. Together, he, Enrique and Lionel marched through the apartment to the chap's room. One can only imagine his parents' distress, wondering what was going on with this invasion. Enrique's grip remained like iron on him till he fetched the money; the entire amount untouched. Nothing was missing of Lionel's hard-earned savings, thanks to the immediate, decisive action of his friend. So, thank God, Enrique let the boy live… Satisfied, he shoved the money into Lionel's hands. He wanted none of it, even when Lionel later offered him a share. He was a true, devoted guardian, watching over one he considered his own.

With time passing, this nagging something, which made Lionel unsatisfied with his life, became more insistent. He needed to move on to greener pastures, to explore other avenues. Not so much for the sake of exploration itself, but more to find an answer to his eternal set of questions, *"What is the meaning of* 'me'? *Where is my direction?"* or, *"What do I have to do to find the purpose of my life. Is there a purpose at all?"* Reselling hash and getting stoned, as fun as it was, was not a satisfying answer. Since quite a while, he had in his mind – or was it in his heart? – this persistent feeling of life being a strange, impalpable illusion he couldn't get a hold on.

And then there was this other brilliant cinema director, Jean Luc Goddard, who had set one of those dialogues which haunted him. So it goes, in a scene of *À Bout de Souffle – Breathless.*

An acclaimed author is being interviewed by a journalist.

"What is your dearest ambition in life?"

"*Devenir Immortel, et mourir* (Turn Immortal, then die)," replies the author.

Lionel appreciated the quote even more because there was a twist to it: the cream of the cream of French literature, the exclusive Members of the *Académie Française* are also called *'les Immortels'*.

Lionel's inner compass was stirring, and he knew that his next step in the big journey of life was all set and inevitable. The compass needle that would give him a sense of direction was, however, still trembling, not yet pointing towards a well-defined azimuth.

But then, Destiny herself got impatient and gave Lionel a decisive kick in the ass. He was locked in this very nice, ultra-clean Swiss prison, but he quickly realised that, as neat and clean as it was, the suppression of freedom is guaranteed to be an experience that will shake anyone's foundations of life.

There was a decent library though, with many science-fiction books – Lionel's favourite genre. He found there excellent novels by Asimov, Heinlein, Frank Herbert, Arthur Clarke, and others. But more remarkably, he picked up one particular book written by the eminent British scientist and prolific sci-fi writer, Fred Hoyle, titled *The Black Cloud,* and took it back to his cell.

And so, that first evening in his new habitat, he was half-way into his book, when the lights suddenly went off. *Okay...that's what they do in jails,* he thought. Tired by the long ride and eventful day, Lionel slept well the first night.

At seven the next morning, he was still sleeping like a dog, when he heard a loud noise. Slam! Bam! He opened his eyes, turned over and looked at the floor. The piece of bread that was his breakfast had landed on the worn wooden floor. The next thing to appear was a mug of hot chocolate, mercifully held out by a gruff Swiss warden at the little opening cut into the thick wooden door. That was the precise moment when Lionel realised *this is not a bad dream. I am truly in jail,* and suddenly it was no longer fun.

Thus, on his very first day he learned that he had to watch out for that loud morning call of 'chocolate-chocolate!' and be prepared to bolt for the door. He would catch his bread before it went into its ballistic flight onto the floor, and then receive gracefully the nice mug of hot chocolate. He was however disappointed that chestnuts weren't on the menu...

What came an hour after the chocolate, was not so nice, however. The warden took him from his cell down to the ground floor. A pair of constables had come for him. They dragged him in handcuffs through the town towards the railway station, half a kilometre away. Along the way he noticed the looks of disapproval and disgust on the faces of the honest, well-behaved, tax-paying Swiss citizens when confronted with this long-haired hippie in handcuffs. Probably a mass-murderer. Another Charles Manson? Here in our wonderful, bright little country?

Soon after, he found himself locked in a special prison carriage on a train going to Lausanne, the nearest city of importance on Lake Geneva. On arrival, he boarded a transfer-truck with barred windows, through which he could see little of the beautiful old town. He felt all this to be uncharacteristically inconsiderate when compared to the attention paid by the rather pleasant staff of his little deluxe jail in Vevey. With no ceremony, he was delivered to the Lausanne jail and locked into another cage, this one without windows. Finally, he ended up in a sizeable room, with windows, where a constable removed his handcuffs. It was the interrogation room of the judge handling Lionel's case, though he still didn't know precisely what the case was about.

He soon got confirmation that they were indeed digging into his trafficking business. After a lot of useless questions about when and where he had met certain individuals while handing over or receiving illegal substances, he was shipped back in the same manner, in reverse, to his geranium-adorned Vevey jail. This strange routine went on many times, day after day, always following the same cheap movie script: handcuffs, people gazing at him in disgust, train, Lausanne, truck, countless questions, then back to Vevey.

Nobody was getting any closer to the truth. He discovered, however, that the whole affair had resulted from the cops having caught one of his trade acquaintances who, being a pitiable spineless junkie, had unrestrainedly spilled the beans, wreaking havoc in their small community. Even his dear friend and protector, Enrique, had been dragged into the mess. But he, of course, would have preferred to be cut into tiny little pieces than rat on his close friend Lionel, the object of his protection.

These countless interrogations, leading nowhere, reminded Lionel of Kafka's depressing novel, *The Trial,* which he had read in his student days.

Now, many years later, with much water having been spilled by the Rhone into Lake Geneva, it would perhaps be interesting, even amusing, to read the faded script of those cross-examinations. Dutifully recorded with two fingers on an Olympia typewriter by the heavily bearded court scribe who looked like he had just come down from the *Alm* – a guardian of fifty cows still attired in his *lederhosen* – the interrogations went something like this:

Judge: "You have been seen at The Strobe on this and this day, with so and so, and on these occasions you have handed over many doses of a strictly prohibited substance, namely lysergic acid diethylamide, commonly known as LSD. Will you confirm these facts?"

Lionel: "I am sorry Sir, but I can't really remember. You know, I was going to The Strobe every day, and I was so stoned…"

"No cheap excuses, my boy! I don't have time to waste. Tell me now, if you want to get out of this jail anytime soon!" bellowed the judge in a serious attempt at intimidation.

Lionel mumbled again with sincere humility, trying hard to jolt his memory: "On which day did you say, Sir? March 25th? Hmm, let me think... I'm afraid I can't remember any of this Sir, it was a long time ago. Besides, how can you expect me to recall such details since I was so stoned? The truth is Sir, I was stoned all the time…"

The net result was that the judge was pulling out his hair in despair, and the cross-examination was going nowhere.

Water-boarding had not been introduced to peaceful Swiss interrogation rooms yet, and so, when the judge finally tired of the game, Lionel was released, on probation till the court hearing.

By then, Lionel had read enough science fiction and he craved Freedom with a capital F, like the big capital F on his Honda CB's French registration plate. It became as clear as the light reflected on the ice of the Aletsch glacier that, as much as he had loved the friendly atmosphere and attractive scene in Vevey-Montreux, he ought not to linger any longer in the land of chestnut-loaded chocolates.

Although the judge had instructed him to remain in town and not leave the canton without prior notice (a directive that was alarming enough in itself), Lionel's plan called for spontaneity. In no time at all, he had packed his little bags and rigged them onto the Honda. It was cold and a few snowflakes were floating in wisps on a North wind. But there was no question in his mind. Suddenly, the needle of the compass was steady: Rome, Italy.

He started the motorcycle and warmed up the powerful 750 cc engine for a minute while he threw a quick glance at his map. Then he zipped the map in the tank bag, adjusted the Climax goggles under his helmet, pulled on his gloves, and shifting into gear, headed straight for the Grand Saint Bernard Pass, the gateway to Italy across the Alps.

Just before hitting the freeway, where the ramp began, Milien stood with a backpack, waiting for Lionel to pick him up.

As the Honda gathered speed on the freeway, they both had wide grins across their faces.

7
SHANGRI-LA

1970, IRAN - AFGHANISTAN

On the Road, Part 2

Emerging from his reverie, Lionel looked through the bus window to see the masts and flags announcing the Iranian border coming into view at Bazargan. From that point on in the journey, each border crossing would be a long ordeal, requiring several hours of queuing in front of one petty official's office window to the next, and the next, till every passenger in the bus had collected the many stamps and flyers required in their passports. Only then did the bus reload its human cargo and move on. One positive point though, unexpectedly brought by the Terminator himself, was that with the stash of charas stolen, everyone could feel relaxed; no amount of frisking would have yielded anything. And so the trio, in a rare occurrence of peace at a border crossing, killed time chatting with local Iranian fellow passengers and drinking hot *chai* from street vendors.

Finally the bus took to the road again, towards Tabriz.

Iran was in turmoil. The Shah was running the country with an iron fist, prior to his forced exile some eight years later. It was a time of disorder, contained through fierce political repression. Teheran, in particular, was a scary, unwelcoming, city. Max, Milien and Lionel wished they could move on quickly, but they had to get an Afghan visa, and for this they had to stop in Teheran. There was no other way. They felt more insecure than they ever had during their lengthy journey. Foreign travellers were not welcome; those with long hair even less. Being French didn't help either, because the unpopular Shah had a known inclination towards French culture that had developed during his educational years in Switzerland. They felt hostility oozing from everywhere.

They went straight to the Afghan Embassy to get the visas, and had to wait a few hours for them to be processed, so they slipped into the adjacent public park to kill time. Lionel sat down on a public bench. Strangely, the ill-maintained lawns of the park were littered with old newspapers. After a while, Lionel figured out what was going on. The newspapers were used by rotating, temporary tenants. A man (there were no women in this park), was lying on a newspaper nearby, slumbering, apparently enjoying a siesta. Some newspapers were vacant. Then another man came from a nearby office, targeted one of the available papers, neatly removed the kinks with one hand, lied down on it and went to sleep. More people came and others went. The newspapers stayed.

When a newspaper inevitably turned to tatters, it was abandoned like an old apartment and remained there forever unused, forlorn. The large majority of the tenants were shabby-looking, not because they were homeless or gangsters (they were essentially Government servants working in the surrounding offices), but because that seemed to be the fashionable style – looking European, dressed in Western apparel, but unshaven and shabby. One never saw a smile. Sometimes, a smart ass, likely a well-off chief of section, brought a fresh newspaper.

Always keen to adopt local customs, Lionel was tempted to pick one of the least worn newspapers and take a nap, but hesitated. He was unsure of the reactions it would provoke; everything in this city seemed to hang by a thread, and a small inappropriate gesture could trigger a riot, so he gave it a pass. He couldn't help thinking: *what a mess the park would turn into if it ever rained.* Sheepishly, he asked the question to his neighbours on the bench. Someone told him with tight lips, "It never rains in Teheran."

As soon as they got back the three passports, duly stamped, they moved on, full steam to the railway station; no tourism in Teheran! No charas, either. Oh God, no! Too risky, far too risky. As soon as the train left the station, they felt like they could breathe again, away at last from this grey city packed with grey people dozing on grey newspapers spread on a grey lawn. Farewell, Teheran. The dominant feeling was one of relief at escaping the oppressive atmosphere.

Trains ran up to Mashhad only, after which there were no railway lines to Afghanistan, possibly because of the mountainous terrain. Interestingly, there was no railway system in the entire country of Afghanistan; the all-Asia-invading English railroads had failed here completely. Switching to local colourful buses was the only option to get to Herat, Kandahar, and last, Kabul. And weren't these buses beautiful? Of all the Middle Eastern and Asian countries, there is little doubt that the Afghan truck (or bus) wins the Oscar. Lionel was astonished at the effort, time and artistic love that went into creating these marvellous museum exhibits on wheels. The intricacy of details in the paintings, the multicoloured hanging pompons, the imagination displayed, it was awe-inspiring. His opinion was set: in terms of look and feel, no truck in the world could compete with the Afghan truck.

Despite the fatigue of the long, uninterrupted journey with no proper sleep, except dozing in trains and buses, Lionel could feel the excitement of getting close to his goal. Everything looked different and alien – the deserted landscape, the quality of the air, the animals, the people and how they dressed, the language, the food. Europe had disappeared into the recesses of his mind like an old, forgotten dream. His new life was taking shape in front of his eyes as the bus forged ahead with deafening motor and rattling sounds. It was magical.

Sure, it was winter, and freezing in the desert, but Lionel didn't care. The sky was perfect and the air crisp. There were vast expanses of frigid unpopulated desert everywhere, extending almost all the way between Herat and Kabul. Sometimes, the bus stopped in the middle of nowhere, for a pee break. That was interesting. All the men lined up squatting on one side of the road while the women walked somewhat further away on the other side. Since there was nowhere to hide in this frozen bush-less, tree-less wilderness, the men pretended to look the other way while returning to the bus.

A thick silence loomed over the desert; its splendid vistas suggestive of a crater-less moon. At other times the bus would stop at a roadside *dhaba*, for tea or some food. There were no other structures on the horizon. Lionel wondered how people lived here, so isolated from each other. The buildings were made of thick grey-brown mud walls, rounded off at the edges, as if shaped by a giant child's hand; with tiny windows openings. Inside, it was like a cavern, but comfortably warm. These traditional houses were adequate to protect from the winter cold and summer heat. Lionel, squatting in a corner near the wood fire, slowly drank his hot tea, one sip at a time, with great satisfaction.

Finally, they arrived in Kabul. For Lionel, it was paradise found! Not so much because of the highest quality charas openly available, but because there was a prevailing atmosphere in that wonderful land with its extraordinary people, that embraced him like the arms of a long-lost friend. He felt like he had been climbing for a long time along a steep cliff, beset by difficulties, and suddenly he had reached the peak. He could breathe in sharp clear air! He was enjoying the view from the mountain top. There were camels and horses and more goats and sheep than humans. All the people were unobtrusively hospitable, without ever losing their pride.

This was well before the Russian war, well before the Taliban era. Fear, hate and extremism had not gripped the country, and the Buddhist statues in Bamyan were still intact in all their ancient glory. In those days, these gentile people (in the noblest sense) would leave the traveller alone. They never approached him if he did not wish it. But if help was needed, he only had to ask, and all the support he could want would arrive. If one wished to be left alone, one could die in a ditch and not a soul around would forestall the poor devil in his endeavour. A proud people with a perfect attitude.

Through those vast expanses of desert and the barren mountains, Lionel rode buses in any direction for hours and gazed in wonderment at the ever-changing vistas, the silhouettes of the high snow-clad peaks, which seemed so deceptively close in the crisp air. At the bus-stops, he would mix with co-travellers, but not even they looked at him. However, if he needed any information, he would just have to approach someone and ask, and they would turn into the most helpful people on earth. Simple, honest, detached hospitality everywhere. Lionel was amazed. He felt an immensely strong inner connection with the proud Afghan people.

The only trouble was that upon reaching Kabul, he had run out of money, completely. But he could handle this. The common people here lived a simple, harsh life. If one was sincerely looking for minor jobs and didn't mind hard labour, there was always the possibility of helping a farmer with his truck-loading for shelter and food. Besides, it was the high season, with fresh hippies arriving. He could use to his advantage the fact that he had been in the country a little longer, had learnt a few keywords of the local language, and made friends with several Afghan families.

Dressed like an Afghan in *perahan tunban,* with a *pakol* on the head, day by day, he merged more with the local population. He acted as a guide and mediator for the recent arrivals, helped arrange accommodation, excursions, got them charas, arranged for them to meet up with missing friends, and thus he made a few Afghanis. That was enough. The basic amenities needed here were a bed in a dormitory for a dime, some food, and the world's best charas, with no need to hide.

The food was simple too. He was utterly fond of the unique taste of the Afghan *naans* (the local wheat bread prepared in a *tandoor* oven and served burning hot), available in the street. He would get one of these very long naans and wrap it around his neck like a warm scarf in the harsh winter cold before eating it plain after it had cooled somewhat. It was delicious.

What more do you need? Lionel mused. The world seemed perfect right then. He had definitely reached the closest thing to the Shangri-La he had dreamed of.

8
KALASHNIKOVS IN THE KHYBER PASS

1971, PAKISTAN

On the Road, Part 3

With the weeks and months passing, Lionel realised he was gradually settling into Kabul. But no sooner did he come to this realisation that he noticed, with surprise, that the needle of his inner compass trembled anew. It was a peculiar, unexpected feeling. A hint of dissatisfaction was creeping in – again – like a soft voice murmuring at the back of his mind: *You are fine, yes. Most of your not-so-demanding needs in life are satisfied for sure, but is* that *the point really? Is there no deeper meaning to existence? Is there not some missing creativity, some higher function to it? Is* that *all there is to expect from one's fleeting passage on this earth?*

He didn't observe it at first in his day-to-day activities, but there was that moment when the more sensitive part in him seemed to react, like a good Shepherd dog cocking his ears when he heard the signal.

Parasite had been missing for a while, minding his own business for once. For Lionel, it was a relief. His Italian friend Max, however, was very present. One couldn't help noticing he always had a decent amount of money. He kept himself safe with all that dough. He was receiving regular transfers from his family, but at a cost. Max spent a lot of time checking, waiting and standing in a queue at various post offices and other cash forwarding agencies. Ironically, in some odd way, he had to earn his money. Max's case and

Lionel's differed to a great extent: Max was an exile, and his loving family was helping him; Lionel was a fugitive who had rejected his family. Their circumstances were diametrically opposed. But somehow they got along well, particularly since Max had gained considerable maturity in the past few months.

Adversity is an efficient teacher.

Both Lionel and Max had been walking along a dusty road on the outskirts of Kabul that day, in an area called Paghman, where the nomads from Kunduz in the North came to trade. Having gone to the area on some errand, they were roaming through the open-air market from another age, which sprouted from an amalgam of tents of all sizes, crowded with people, camels and horses. Suddenly, a small troupe of proud Afghan horsemen, looking like old-time warriors with swords at their sides and antique rifles slung across their shoulders, passed by at a canter, in a commotion of hooves and loud neighing, leaving behind a rising cloud of dust. It all looked adventurous and beautiful and seductive, in a romantic way, just like an image pulled out of his teenage book, *Land of Swift-Running Horses*.

Something was screaming in Lionel, and he longed to catch hold of the riders and ask them if they had a spare horse for him to ride along with them. He was so absorbed in this vision of himself riding one of those small, strong-looking horses that he didn't hear Max talking to him at first. Jolted from his reverie, he asked Max to repeat what he had said. He learned that for some absurd reason Max was considering travelling further East, on to India, and he was looking for a companion. What a dumb idea when you have just found Shangri-La!

"You want to increase the distance between yourself and your girlfriend waiting back in Italy?" Lionel couldn't help joking.

Max retained his newfound composure, merely insisting that he didn't want to travel alone.

"No way man, I'm fine here," Lionel replied. "I have no business in India that I know of (or so he thought), and no budget to travel!" That part was true.

Later in the day, Max persistently brought up the subject, elaborating on his plan, making it more interesting by pointing out that he would take care of all the travelling expenses. That finally got Lionel's attention. *Hmm...why not? A few hundred kilometres eastward wouldn't be a big deal, and he could always return to Kabul later*. The needle of his inner compass had turned towards India without him even noticing.

Then, call it fate or not, Milien suddenly resurfaced. So, for better or worse, the team was complete once again.

Soon they were back on the road: another adventurous, dusty bus ride to Jalalabad, and then all the way across the mountains to the history-laden Khyber Pass, the gateway to Peshawar, Pakistan.

Though Lionel and Max wondered if it was a wise choice, given past experiences, Milien carried the bulk of their generous charas supply for weeks to come, stashed in his now very bulky underwear. Max and Lionel had small chunks with them too, but Milien had offered to take the bulk. Who in his right mind left Afghanistan without a decent provision of the black Afghan honey-hued marvel?

Besides, it could be a substantial source of revenue in India, and a means to offset expenses, if needed. A kind of financial insurance, they thought.

It was a hot day, all passengers were sweating in the overheated bus. At last, the bus reached the border. At the Torkham Post, it stopped and everyone stepped down under the fierce sun. The usual border-crossing ordeal awaited them, which took a good hour. Past a succession of counters they walked, attended by as many customs officers, collecting an equal number of stamps or loose forms in their passports. At the endmost counter, a medic sporting a stethoscope, scrutinised the non-locals' vaccination booklets. Then the luggage of each individual on the bus was checked. Finally, the bus itself was inspected and searched from roof-rack to bumpers.

They finally cleared the Afghan border-post without further hinderance and the bus moved on to the Pakistani post, a few hundred metres down the road, traversing a stretch of no-man's-land in-between, where the same song was played in its Pakistani version, for entry into Pashtun land. Another hour passed, processing passports, visas, stamps from one counter to the next, searching the bus and so on.

At last, the border was crossed, slowly, patiently, without incident, and left behind. They were now in Pakistan, cruising at the best speed this museum-worthy artefact of a bus, adorned with extravagant paintings, was capable of. Parasite cheerfully boasted about his brilliant charas smuggling performance.

Having reached the hill road, the bus began to painstakingly negotiate the steep hairpins on the slow, winding, pothole-ridden track that led to the top of the Khyber Pass.

Meanwhile, in a subtle, invisible world hidden behind the veil of Maya, those strange scheming entities that take extreme pleasure in pulling the strings of human fortunes, were busy at work. To a visionary passenger (that excluded the three materialistic Western travellers), it might have seemed that they would be preparing the ground for another hair-raising situation, even more serious than the Midnight Express episode, adorned with AK-47 assault rifles and angry border troops. When all was set, in a low, inaudible voice, they whispered a few insidious words in the left ear of a resolute, trigger-happy Pakistani officer, somewhere high up the mountain.

It was past mid-day and sizzling hot. The breathtaking vista, the lunar landscape stretching all around them was out of this world and Lionel was absorbing it all in fascination. He took note of a Buddhist monk on the bus, in his classic attire of dark-red robes, such as the Tibetan monks wore. His head was shaved, but he was neither Afghan nor Tibetan. He appeared to be a weather-and-sun parched Westerner, dusted over. It was an occasional sight here. Some Westerners, with a mystic strain written into their genes, went to stay in the monasteries for a sabbatical period, to familiarise themselves with Buddhist teachings.

Milien was sitting next to the monk, to the left of the aisle; Max and Lionel were on the right, one row forward, Max at the window. Oddly, Milien kept discreetly gesturing at them, touching his nose. Again and again. Something seemed to be amiss, but Lionel was too tired, hot and bus-rattled to get the meaning of his miming. Local villagers and merchants populated the rest of the bus, and there was a pair of long-haired goats at the back. Another lone Western traveller sat near them, undaunted.

They had reached a point well past the border into Pakistan, near the top of the Khyber Pass. There were still innumerable check-points, all heavily guarded by army personnel. Suddenly, for no clear reason, the bus stopped. A soldier, a Kalashnikov slung across his chest, boarded the bus and barked a few words to the driver. The passengers were ordered to get down from the bus, go to the check-post on the other side of the road, show their travel documents, and sign the book.

Having completed this formality, the passengers proceeded to climb back into the bus. Lionel sat down again on his uncomfortable bench. Almost everyone had boarded, including the goats (they weren't required to sign but went with the owners nevertheless), and a few new locals had settled on the roof, amid the bags and boxes. But the bus did not move. No one knew why. There was not even the wisp of a breeze. The heat in the bus was stifling. Strangely, the monk was still missing, his seat to the left of Milien vacant.

Suddenly, there was a big commotion! Heavily armed border soldiers stormed into the bus, Kalashnikovs raised, loaded, primed and pointing at the passengers. What was this? What was going on? They dragged a man, naked but for his underwear, down the narrow aisle of the bus. Was it the monk?

An AK-47's barrel pointed directly at Lionel's chest and the officer screamed in Pashto, *"Dagha saray pēzhanē?* (Do you know this man?)"

"No, Officer, never met him before!" Lionel replied hastily in English. It was the truth.

The soldier moved to the opposite passenger. "Do you know this man?"

"N-nehi! (N-no!)", stammered the man, terrified.

The soldier reached Milien and shouted the same question. Mad Max and Lionel prayed silently, hoping that for once Parasite would not mess up. Their hearts stopped beating for a moment.

"No, Sir! Not travelling with him, Sir!" replied Parasite firmly, with not even a tremble in his voice. He could feel the pack of *hash* pressing down on his intimate parts, but having learned the hard way how to survive challenging situations, his answer was convincing enough.

The officer moved on to scream at the next row of passengers. Finally, the naked monk and all his belongings were dragged back to the military post. Max and Lionel's flat-lined hearts resumed pumping again. They looked at Parasite. His face was as white as a well-pressed bedsheet. All the soldiers had left the bus.

A now cool Max whispered in Lionel's ear, "I hope he didn't pee in his pants onto our charas!" Lionel, still shaken, could not laugh.

At last the bus moved on and Parasite leaned over to them. Max couldn't hold back any longer. "Did you pee in your pants?" he asked with morbid curiosity.

Milien shook his head in denial. A sigh of relief! Parasite has not rendered their charas useless by contamination; it was well wrapped in plastic, but one never knew...

Parasite kept on, "Sitting next to him I could smell the big load of hashish under his robes. That's what I was trying to communicate to you!"

It turned out that the stripped-down monk had been audacious enough to board the bus to Peshawar with an astonishing ten kilos of black Afghani taped all over his body, well hidden under his loose, all-covering blood-red robes. Obviously, the guards had got a whiff too. Although it was carefully sealed in plastic, Afghani stuff is strong-smelling and potent, and our unfortunate monk had not accounted for the exceptional heat that day, which intensified the smell and caused his downfall.

In retrospect, considering they had looked straight into the barrel of a Kalashnikov, the trio considered themselves, once again, lucky. But again, the situation was paradoxical: one of three Pakistanis perhaps smokes charas, yet no foreigner can carry dope into or across Pakistan. Here was another of those wonderful countries where this offense could land the ignorant traveller in the worst prisons for many years. The punishment in Pakistan could be even worse than in Turkey, and there were terrifying rumours circulating of occasional death sentences carried out for the crime of drug smuggling.

The three friends were filled with sympathy for the tragic fate of their hapless fellow passenger, caught before their very eyes. The magnitude of his crime, seen from the Pakistani authorities' point of view, had landed him in this situation. On the bright side though, the man had saved them; the soldiers, concerned and busy with this big haul, had neglected to search anyone else. Here again was another vivid example of how thin the line could be between uninterrupted life-flow and ultimate catastrophe.

The nerve-wracking episode had shaken Lionel so forcefully that he decided he had played Russian roulette long enough. He had to quit smuggling dope across borders once and for all. His baggage of luck was fraying too fast at the edges and probably wouldn't last much longer. If they were ferrying big loads for money, like the monk had been doing, it might eventually have been worth the gamble. But to risk a similar conviction for smuggling the single kilogram they carried for their personal consumption was definitely not worth the trouble. It was best to leave this activity to the professionals on the drug route – the local Pakistanis, smuggling half a ton at a time in a truck with no risks taken, having lavishly bribed all the officials on the way; and then reaping immense profits. Lionel and his friends, as well as the ill-fated monk, were foolishly operating at the wrong end of the spectrum. Lionel considered himself an absolute, thoughtless imbecile.

Acting in parallel, there was pushing from the top of his head, a *force* working inside him – the same force that was moving the needle of his inner compass to show him without ambiguity where to head to. The pressure was definitely increasing. It was becoming crystal clear that something on the drug front had to end, *now*. Overcome by a surge of anguish at the thought of his stoned days coming to an end, Lionel foolishly resisted the change.

On a dizzy verge where all disguises fail
And human mind must abdicate in Light
Or die like a moth in the naked blaze of Truth,
He stood compelled to a tremendous choice.
All he had been and all towards which he grew

Must now be left behind or else transform
Into a self of That which has no name. [III-1]

What of Pakistan? Well, there was no time for exploration. Feeling too insecure to linger or roam, the trio chose to move on. The discomfort was not caused by the people but the political situation of the time, which, like in Iran, was unstable and volatile. To make matters worse, India and Pakistan were on the brink of war and there were rumours circulating of a possible closure of the border.

Lionel had to admit to himself that the Khyber arrest affair had seriously rattled him and he thought they should move into India as soon as possible. From what they had heard from returning travellers, there was no rigorous law enforcement going on there unless you were a large-scale dope smuggler. They mostly left the casual consumer alone and in peace.

Sadly, he had left Shangri-La behind, but India, in those days, still held a reputation for being a land of tolerance.

9
HOME

1971, NORTH INDIA, WAGAH-ATTARI BORDER

Without a moment of rest, they kept travelling through Pakistan, from Peshawar to Lahore, and the final leg of this tense journey, to the Indian border. At last they arrived by train — an authentic British Raj period train hauled by a screeching and puffing steam engine – at Wagah, the border town on the railway line connecting Lahore, Pakistan, to Amritsar, India. The train didn't cross the border. Cows lazily grazed on a two-kilometre long stretch of track, possibly closed since Partition. The border had to be crossed on foot.

Thus, Lionel and his friends got off the train at the Wagah railway station, on the Pakistani side. They walked to the border post and in the course of an hour, made their way past the Pakistani bureaucracy. Then they hauled their backpacks on again and walked the long stretch of no-man's-land between the border posts. Sweating profusely, they arrived at the Indian side of life. There, they repeated the process over another hour with the Indian version of the same bureaucracy. It all looked like another iteration of the Torkham exercise, even more complicated and with more trekking involved. The escalating political tension between the two countries might have been the cause for the extended ordeal.

Wondering if they were still in control of all their senses by the end, they were allowed to proceed. They tramped the fair distance to an identical train, this time Indian, its engine steaming and at a standstill at an identical railway station, called Attari, but Indian. It all looked the same as the other side of the border, but it was now Indian.

That was in itself a strange experience. As if the entire Partition construct had been an absurd exercise in futility, having divided at great cost a country which was historically and culturally one. Today, as then, the Muslim population of India exceeds that of Pakistan, thus defeating the very purpose of the operation. An ill-conceived political scheme, nurtured by the division-savvy British on the eve of their departure from the sub-continent, and heavy with unfortunate consequences that would be far-reaching in the scale of time.

At this time, Lionel's life journey was reaching a crucial point, as crucial as the disturbing dream he had experienced in Corfu. Except that this was no dream but a real-life event.

He was dog-tired and utterly exhausted. He had crossed the no-man's-land. He had braved and conquered all the border officer's cubicles. He walked past that last, red-and-white striped barrier of the Indian check-post, manned by an impeccable, smiling Jawan dressed in a crisp, colourful uniform, his turban featuring an impressive red-and-yellow crest, spread like a Japanese fan.

Lionel marked his first step on Indian soil.

He looked around. From a purely physical stand point, it looked like an exact replica of the Pakistani side. He saw the same trees – *neem* and banyan. He saw the same little barracks housing the guards. Another railway track; another similar-looking train; the British Raj influence on both sides. Yet, everything was subtly different... He took a deep breath; it felt like honey. Everything shone and sparkled around him. One thought, and only one, came to his mind: I AM HOME!

He could not believe it! But yes, there was no mistake, he was home!

He entered the railway station and sat down on a wooden bench on the platform. The Station Master came and sitting beside him, began a conversation, asking him the customary 'Where are you from?' With elegance he offered Lionel a cup of tea, served in a white china cup set on a white saucer, and some biscuits.

At last, and for the first time in his entire life, Lionel felt at home. Instant recognition. Everything was at once scintillating and intimately known.

For a while he just sat there, choking on his own tears.

He had not planned for this, never expected it, not even hoped for it. He had simply followed the guy who didn't want to travel alone. Lionel realised that he was still carrying in his backpack the book he had found in the trash pile down in the squatter's house basement in Rome. He had kept reading the book, and admitted to feeling a kind of curiosity about that place referred to as *La Ville Blanche,* in India, and nothing more. But in that moment, something of an altogether different magnitude had happened: so unexpected, so unthought-of. It was like Destiny having grabbed him by his long hair and forced him to turn his head in another direction. Maybe Destiny was just playing with Max, the Station Master, Parasite and him.

Even as the experience slowly faded, he sat stunned by the formidable mystery of the universe and all these intertwined beings. He realised so much remained hidden, yet to be revealed, and that he had much to learn.

And perhaps, to this end, he had reached the right land…

10
AN UNFITTING BACTERIUM

1966, FRANCE, LES CÉVENNES

Here was the strangest thing.

Lionel had travelled some ten thousand kilometres in the last few months, finally reaching a remote land where everything should have been alien to him – the people, their looks, skin colour, the way of dressing; habits, religions and languages; the culture, the landscape, the climate; even the animals – monkeys, camels and elephants. Monkeys? Elephants? In Europe, one had to go to a zoo or a circus to find an elephant or monkey. Here, there were elephants and camels standing at the traffic lights! The subcontinent's topographical features too, displayed an enormous scale: rivers like the Ganges, as wide as a sea, the giant Himalayan mountains (highest on planet Earth), the seemingly infinite, flat, mind-dulling plains.

But he was home.

All these creatures surrounding him, including the shocking multitude of humans, living in such close proximity, something he could never have imagined, were friendly to him and welcoming.

This was when he realised that in his whole life till that day, he had always been a stranger, a pariah, wherever he was, even in his hometown. All this time he had been an unfitting bacterium, a trifling, exasperating growth on a society allergic to him and his kind. Wherever he went, people and systems wanted to get rid of him or squash him, as if he were some kind of irritating bug.

When he had reached seventeen years of age, he found himself in a new college, lost in some little populated, remote mountains in the South of France, *les Cévennes*. His mother had discovered the place for him (befitting a PHS adolescent), and he really liked it. He had the best intentions of being well-behaved. They had overlooked his record of having been expelled from so many previous schools, always for the same reason – insubordination. His mother was happy, and he was happy. The atmosphere was free and relaxed, ahead of its time in terms of student freedom; one that encouraged self-responsibility. Students above the age of sixteen, boys and girls, could go after study hours to a little café – Koko's, at the centre of the campus, for a coffee or non-alcoholic drink, smoke a cigarette and listen to nascent rock music (it was 1966). This was tolerated in a positive, open-minded way, and cute adolescent romances flourished at Koko's.

But back in Lionel's room, and not at all tolerated by the college authorities, was a bottle of rum which he kept hidden in the depths of his cupboard. No one knew except his roommate. In his quest of knowledge, Lionel set out to experiment; he wanted to understand what it was like to be drunk. He considered it a legitimate research project. Thus he began attending quite a few classes – maths, philosophy and so on – drunk.

And this was how, at an early age, he learned (and later mastered), the art of behaving sober in an intoxicated state.

Unfortunately, in the middle of these experimentations, something unexpected happened, which turned out to be reason enough for him to be expelled in the middle of the school term. Something the college stewardship perceived as so outrageously blasphemous that it couldn't wait; he was to be executed at once, against a wall, shot without judgement. It was equivalent to what they called in wartime, a summary execution.

One fateful day, the Principal of the school died. He had been unwell for a few days and then, a massive stroke brought him down suddenly. This was a catastrophe for the school. Classes were disrupted, and the funeral was announced for two days later. It was a scorching day in May. All the students and teachers were standing in the schoolyard, lined up and attired in their Sunday best. There were no trees to cast any merciful shade as they stood in the mid-day sun. They waited for the black hearse to bring the corpse to the village church for the service, and afterwards, to the adjoining cemetery.

The hearse came and the casket was loaded into it. Yet no one moved. They waited, and waited... sweating under the blistering sun. It became known that one teacher, the Professor of Geography, was missing. The entire assembly, including the college staff, began to get restless. The situation grew increasingly unbearable. The inner pressure was building up not only in Lionel, but all those gathered. Social convention and etiquette demanded that they remain still and silent, mourning the death of their beloved Principal. He had been a nice man, and Lionel had liked him too. For once, no one had ever dragged him into the Principal's office to face trial, as had happened everywhere else. But it was surely time to be sensible and move everyone into the shade till the geo-sucker showed up? Sweating in his navy-blue suit, Lionel considered leaving the aligned rows of students to go over to a teacher and request relief. The whole scene reminded him of the classic movie *Bridge on the River Kwai,* where the Japanese camp commander tortures the prisoners by keeping them standing at attention under the tropical sun till they collapse. If this went on much longer, they could have a casualty here too.

The boy next to Lionel was a close friend, with the same liberal-minded tendencies, if somewhat less radical. Lionel looked at him out of sweat-tinged eyes and gave him a meaningful nod. They focussed their attention on the road leading from the village to the school, where the sound of an approaching car was audible. From afar, it looked like one of those common Peugeot 203 models. Their whole attention turned towards the incoming vehicle – the missing teacher was arriving at full speed, pedal on the metal. The inner mounting pressure, sweat and all, had had no time to subside.

At first they wondered what on earth was on the roof rack of the Peugeot, protruding front and back. Then as the car came close, they realised that three ridiculously long pairs of skis were rigged on the roof-rack. It was somehow utterly preposterous. Like some absent-minded professor had mixed up the times, the events, the seasons, the temperatures, and had forgotten that he was arriving at a solemn occasion, the funeral of his respected boss. Maybe the car had not been used since the winter before and had refused to start, hence the late arrival. Who knew? Lionel and his friend gazed in disbelief at the unspeakable incongruity of the scene unfolding before them – the well-aligned assembly on one side, and a guy equipped for winter sports on the other, at a funeral in the middle of a late May heat wave.

There was complete silence.

The door of the Peugeot 203 opened abruptly. Like a puppet springing from a box, the dazed teacher, dressed not in politically correct black, but casual attire – a bright red chequered shirt and heavy trekking boots – stepped out and joined the sombre ranks. The entire congregation was aghast!

For Lionel and his friend this was the last straw. They looked at each other and their eyes locked. In that moment they knew they would pee into their sweat-stained, black, freshly ironed pants, unless, unless… They cracked up with laughter. It burst from them like the million gallons of water when a dam breaks, with no chance of control or restraint. All the accumulated tension was released. Ah! It felt good!

Lionel and his laughing friend understood that this laughter did not befit the serious business of a funeral in progress, and would seem blasphemous. That thought only made matters worse. The well-aligned group of students and teachers around them lost its alignment as they shuffled closer to hiss sharp reprimands: 'For God's sake, stop it!'

Both boys harboured a painfully clear awareness inside their laughing selves that their behaviour was totally out of sync with the solemn occasion, but that thought only increased the urge to laugh even more. The entire congregation stared at them with disdain. That too, made it worse. The hissing continued; so too did the laughing. As the hearse finally started on its solemn journey, the assembly settled into a funeral march behind it – a funeral march of the worst kind, for two members of the procession remained engulfed in insane mirth all the way to the church.

Lionel thought, *Oh Lord, I can't help it! If you exist, please be with us! You know that there is nothing malicious in this!*

The Lord in his all-embracing love understood perfectly. Less so the college authorities. When it was all over, there was no summons to the disciplinary council, no judgement, only a straight dispatch to the firing squad, blindfolded, back to the wall.

The very next day Lionel's father arrived, summoned to the school (*déjà vu*), all the way from his home five hundred kilometres away, to take his errant son out of the school. Meanwhile, Lionel could not attend class and had to remain confined to his room at all times, like a pest.

Lionel was irate. In his mind, he did not deserve this. But then, could the whole thing not have been some strange, instant karmic retribution for his experiments with being drunk in class? Who knows? Having abused the exceptional freedom he had been offered? Rightly punished, but for the wrong reasons?

In an amusing observation, his friend did not get expelled. Why? He had been laughing as hard. As usual, the teachers had concluded that Lionel was the ring leader and hence the harsh, instant banishment was meted out to him.

In the end, it amounts to the Establishment exorcising its fear of the unknown, the unconventional, the non-aligned. The social system with all its conventions, its self-perpetuating ground rules, was only expressing fear. Fear of being confronted with something that did not fit in. So, in an act of self-defence, the system did its best to eliminate that which did not fit the conventions, like an organism getting rid of an unknown germ, be it detrimental to health or not.

Lionel had spent his entire existence being that kind of bacterium.

11
CALL OF THE ROAD

1966-1968, FRANCE & SWITZERLAND

Blowing it all up

It took a long time and many tacks through an ocean of possibilities to find direction. Having been expelled from so many schools and colleges, Lionel had to decide in which direction to proceed. What interested him? Where was the *sparkle of life*? Maybe something in him even wanted to make his parents happy after all their successive disappointments.

Lionel worked hard in his last year in college to earn his baccalaureate, ending at last those wretched schooldays he hated. Being a university student appealed to him and seemed to offer a new life much closer to freedom than the past educational years. Thanks to his diligence, he gained admission to an Engineering High School in a university town in Lorraine. It specialised in Information Technology (the early beginnings of it) and Aerospace. He had a keen interest in the subjects, but found the approach boring. For some unfathomable reason, he could never adjust to the normal systems of academic education. It just didn't work for him. He always ended up with the distressing feeling he was wasting his time, wasting his life. He wanted more.

The next wake-up call came on the day when, desperate to kill his boredom, he went in idle fashion to see a movie called *Blow Up*, directed by the iconic Michelangelo Antonioni. The film became a contemporary classic, calling into question the boundaries of the Real in our day-to-day life. When

Lionel came out of the theatre, there was a new intense feeling in him that he could look at the world differently. His mind had been hovering in stasis, but now he realised that life as we perceive it, could as well pass for an illusion. What exists, and what doesn't? This was amounting to a quasi-oriental way of looking at life.

But Maya is a veil of the Absolute;
A Truth occult has made this mighty world:
The Eternal's wisdom and self-knowledge act
In ignorant mind and in the body's steps. [X-1]

This question became powerful enough to make him interrupt his engineering studies. He realised he did not want to be an engineer; had never wanted this. He knew it was his parents' dream, not his, that one day he would get a job in some prestigious company such as IBM, British Petroleum or the like, or even better, take over the family business. To make money, get married (preferably within the PHS community), settle down and have children, was the logical progression in their mind. But, to Lionel's way of thinking, this picture of life was an unbearable prospect. He shuddered at the thought of such an unromantic, ordinary future.

He could not conceive living his life based on the ideas of other people. He had to find his own way. In his student room he had taped to the wall, a quote in large, flourishing type, from an intriguing oriental book he had just discovered, called the *Bhagavad Gita*. It read:

Better is one's own law of works, though faulty,
Than an alien law, well wrought out.

Relaxing on his bed in his tiny room just below the roof at the Pension Choley, a posh student's home, hands clasped behind his head, he mused on these words. He would make sure they became his ground rule in life. Given time, it became clear that the engineering path was not for him, at least not in the conventional way.

Under the *Blow Up* influence, in another dramatic turn of mood, Lionel took a decision to study photography. Somewhat childish, but again, he wanted more.

Thus, into his life tiptoed the Swiss period.

It was a beautiful place on Lake Geneva, with a magnificent view on the Alps in the distance, and the kind of peace permeating an entire country that had not known war in centuries. That's where his school of photography was located; the playground for his latest fancy. Having overcome the tough entrance examination, he was ready to settle into his new, self-chosen student life.

Satisfied, he got a place to stay a stone's throw away from the scenic lake shore. His caring mother (in what was to be her last intervention in his life), had concocted a student room in the house of an old lady, a spinster, fussy like a cat, who insisted on total silence, no music, no visitors (male or female), and more important than anything else, no pubic hair left in the bathtub. In this smothering, restrictive environment, Lionel readied himself to get started on the three years required to get his Photographer diploma. Predictably, he soon left the old witch's cage to share an apartment with a fellow student, where loud music could be played and wild parties held with impunity.

Shamefully though, he entered a new phase of life (everything was moving fast in these early years). Soon after he started the course, his attendance showed a lack of enthusiasm. As usual, he had trouble adapting to the rigid academic system, and his new lifestyle brought different priorities. He still attended lectures and classes, learning as well as he could, but his primary interest was elsewhere – where he could find the spark of life. It was in the spring of 1968, when the winds of change started blowing, first in France, then spreading all over Europe.

Lionel was not the only one sensing the absurdity of excessive consumerism and wishing to revolt against a system perceived as oppressive. A fresh rejuvenating wave of rebellion was sweeping over the youth, and in May '68, the students' revolution erupted in Paris. Although Lionel supported the cause in his heart, he did not take active part; his individualistic nature would always resist involvement in collective movements.

Meanwhile, the spirit of freedom and experimentation was conquering youngsters in Europe and America in an ever-widening sweep. In music, great gigs were taking place, featuring future superstars – Led Zeppelin, Santana, Pink Floyd, the Rolling Stones, Jim Morrison with The Doors. Morrison in particular, influenced Lionel deeply because he was burning so wildly.

I see myself as a huge fiery comet, a shooting star.
Everyone stops, points up and gasps 'Oh look at that!'
Then — whoosh, I'm gone...
And they will never see anything like it ever again...
And they won't be able to forget me – ever.

James D. Morrison

It was a revolution and its impact on youth phenomenal. Parents tried to shrug it off with remarks like: *Well, it will wear out soon. It's just another fast-fading fad.* Deep down, they were terrified because they could not comprehend what was happening to their children. But the children knew that fifty years later and more, the indelible imprint left on history by these artists and their work would be unequivocally acknowledged as classics in music. None in the elder generation then believed that the words *Classic* and *Rock* could ever be associated.

This went hand-in-hand with the discovery of recreational drugs of all kinds, from mild hashish and marijuana, amphetamines and other bizarre chemicals, to powerful hallucinogens like LSD. The more addictive substances – opium, morphine and heroin – soon followed. As a by-product of this movement, there was an unfortunate proportion of collateral damage, but this wild wind carried an entire generation towards the next millennium, setting its deep impress on the decades to come.

An entire year flew by and Lionel was always in a rush to tackle real life, not an academic facsimile. He decided he had learned enough theory and now needed to find some field work. He would always doubt the value of some elegant piece of paper, framed and hung on the wall; that a diploma could make a difference in life. Taking a leap of faith, he sought a job as a photographer and got his first employment at the Studio Molinari, in Paris. This was not his city of predilection, but he was determined to earn his living and put an end to parental support. Since the *Blow Up* experience, the conventional pattern of life had seemed obsolete. He observed the world and himself as if he was his own witness. Inside each individual was the chemistry of life – brewing, cooking, fermenting. All it needed was a minor incident on the outside for something undefinable to be triggered.

In his case, the blow-out occurred in two successive salvoes, in a two-stage crescendo, with a pause in-between.

Phase One

The incident had happened a few years earlier when he was about sixteen. The Kalmer family had gone to Paris for the weekend, crammed into a Peugeot 404. His father was a hard core Peugeot devotee, and he was at the wheel of his latest acquisition, with Lionel's mom sitting next to him. Lionel sat in the back, bored, along with his younger brother. The two adolescents studying in different boarding schools, it was one of those rare occasions when the family was complete. In spite of this worldly separation, the two brothers were aware of a strong kinship bonding them. With just a few years difference in age, when circumstances prompted, they would always turn into a tight-knotted, powerful team.

They looked at each other with the kind of silent expression that screams, *what the Hell are we doing here?!*

The 404 cruised along the River Seine, on the Quai de Seine. There were bridges spanning the river, under which one could see the occasional *jaja*-addicted *clochard* taking a nap. The car stopped at a traffic light, purring idling in the front row, facing the zebra pedestrian crossing — and suddenly, in blew the wind of destiny.

A group of six young guys and girls traversed the street, just in front of the car. They had rucksacks on their backs, frying pans and cooking pots hanging to the side, making *clonk-clonk* sounds, and they all had long hair! Boys as well as girls. The girls could hardly be distinguished from the boys, wearing the same dirty jeans and worn-out jackets. One girl had a guitar slung over her shoulder. And they were laughing, in joyous crystal voices. They were young and dynamic, not aged, desperate, drunk *clochards,* and they briskly crossed the street with youthful energy.

During that brief instant of glory, they were as splendid as the Sun. Lionel had never seen anything like this.

The entire appearance lasted only thirty seconds, while they sprang from behind a corner, crossed the road in their relaxed fast stride, reached the opposite pavement, and disappeared down the stairs leading to the Seine. There was a *légèreté* about them – a lightness of being. They were just themselves – untainted, pure, free. And in that same moment, Lionel's soul screamed to be part of that scene instead of sitting, bored as hell, in the back seat of the family Peugeot. It lasted an instant, then they were gone.

It had felt like a dream. But it was so painful that he found it hard to breathe afterwards and he had tears in his eyes.

Later, he came to know that this generation of tramp-like, nomadic youth – the authentic precursors of the better-known Hippies – had been given a label, for society never feels at ease as long as an emerging section of it remains undefined; they were referred to as Beatniks – the beautiful, aspiring Beat Generation, the first wild and fearless children in line for transformation. The Beat was a movement said to be influenced, among others, by American writer Jack Kerouac, author of the immortal essay, *On the Road,* published as far back as the '50s.

These few illuminated seconds were enough to distil a clear vision inside Lionel's head, or was it in his heart? Around these girls and boys he had seen a love-light sparkling vividly, and he had received this as a clear message: *Yes, this is for me!*

In that instant, Lionel realised with utter certitude that he did not want to become an engineer, or indeed *become* anything else for that matter. All he wanted and yearned for was a taste of this sparkling freedom.

> *...the only people for me are the mad ones, the ones who are mad to live, mad to talk, mad to be saved, desirous of everything at the same time, the ones who never yawn or say a commonplace thing, but burn, burn, burn like fabulous yellow Roman candles exploding like spiders across the stars and in the middle you see the blue centerlight pop and everybody goes 'Awww!'.*
>
> *Jack Kerouac, On the Road*

But the machinery of life insisted on grinding on. The red light at the crossing turned green, and the car moved on. Obviously, he couldn't say a word to his parents. He had to digest it alone, the tremendous impact this vision had had on him.

Six months passed, or was it a year? Lionel did not forget that moment of light, but could not at the time make the bold and drastic move of abandoning his present life altogether. He was still too young and dependent on family, from both financial and emotional points of view. Ironically, he had not yet realised that the financial part didn't matter, since he was yearning for the life of a tramp!

12
EMBRACING THE ROAD

1967, THE NETHERLANDS, AMSTERDAM

Phase Two

It was the summer holidays. His parents had had a fight over God knows what. His brother had been sent to a youth camp while it was decided that Lionel and his father would go to Holland for a vacation. So there he was again, sitting bored in the car – a newer Peugeot – his father driving, the only noticeable difference this time being that Lionel was sitting in the front seat. His mother was not there, thankfully, because there would otherwise have been endless arguments. Besides, she would have fought like a tigress to prevent him from doing what he did a little later.

Lionel and his father went to all the usual sightseeing spots, like a pair of typical tourists. It was boring – all of it. They visited countless museums, more museums, and yet another museum was coming up, this one the *Vincent Van Gogh Museum*. Oh, boy! Was there no end to this?

They parked the car, bought tickets at the entrance and walked in. To his own amazement, once inside the museum, Lionel was suddenly jolted wide awake. The moment he had his first glimpses of the original Van Gogh paintings, his world changed. Here were the originals, the genuine thing, the actual canvas in front of which the artist had stood, had worked upon during long, gestating, aspiring hours.

Published reproductions of an artist's work may convey the aesthetics, the message, the balance of the artwork perhaps, but no reproduction can pass on the *light-force* that emanates from Vincent's paintings. It was even more of a shock because Lionel was expecting nothing of the kind. He was just an atheist adolescent, bored to death, who had been dragged into a museum. For the first time in his life he was seeing something he later elected to call 'the Divine', a vibration emanating from a source that some may have called God, though Lionel did not use the name. He despised the 'God' word, worn by centuries, if not millennia, of abusive utilisations, interpretations and manipulations. But whatever it was, it pulsated within those paintings, hitting him straight in the chest like a lance of light. It was breathtaking, and he stood in awe.

In a hall bathed in natural daylight provided by a transparent glass ceiling, the Van Gogh paintings were sparsely displayed on the walls. In awe, Lionel could see another light, not a 'normal' light but a light that did not belong to the physical world, a light that overlapped the material object made of canvas and paint. And this light sparkled for an inner sense of vision infinitely more sensitive than mere sight, going straight to the heart and caressing the soul. It could not be captured by artifice, photographed or reproduced; no one could point a finger at this light; either one saw it, or one did not.

Some would never see it.

Such is the power of a true work of art: to incarnate and express not just beauty and harmony, but much more – the light that originates from the Realm of the Gods, the light of the Over-mind. And perhaps, one day we will see emerging in art, even higher planes of consciousness.

Was that moment of grace in the Van Gogh Museum a factor leading to the events that followed a day later? Lionel would believe so. A calm had come down on him, a peace which grew from having realised he had been right all along in his premonitions; there was more than what met the eye. How deep it went he had no idea. But something in him had disconnected itself from the chains of consequences; he knew he could never live a life of freedom if he was not free within.

Driving at a leisurely pace through Amsterdam, Lionel and his father had reached the Dam, a well-known square in the heart of the city, featuring circular stairs around a tall monolithic monument. They were cruising along the periphery when it hit him like the entry into another world. Scattered all over the Dam, there were dozens, hundreds perhaps, of the long-haired Beatniks or Hippies — whatever the label was he didn't care — just like those he had caught a glimpse of in Paris, along the Seine. Relaxing on their sleeping bags, playing the guitar, smoking joints, trading things, reading, discussing, hugging, kissing! There it was again: this small world was sparkling like the bubbles in a glass of champagne, only there was light inside the tiny bubbles instead of gas. In Lionel's mind and heart, invading all his gates of perception, he heard a loud cry: *This is for me!*

He turned to his father, driving past unimpressed, and with no trace of hesitation, said, "Can you stop the car a minute, please?"

Not knowing what this was about, his father complied. Lionel grabbed his bag, opened the door, got out of the car and through the open window, addressed his dad, "You go to the hotel. I will sleep here."

The poor man almost had a heart attack on the spot. "No, no, no! This is ridiculous, get back in the car and come with me! You can't do this!"

But Lionel insists. He is adamant.

His father sees his unbreakable determination and yells, "You are out of your mind! What has got into you?"

Something within Lionel was smiling. Maybe he had got out of his old mind indeed! Something nice was getting into him, keeping him calm. He replied in a firm tone, "Look here, you go on to your hotel and see whatever you want to see. I am getting out and I will sleep and live here. I will meet you again after a few weeks, okay?"

His devastated father realised this whole thing had come to a point of no return. He kept mumbling about the madness of unpredictable adolescents and then, showing a trace of fatherly concern, took out his wallet with intention to offer Lionel a wad of notes.

Lionel raised his hand in a gesture of rejection, objecting, "No, no, I don't want your money! I don't need your money. That's the point."

Thus did Lionel live and sleep on the Dam. In the following days, his father even came twice to check how his son was faring. He had broken the news to the boy's mother on the phone, and after a severe blasting, she had given him specific instructions.

But one day, returning to the Dam, he found his son gone.

Years later, Lionel realised he must have been a cruel child to his parents, who had been doing their best to give him a proper education. Yet what was their reward? Their son's only ambition in life was to become a wretched tramp!

The new life had a rhythm, a pattern to it. Every morning at 6 a.m., the fire engines came in and everyone had to pack up and leave. The entire area was flushed and cleaned. Soon the warm sun dried it again and after a while, they all returned.

After a few days of this, Lionel met a boy and a girl, and they ganged up to hitch-hike to Denmark, and then Sweden. In Copenhagen, on the wharf leading to the ferry that crossed the strait to Malmö, Sweden, they met this bloke with long hair, jeering face, wearing a faded denim jacket, who distributed packets of cigarettes to smuggle onto the ferry. It was some kind of legal smuggling, linked to a different rate of taxation; each passenger was allowed to take in a certain quantity of cigarettes into Sweden. The guy gave them each five cartons (the maximum permitted), and they understood that all this was well known to the customs staff. Under the tolerant and watchful eyes of the authorities, they sailed with the tobacco load to Sweden. On arrival, they received their share from the pirate operation, and had some pocket money to go on with their journey to Stockholm.

The Sweden excursion was short. Denmark, with its unparalleled freedom and spirit of tolerance, had made an impression on Lionel, so he bade farewell to his friends. A week later, having returned to Copenhagen (same ferry but no cigarettes), he came across a nascent hippie commune, within which he mingled for a while. There was something remarkable happening here in Denmark, which, from a social point of view, was very much ahead of its time, when hippie communes were sprouting all over Europe. This was in stark contrast to his life experiences in France and other European countries. In Paris, the police were hunting down marginal youth, just for the crime of wearing long hair. But here, he found a friendly, positive atmosphere. Not only was there no Government interference, but the municipality of Copenhagen provided them with social aid in the form of free apartment buildings to live in; not five-star, but decent, and in a non-posh area that attracted no high value in real estate. They were not only left in peace but (unimaginably!), received a Government allowance towards the basic needs of life. It was a small allowance, but a kind, thoughtful gesture indicative of a diametrically opposite social attitude from what Lionel was used to.

Officialdom's attitude in Paris or Rome was: *These brats are perverted, bad rowdies; we must tame them and teach them a lesson, preferably in jail.*

In Denmark, it was more like: *What's wrong with our children? We have to help them and give ourselves time to understand why they behave like this; let's give them some freedom to do their experiments and watch the outcome.*

What a world of difference!

This was an interesting phase in the experiment of finding alternative ways of living together in a commune. Lionel shared the humble room of a young fellow named Tommy, who tailored those colourful dresses that were *en vogue* then in the posh hippie circles (true hippies wore genuine rags because they were broke). Tommy himself was the living embodiment of the new fashion, with his long, blond Viking hair tied with a red bandanna, patched jeans and furred jacket, ornate with multicolour ribbons and laces. A fringed leather purse hung from his shoulder. There was always a *chillum* inside, and one or two packets of original *Ganesh beedies,* imported from India.

By character, Lionel was a hardened individualist. He never felt he truly belonged to any group, clan or party. He loved to relate to individuals, but always found it difficult to integrate himself as a cog in a collective machine. However, he appreciated the atmosphere he had discovered in this commune – the peaceful togetherness, the sharing of whatever little one had to offer. It possessed something of the new consciousness that was attempting to manifest itself in the world, perhaps indicative of a golden age yet to come. There was renewed hope in mankind, along with a belief in simple values like honesty, simplicity, compassion, and turning away from greed and excessive consumerism.

And love was acknowledged as a powerful creative force.

A month later, give or take a week, since time had lost its meaning, Lionel had fulfilled his need to live this free-flowing life. He had embraced the glimpse of sparkling light in that moment on the Dam in Amsterdam; he had kept up with the signs and was glad for the enriching experience that had followed, like a test run for a more radical migration to come. He hitch-hiked back to France, to his small town in Lorraine, and the house improperly called 'home'.

His parents heaved a sigh of relief as they opened the door to him. He was intact and had not gone mad.

One thing he had grasped with certitude from this brief experiment was that all that was happening among the controversial youth during the years around '68, was sowing the seeds of something destined to grow in the perhaps far-off future. It was a key period in the flow of time. The Beat Generation had the unique privilege of being the early pioneers riding the crest of this wave of new consciousness which swept the world in its first burst of wild frenzy.

It was often anything but a smooth ride, though.

13
UNIVERSAL ONENESS

1971, NORTH INDIA, BENARES

Merging with River Ganga

They rattled on by train – Attari, Amritsar, Old Delhi. Good old-fashioned steam engines *tchook-tchooking* at a slow pace, spitting clouds of black soot, stopping at every station on the way, allowing plenty of time to watch and absorb the *alien-though-intimate* scene. Seated on the foot-step of the carriage, door wide open, Lionel became immersed in this world of new sensations; overwhelmed by the scale of everything. The broad gauge train carriage itself was almost twice the width of an European train, packed with people, luggage, bags piled everywhere... There were bars at the windows (which explained the newspapers reporting hundreds of fatalities each time a train derailed), and the bogs at both ends of the carriage stank terribly.

But it was only one of a million smells assailing his senses in a mad succession of fleeting whiffs: spices in baskets, the sweat of the crowd, jasmine and coconut oil from the ladies' hair, pats of cow dung splashed on the walls to dry and use as fuel, red dust and coal smoke, all wrapped together in the air drafts traversing the train. Destiny had been whirling around him all the time, and in that timeless moment, she had caught him in her arms, squeezing him, leaving him breathless.

The team was still around, including Max, who met all Lionel's expenses en route and Lionel returned the favour by making himself available as Max's shrink, displaying a benign smile whenever he began howling, for the umpteenth time, about how he would never see his mother or girlfriend again. Parasite was there too, forever sticking to him like a well-chewed blob of chewing gum. And surprise, a true gentleman had joined the party – a Frenchman who had been on their trail since Kabul. Lionel had been watching him on the decorated bus from Jalalabad to Lahore, and no doubt he had noticed the casual glances. Unobtrusively he got closer, landing in their midst like an UFO from a different planet to their untidy, tramp-style, long-haired beatnik environment.

But the point was that the wave of new consciousness was just looking for instruments to help spread itself. It would sweep away whoever was ready to ride it, regardless of origin, profession, colour or class. It did not care about such matters, it had no preference, it would just pour a small portion of itself into any vessel apt to receive it. And lo! The chosen ones would cross half the world on wings of joy.

But why did this particular man stick out? Well, imagine a Government employee stepping out of his office in any Paris street, well dressed in black, impeccably ironed pants and white shirt, beige corduroy jacket and well-polished brown leather shoes, but sitting in the back of a country bus, next to the goats, on the Kabul-Lahore haul. Hair short and neatly combed. At first the beatniks were speechless. The man carried only a small hand bag, like a diplomat's attaché case. They discovered later that, among other personal articles, he had one of those super-light, super-small, high-tech sleeping bags packed into that case. Something in Lionel admired the man; he smiled at him, and perhaps the man felt he was not being judged for being so different from the usual backpackers.

After a period of respectful, silent co-existence, Lionel addressed him. He was indeed French, and about thirty-five years old. His name was Serge. It transpired in conversation that one day, in his routine-laden, boring government-servant existence, he had decided that enough was enough, and walked out of his office, with just what he had on him – his office clothes, including the corduroy jacket, and his attaché case. On a whim he had bought the special sleeping bag the day before, not yet knowing why. He had enough cash on him, and with minimal equipment, or lack thereof, he went straight to the railway station – *la Gare de l'Est*. With no further ado, without formally ending his job or informing his family, he bought a ticket, walked down to platform number 9, and boarded the Orient Express to Istanbul. Serge enjoyed this new free life in full, making up for the many years of being tied down in boring, clockwork functioning.

Lionel was impressed. He developed a genuine liking for Serge, who came from a different background than the rest of the little group, and yet he was on the same quest.

The motley troupe arrived in Delhi, where one first unnerving impression stuck out. It was the month of April, and the mercury had been rising sharply; an exceptional heat wave had been sweeping across the Indo-Gangetic plain for several days. To call it blazing hot would have been an academic understatement. Flooded with an overdose of sensory input and numbed by the furnace-like heat, after two sleepless nights spent in the Crown Hotel, a cheap den for junkies in Old Delhi, they hastily moved on to Varanasi, then called Benares or Kashi. They hoped that the legendary river Ganges would cool the atmosphere somewhat.

Lionel had insisted on not wasting more low-quality time in Delhi, as he had read and heard a lot about the holy city and had an odd intuition that ancient Kashi had something in store for him. As a student, he had once browsed through an old issue of *National Geographic*, with an extraordinary picture of an amphibian Jeep, and a German Shepherd dog standing on the deck, cruising down the Ganges along the *ghats*. It was one of those images that had remained indelibly etched in his memory.

Maybe those little scattered bits of impressed memory are the faint links, the threads between past and future, at play in the background, weaving together the canvas of life.

The group of four arrived at the Benares railway station at first light. By 6 a.m. they were moving at a slow pace towards the ghats in two cycle-rickshaws, propelled by two equally skinny *rickshaw-wallas*, who sometimes turned back to flash wide, joyful smiles at them.

The town was waking up, but the shops were still closed. When the narrow alley turned into a dead end, the rickshaws came to a halt. They stepped down and the ghats appeared just below them, bathed in the morning light. There, stretched the immense River Ganga, like a brown goddess shimmering with golden reflections, lazily flowing right in front of them. What a sight! For a while Lionel and his friends stood immobile, in awe: none of them had ever seen, or even imagined, such a vast, powerful river. The distant opposite shore was faintly visible through the morning mist, under the violent red-coloured disk of the rising sun. Far away on the left, there was an endless bridge flying across the river, and a long freight-train crawling across it with a never-ending *thud-dud, thud-dud* sound, muffled by the distance and mist.

Down below, where the long flight of steep stairs reached the muddy water, early devotees were already having a bath in the holy river. A line of imposing buildings and temples topping the steps stretched far towards the cremation ghats on the left, and to infinity on the right. Most of these buildings bore the mark of timelessness, flanked by huge walls of enormous stones. Through the multiple orifices, windows, and gates of the buildings, and from loud-speakers located on the roofs, ear-splitting temple music – shrill *shehnai* and wall-shattering drums — saluted the rising of the sun. Pungent odours of incense, flowers, fish, and humid rot swept by, one after the other, or mixed with equal abandon, in the gentle breeze.

All this together turned the panorama into an awesome experience involving all the senses; it seemed to belong to another age, having surged from some undefinable yet somehow known past.

Lionel broke out of this long moment of stupefaction and walked down the steps till he was standing just above the water. There were already a significant number of people taking a dip in the sacred river. Somehow, he felt that this, and only this, was the right thing to do in that moment. He left his bag in the charge of a friendly *jalebi* merchant sitting on a rectangular granite slab under a large umbrella, with his baskets of sweet goodies around him. Lionel took only his towel, and a rectangular, sharp-edged piece of soap – the cheap brown kind reminiscent of hardened molasses. Removing most of his clothes, he kept only a loincloth, as he could see all men were doing (the woman bathing wrapped in their saris looked odd to him).

He went down the steps till he was waist-deep in the murky water, then dipped himself in full in the cold water before proceeding to soap his body thoroughly and vigorously to dissolve twenty years of unwanted life, with all its deeds, stains and sins attached. He placed his piece of soap on a small slab protruding from an adjacent stone wall and, walking down the steps into deeper water, immersed himself completely in the cold current, again and again.

He had the strange feeling that the water of the Ganga was oozing into his body through each and every pore of his skin, producing a kind a sizzling effect, not so much on the surface as reaching deep into his cells. It filled his entire body with a refreshing bliss all the way to the marrow of his bones. It was an amazing, physical feeling he had not expected. He remained in a state of weightlessness in the water for a while longer, savouring the moment and watched the sun getting higher in the sky. The River Ganga was doing her marvellous divine work. Feeling like a new man, he came out, shivering in the brisk morning air, and walked up the steps to where he had left his soap. He looked all around: the soap had vanished.

The river was divine, but mankind was mankind.

Max and the others had decided to check-in and share a room at a small fleabag lodge nestled in a narrow lane parallel to the ghats, just behind the line of temples. It would be a plain bare room with whitewashed walls, where they would each spread their sleeping bag, establishing their private territory of a few square feet. Lionel wanted nothing of this. He had not travelled ten thousand kilometres to reach the mighty River Ganga, only to bury himself in a crowded cement cube with one narrow window looking onto a back alley, and a ceiling fan roaring above his head.

Instead, he kept on walking upstream along the ghats. After a kilometre or two, the buildings on the shore gave way to open ground, sloping directly into the water. There, he found at anchor against the steep clay beach, a tiny houseboat with freshly painted blue side panels. It was not something one could justifiably call a houseboat, no; it was just a small wooden boat with a little roof and a few shutters, empty inside. Lionel thought this boat could be a perfect base for living a life woven in intimacy with that of the Goddess Ganga. The boat owner, an old dark fisherman in a loincloth, greeted him with a wide smile, showing his many missing teeth, and promptly agreed on a bargain. Few travellers came this far upriver, and he was happy to get a guest for his boat.

A narrow gangplank between two mooring lines connected the boat to the shore. There was only a slanted, planked deck, covered with the wooden roof, flanked with side panels that could be lifted and held open with a stick. Nothing else, not even a bed. But he needed nothing. He had his sleeping bag, the Ganga provided free water for bathing, a municipality hand pump stood on top of the slope for (dubious) drinking water, a few bricks topped by a metal grill on the shore served as a kitchen stove. The Ganga also dispensed floating drift wood for the stove. What more could anyone want?

It suited Lionel well. He slept and lived on the boat, and found himself again. He enjoyed being completely alone in his own space, rocking gently on the moderate waves. He cooked his own food on the improvised stove on shore, he lived on rice and *dal*, a few *rotis* prepared on a *tawa*, and curd. He was learning to extract the *rasa*, the nourishing energy out of his scant food.

He enjoyed his solitude, floating on Mother Ganga. The contentment of being on his own was, in part, compounded by successfully bidding farewell to Parasite. He had finally arrived to the point of no return with that guy. Bluntly, Lionel told him: "Look, you have remained glued to me long enough. You are now in India. You have been sticking to my ass like a famished leech all the way. That was fine, but now the time has come for us to part. Be on your own. I want to see you no more."

Though Milien had been shocked and taken aback, perhaps disappointed too, he took it surprisingly well. Lionel saw him grab his little bag, mumbling, "Maybe you're right." He had then walked a few hundred metres to a raised platform under a sacred *neem* tree nearby, set in the centre of a small square, close to the ghats – the home-turf of a group of colourful *sadhus*. He settled there, soon passing the chillum along as if he had always belonged to this landscape. So Milien finally took the responsibility of his life into his own hands, and Lionel, who had been fighting feelings of guilt, realised he had thus rendered him a favour.

They never crossed paths again.

Left to himself on his tiny boat, Lionel discovered and started practicing yoga and *pranayama*. Having read a great deal about the mysteries of Indian sages, he thought that this mountain of literature couldn't have all been built based on pure invention; there had to be some amount of truth behind the tales, and he intended to find out. He felt *he had to know*. So he practised concentration, alone on his little boat, most of the time.

The unique atmosphere of Benares was remarkably conducive to this experiment. He perceived that Kashi was one of those rare blessed spots on Earth, where some strange confluence between the occult and the real created conditions wherein the physical world was separated from the untold dimensions only by the most fragile veil. In this exceptional place, it only required a minor effort from oneself to tear through the veil and glimpse the beyond. The question was though: *Was he really ready for this?* For, in fact, he had not the slightest idea of what immense powers might lie beyond.

Lionel had finally said good-bye to all varieties of dope. It may seem strange that it happened in this place where so many sadhus were roaming everywhere, always carrying with them a well-used chillum made of clay, which they were prone to use at any moment. Yet, something within him was becoming clearer, pointing him to a different path: *I have to explore those realms and further, but through a different gateway*. There was an intensity within him, present at all times, burning like a flame inside, as if nothing else mattered: *I want to know!*

Kashi was such a powerful place! From the moment he had arrived he had fallen under its spell. Something in him was fiercely determined to find out what *that* was. He *had* to dive into the core of what was going on here. There was no doubt in his mind that *something* had been happening in this place for centuries, millennia perhaps. And again, *he had to know*...

One beautiful evening, he had been walking along the ghats, practising an exercise in yogic breathing. When night had settled in full, he had sat down in a quiet corner on top of a ghat to relax, his back close to the massive stone wall of a temple. There he sat, looking out over the seemingly endless river. Despite a thin crescent moon, the water was black and only a few scattered lights shimmering on the opposite bank indicated the far shore.

It was quiet; he was alone; there was nobody nearby. The waves in the river made a gentle, soothing, lapping sound on the ghat steps. The stars overhead were doing their best to sparkle in a pure black sky. Suddenly, with no prelude or warning, out of nowhere, for no apparent or specific reason, there came to him an overwhelming experience.

He had been sitting there thoughtless for a while, when he abruptly realised that *he had become ONE with the entire Universe.* He looked around with the wide-open, love-filled eyes of a newborn child. His mind was blank, no single thought disturbed this timeless moment; there was only a single self-obliterating perception: *I am everything that is around me. I am the Ganga and the boats on the Ganga. I am the ancient stone buildings, and the chants in the temples, and the lapping of the water below; each and every sound, I am. And I am the whole Earth, every atom is me. I am the breeze, the crescent Moon, I am every star in the black sky, and each star is me! The concept of distance, abolished: the whole Universe is here. And the 'I' itself has become irrelevant because I am All, and All is me...*

The crushing revelation translated into one single thought within his absolutely vacant mind: *Oh! Maybe THAT is what they call God?!*

For a while he was filled with inconceivable bliss.

From early childhood, Lionel had always been a hard-core atheist, and maybe he still was, though in a different way now, without borders or limiting concepts. The Divine he sought alright, but without the bullshit attached. Despite this, or possibly *because of it,* he had been granted this moment of Grace, when he had realised the Divine in everything. Formerly, he may have had glimpses, beautiful moments, like seeing the sparkling light in the paintings of van Gogh, the beauty of a snow-covered high mountain, but nothing could compare to *That*. *That* was integral. *That* was all-encompassing. *That* was something he had never experienced. Something he could never have conceived.

For ever love, O beautiful slave of God!
O lasso of my rapture's widening noose,
Become my cord of universal love. [XI-1]

After this mind-shattering experience, life would never be the same again.

O word, cry out the immortal litany:
Built is the golden tower, the flame-child born. [XI-1]

14
THE FALL

1971, NORTH INDIA, CALCUTTA

As mad as can be.

In the aftermath of this stunning moment – of being one with the Universe – Lionel understood he had been relying on drugs for so long for no reason. Charas, acid, opium and more... what on earth for? There was no need for any of this stuff! Drugs were only obscuring the real thing. He could see it now and he knew there would be no turning back to that world of artifice.

A few days went by. Following this experience, life on Lionel's houseboat returned to normal, but something seemed more and more amiss with each passing moment. For the first time, he began to experience a serious instability within his mind, linked to some nagging anxiety deep inside. He couldn't figure out the reason or the source of this anguish.

In an effort to resolve the issue, he convinced his remaining friends, Max and Serge, to move with him to the Buddhist settlement built around the ancient ruins of Sarnath, a small township on the outskirts of Benares. A short ride in a ramshackle country bus took them there. The place was uncrowded compared to the bustling city and appeared peaceful. Peace was what Lionel needed and he thought Sarnath could be a better location to channel the tremendous pressure he felt building up in his head.

Never before, had he been exposed to Buddhist and Tibetan cultures. They fascinated him. Buddhist monks were omnipresent, dressed in the traditional ochre robes, with one shoulder and arm exposed. *Thukpa*, noodles, and *momos* became staple foods. It was a total change of atmosphere. An ancient, massive *stupa* stood near a generously shaded garden. When the sun got lower on the horizon and the heat of the day receded, Lionel enjoyed walking in the Deer Park, remembered as the spot where the Buddha, having received Enlightenment, delivered his first sermon.

Lionel still had the more or less pleasurable company of mad Max and Office-wallah, as they had nicknamed Serge. The latter was quite a character. He had never touched a joint in his whole boring office-life, and it created in him an urge to catch up wildly with everything he had missed out on. The guy was stoned twenty hours a day, yet he remained a gratifying presence, writing and reciting poetry, and doing other extraordinary things with real entertainment value. He was one of those uncommon, interesting people, driven by a great aspiration to learn and change.

They stayed at a shabby government-run guest-house next to the Tibetan temple. The rooms were large, hot and barren, except for a few sagging *charpoys*, and teemed with ferocious mosquitoes at night. The monks held Lionel spellbound while chanting and reciting their holy verses. He could hear them through the window, and sometimes he joined them in the prayer hall at the temple. The simple act of sitting among them bought him a profound peace.

The first few days had been interesting and educative. Unknown cultures had always attracted Lionel, and he yearned to immerse himself within them. However, something new crept into his life, something so unexpected he never could have imagined it would happen to him. Instead of a haven of Buddhist peace, Sarnath soon turned into a scene of nightmare.

Terrified, he realised his mind was slipping away.

Since that experience in Benares, something was pulling with an exacerbated intensity, hammering at him without pity. Viewed in its soft form, it was like a poking finger, telling him in blunt thought waves: *Go! You must go! There is no postponing this; don't even think of it.*

Go? But go where? He didn't understand what this was about; it seemed crazy. He had met so many mad people on the Route, but he had always been the level-headed one. How could such a thing happen to him?

Adding to his frustration, he couldn't go close to any kind of drug; couldn't even touch an inoffensive joint. He had thought this might calm his runaway mind. On the contrary, the effects were out of proportion and disastrous. Was it not the height of irony that here, in the land of omnipresent charas, smoking had turned into a prohibited refuge? But the inner voice kept insisting: *No! You must leave all this behind! Go now!*

Drug chapter closed. He had navigated the story in full, making the best of it for years. He knew now that he was being led towards something else, of an entirely different nature, far more worthy, but also far more perilous.

When he tried to look at it from the perspective of a witness, he envisioned the phenomenon as if some skilled surgeon had cut out a rectangular segment from his cranium, removed the piece of bone and created something like a window, gaping wide open to the beyond. There was no control over this; it *was* wide open; couldn't be closed, period. *Things*, dreaded things, would slip in unchecked, at anytime, anywhere, day and night, awake or sleeping. He could not close that window. His subtle body was no longer his house. Entities from the nether planes of consciousness, that seemed to have grand fun at his expense, visited him.

That's a hard thing to live with when one is as unprepared as Lionel was, without the guidance of a knowledgeable guru and his reassuring physical presence. He was simply going over the edge! Absolute madness gripped him. Was this a sequel to having been too wildly, and for too long, immersed in the world of psychedelic drugs, and then, unprepared and impure, so to speak, been thrown headlong into this overwhelming life-changing experience in Kashi?

That, by contrast, had been the genuine thing – untainted, pure bliss dispersed by the Divine, at the Divine's own choice of time and place, not some chemically-induced pretence at ecstasy. It had been so powerful, so unexpected, and for a while at least, not fully digestible. He felt with every cell in his body that he had to do something, but what? He was being hit on the head again and again, as if there was a sudden urgency, declared by some occult entity intent on guiding his steps.

The realisation that he was turning crazy terrified him, but he could do nothing about it. One night, it became so unbearable that he passed out under the violence of the attack. Gigantic forces were rushing into him through that open window. It reached a point where he could not contain it anymore, he felt he would explode. His last option was to lie down on the charpoy, let go of all fear, and voluntarily faint – what an outsider would have observed as losing consciousness – to alleviate the body's resistance and allow the furious rush to pass through. Even then, it felt like the entire length of an express train was gate-crashing through his organic structure, with the whole brutality of impact, vibration and thundering sound, and finally exiting, while he was out of his body, watching in awe, hoping to survive the onslaught.

In the morning, he tried to explain what he was going through to Office-wallah, who was, as usual, stoned. In the circumstances, Lionel thought a junkie metaphor would help. "Imagine," he said, "imagine for an instant that you are stuck in a hellish acid trip and there is no end to the darn blotting paper patch's effect. It lasts forever! Just imagine!"

Nope. Serge didn't even look up from his notepad, on which he was furiously scribbling. "Huh?" he groaned.

Lionel felt he was still tied to the same railway track with another express train approaching and shaking the track madly. He talked to a wise, cool turtle, who stood safely away from the iron rails. The turtle would issue some Zen-type koan like, 'Yeah, man, life comes in all shades…'

In despair, Lionel tried to communicate his anguish to the Italian guy, Max, who said, "Let's go to Kathmandu! It's sizzling hot here. In Kathmandu it will be cool. It will do you good to chill out, man!"

At least his intentions were good. He would help Lionel get to Kathmandu, Nepal, and spare no expense in the endeavour, including the plane fares.

So they back-tracked from Sarnath to Lucknow, where they could board the cheapest flight to Kathmandu.

The back-tracking could not have led to a more disastrous consequence. Arriving at Lucknow, more nightmares engulfed Lionel. He was consumed by terror and anguish, day and night; he was restless, incoherent, his body shivering. Max had booked the tickets, but then, time after time the bi-weekly plane to Kathmandu was cancelled. Whether for technical reasons, or poor weather, the expected plane did not show up. Or was it because of him and his nightmares, or by the will of the entity that had now taken full possession of him? Meanwhile, the ethereal yet painful stick came down, nudging him to turn back. Every day it became stronger and harder. Destiny was doing her dance, beckoning him ever so irresistibly.

She was clear about it; he wasn't. What was left of his mind kept slipping deeper into total confusion. He was running left and right, and right and left. He couldn't sleep. He couldn't eat. He screamed for no apparent cause. He learned that there was something worse than anguish: the terror of more anguish to come.

The guys were getting worried, and with good reason. It came as a relief to them when he finally announced he would not go to Kathmandu, for chilling, as he perceived a new truth emerging from his shattered consciousness. The message had been with him all along, printed in black and white in the book from the squatter's house in Rome; the book he carried in his backpack. But his drug-addicted mind had been too hazy for him to see it.

Suddenly, he understood. It was obvious. How could he have been so blind? Willingly or not, he was being ruthlessly taken towards the White Town. That was it. And once his eyes were opened, he saw the overall picture like a vision: there at *La Ville Blanche,* there was this ashram, where he would meet the Mother, as she was called in the book. She would understand and know clearly what was happening to him, and she would have the cure. He now saw with clarity that she could save him.

In the realm of his former crass ignorance, the friction created by the pressure of urgency clashing with his absurd resistance, had manifested itself as madness. Time was running out. There was a trait of inevitability and urgency attached to this call, even as he did his best to escape destiny and stick to his callous vagabond attitude.

As for the book, he had lost it in Sarnath; no idea where or how. It was just gone. Not surprising given his chaotic mental condition. But with it he lost the possibility of browsing its pages, which always had a comforting effect on him. Now, he had only the memory of it, left in his badly messed up mind.

He felt he was going down as inevitably as the Titanic, except in a less spectacular fashion. There was only one lifeboat still floating on the waves of his inner turmoil, carrying a banner with the words: *Go, see the Mother!* Somehow, there was the entirely illogical certitude again that she, and only she, would understand what was happening to him, and rescue him from the psychological misery into which he had been sinking deeper with each passing day. It was his last chance. If this did not turn out to be true, he would soon be gone from this world.

Thus, having given farewell and thanks to his friends, Lionel left Lucknow, not in a lifeboat, but on top of the cabin of a Tata truck, having trekked to the exit of town, to NH 30, the highway to Calcutta. Some angel disguised as a Sikh truck driver accepted him as a free-of-fare passenger. "*Paisa nehi* (no money)," Lionel had mumbled. He was now penniless without his Italian benefactor and because of this, it had taken additional courage to break free again. But come to think of it, what had there been to lose? On one side, extinction was assured in the short term; on the other, it was not much brighter, but at least there was the hope of salvation. Rattled and shaken along the dusty road to Calcutta, his resolution remained firm. It had become a matter of life and death.

On top of every Indian truck cabin, there was a rectangular open box, made of wood, painted with colourful motifs and deities, that contained rope, old canvas tarps, and the odd tool box. The driver had told him to settle up there, with its regal view of the road. Had he not been so shattered in mind, he would have felt like a King surveying his kingdom on elephant back.

In the short span of a few weeks he had lost weight and turned frightfully skinny. He experienced the full implications of what it meant to be mad and all alone in a foreign far-off land, without money, relatives or any means of communication. A land where everything felt alien – the people, languages, the overwhelming density of the crowds (even more so in the over-populated Indo-Gangetic plain), how people squeezed and piled onto trains, the gigantic scale of things, be it trains, bridges, rivers or factories. He recalled Europe as a land of toys by comparison. He felt pounded by the sensorial aggression – the thick red dust in the sunset, the pungent smells, vast clouds of fireflies blinking across the sky after dusk, the omnipresence of loud noises. Silence and peace in India? It didn't exist! Another myth concocted by pseudo-mystic writers...

Lionel was on another planet for sure, and the wrong one; at least not the one he had been dreaming of. This was a realm of loud, omnipresent cacophony, anytime, anywhere. His once found Shangri-La had vanished, left far behind as a fading memory.

Yet, seen from a different perspective, in the middle of his disaster of a sinking life, he realised he had the good fortune of being in this glorious, vibrant land, referred to by its people as Mother India. An amazing, tolerant country, where the mentally insane could prosper on its wild and rough streets. Paradoxically, Lionel still felt in his heart that he was home. Had he been in France or Switzerland, they would have locked him away in a padded cell long ago. In India, however, he didn't stand out so much: mad men and women could be seen, dressed in rags, or even stark naked sometimes, mumbling to themselves or yelling insanely, while roaming freely across the towns. They were considered a normal part of this tolerant society. The only oddity was that he was a white mad man. Although he had been told there were a few of them too; the foreign Embassies in Delhi were busy repatriating them to their countries of origin.

Thirty hours later, his blessed truck reached Calcutta. Lionel struggled a few days there, trying to find his way, living in the streets, harboured by a community of lepers. They blessed him with their hospitality – food and a clean-swept corner of pavement. While he slept, they looked after him. Nobody would ever dare steal any of his meagre belongings. He was just another pariah among pariahs. When one is nothing but a beggar, more often than not it is the poor who extend their hospitality, seldom the rich.

His trials and tribulations across the city took him to the stunning Howrah Bridge, spanning the river Hoogly, an arm in the Gangetic delta, where she reached the Bay of Bengal. Lionel was in awe. Not so much because of the bridge, although it was an impressive, gigantic, multi-storied metal structure glorifying the same technological generation of civil works as the Eiffel Tower in Paris, but by the 'wildlife' it harboured. The bridge itself was a city. In every nook and corner, even in the upper structure, there were shops, stalls, and even habitations. Perhaps a few thousand people lived and thrived on the bridge. It was an astonishing sight, one that could only reinforce his anguish at being lost in an alien world of insane people. For insane, he himself had become.

Soon enough, the stick came down again, making it clear there was no escape. There was only one destination, and he had to go on. It was like being in the army, during wartime, with marching orders issued. Except that he was a soldier in rags, famished and unarmed. Soon he found himself on a train, heading South, in a disreputable third class carriage, without a ticket, sitting near the door of the coach, next to some sadhus. Occasionally, the sadhus lit a mighty chillum and circulated it among themselves with booming exclamations of *Om! Shankar!* Lionel passed on the pipe silently when his turn came.

The conductors came and went. They just glanced at him and the sadhus; the unspoken understanding was clear: *sanyasa* was part of Indian life, and no conductor would ever ask him for a ticket. The silent agreement was that he would sit on the floor, near the always open door, with the most beautiful view one could have from a moving Indian train. The rail track was, for the most part, close to the seashore, lazily linking small fishing towns. Endless metallic bridges crossed wide expanses of backwater. Huge pyramidal white piles of harvested salt waited on shore to be collected by lorries for distribution. From time to time, a monumental railway station, packed with noisy busy crowds, revealed the presence of a large city on the Coromandel coast.

At the end of this epic rail journey, three days and four nights long, loaded with mind-boggling visions of this magnificent new world, sometimes alighting at a station to catch up on a few hours of sleep, only to board the next train, he arrived at Madras Central, at the heart of the big South Indian city, Madras. Mingling with the hundreds of passengers sleeping on the ground, he spent the night at the station, in the noisy main hall.

Early the next morning, he walked all the way to the Koyambedu Bus Stand and boarded a rattling bus, on its way to *La Ville Blanche*. By then he had had plenty of occasions to learn that when the bus conductor came close, he had only to mutter in a bored tone *"Ticket nehi* (No ticket)". He thus asserted the mutually understood, 'I am travelling without a ticket', which was more like a statement of intent rather than an admission of guilt. After a brief condescending look at his rags, the conductor would leave him alone. Strangely, in buses too, there was the same odd, unspoken code: one could not sit on a seat, but one could stand near the door, always left open, or sit on the steps. There was a coherence in the system.

But that was not all. There were greater subtleties he discovered hidden within this non-printed code. He found that beggars were not granted this privilege; they could not board a bus or train. What was the difference? In a nutshell, a sadhu was considered a holy man who begged, while a beggar was just a beggar. The code also defined in great detail the attributes pertaining to each category, which differentiated them to a bus conductor, for instance, and to society at large. A saffron dress (if any dress at all), long matted hair (or a shaved head), a prayer *mala* made of *rudrashka* beads, white ash or sandalwood paste symbols on the forehead, the trident and drum, these were all Lord Shiva-related attributes attached to the sadhu. The beggar's attributes were just the rags, the dirt, and the subservient body language. From Lionel's point of view, the striking difference was not in the dress or the hair (or lack of it), but in the eyes. The beggar cried and whimpered, while the sadhu boldly laughed the laugh of a king.

For some mysterious reason, though Lionel had none of the right attributes except the long hair and rags, some intuitive perception cast him into the sadhu category. Why else would a half-naked white man roam here in such a precarious condition, if not on a spiritual quest? They had no way of knowing, of course, that in that moment his quest was not so much spiritual, as one of survival.

Thus, in a state of extreme inner solitude, he mused on the condition of the swarms of beggars assailing the bus at each of the many stops on the road, while it travelled from one small town to the next – disabled, crooked, malformed men, one-legged or one-armed men, disfigured lepers with bandaged stumps in place of hands and feet, women carrying infants resembling living skeletons. He wondered how such segments of mankind could live such a life. He knew that in comparison, at least from a physical point of view, if not psychological, he was still faring well. The strangest part was that when amongst themselves, these people were mostly smiling, tolerant of their fate. In the shattered remnants of his Western mind, he found it difficult to reconcile these terms.

The bus kept moving. At last, dazed by the long journey and suffocating in the extreme humid heat of mid-afternoon (one could smell the salty sea), Lionel reached his tardy destination – a crowded, noisy bus-stand on the periphery of the modern extension of a little historical town, a former French colony.

Street vendors instantly surrounded the vehicle, shouting at the top of their voices, advertising South-Indian snacks such as *Muruku! Vadai!* Tamil was the local language here and the Dravidian consonants felt alien to him.

He alighted from the bus, looked around to orient himself. Having asked for directions, he walked quickly towards the heart of the town. He walked barefoot, chest exposed, his long hair covering most of his back. By then, his worldly possessions had shrunk to a *lungi* wrapped around his waist, his sleeping bag rolled in a bundle hanging over his left shoulder, and a small rag-bag with a flap clutched in his right hand, mostly empty.

He sat down on the pavement, his back against a wall, to inspect the contents of his bag. In no specific order, he found a piece of soap, a brass bowl, a booklet in which he had scribbled drawings and notes about his travelling experiences, a battered map of India, his passport stamped with a visa which had expired, and three rupees and a few paise – the remnants of some generous soul's beneficence, received on the train two days earlier. That was all. The brass bowl was an essential article to the itinerant mendicant. Truly multipurpose, it served as a receptacle for food and water, for gathering produce or money, for cooking rice over a wood fire, even to carry water to wash after relieving oneself, usually in the open fields.

Lionel rose and walked on again in the scorching heat till he crossed a canal with a trickle of insalubrious water lazily flowing in its centre, in which a company of filthy black pigs were competing for a few scraps of food.

Then, abruptly, there came an amazing transformation. Well aligned, parallel, clean streets, almost devoid of people, with neat villas and colonial buildings on either side, all of them neatly painted in a bright white colour, enhanced with a touch of light grey. Under the punishing sun, it was almost blinding.

He had reached *La Ville Blanche*.

PART II

THE QUEST

15
THE ENGLISH

1429, FRANCE, ORLEANS

A Young Woman as Warlord.

Jean d'Aulon was busy in the stables next to his host's house, cleaning and checking Jehanne's arms, with the help of her two pages. He was meticulous and thorough. Twenty years in the service of the Dauphin, and having survived several military campaigns, he knew well that neglect of one's equipment could spell disaster on the battlefield. He smiled to himself. *As much as she relied on the Archangel Saint-Michel, the dragon slayer, for the divine aspect of her protection, in a similar way he would ensure her safety from a more materialistic point of view. At least, as much as it was humanly possible,* he thought.

D'Aulon was of medium height, still a strong and handsome man at forty. His face was weathered and craggy, the result of many soldiering campaigns. He preferred to keep his auburn hair shoulder length, wisps of grey showed at the temples, and he was clean shaven. His green eyes were always alert, more so when he escorted Jehanne.

He came from a noble household and had a reputation for righteousness, which seemed to be a virtue that ran in the family. Perhaps, it was one of the reasons he had received his present assignment, as Squire and Bursar to Jehanne's detail. Another aspect might have been his military experience. He was fearless in battle and was renowned for having had four horses killed under him in one single battle at Montargis a few years earlier, fighting on the side of the Bastard of Orléans – Count Dunois.

All the components of Jehanne's expensive armour, gifted by the Dauphin, lay aligned on a bench. The pages had patiently polished all the metal parts using a pad of straw dipped in a mix of ash and water. This done, they had applied the rare, high-quality seal-grease that Jean had obtained from a merchant trading with the Northern lands. They had vigorously rubbed every part of the armour with this grease that prevented rust, before finally polishing the metal to a high sheen. The result was stunning. The armour shone in the sunlight like a blinding beacon of light.

They treated the leather parts and straps that bound the armour with the same grease and care. Jean d'Aulon had scrutinised each strap for damage or weakness, but they were all supple and strong. With equal care, the pages had cleaned, greased and polished Jehanne's saddle, and the leather of her charger's harness. D'Aulon had taken a close look at these, too. Satisfied, he had turned and stepped out into the paved street to return to the house.

That was when the first far-off sounds of battle caught his attention. At the same moment, a young squire came running down the street, out of breath. "Sir! Commander Dunois has left the walls with a sizeable party!"

D'Aulon entered the house and ran up the wooden stairs to the first floor, to inform Jehanne of the development. He gave a slight cough before lifting the curtain that separated the landing from the room where she was resting. The room had one sloping wall under the steep tiled roof; the other wall was a tall vertical white-washed partition that separated the room from that occupied by her host's family. In a corner stood her sword, sheathed in its scabbard, leaning against the wall. Her Standard, embroidered with the golden *fleur-de-lys,* shimmered in the shadows. Opposite the small alcove-shaped bed, a narrow window faced the street.

Early that morning, Jehanne had ridden beyond the fortifications for a full league eastwards, to meet Dunois, who had returned from Blois with new reinforcements. She was having a respite when one of the English Commanders, Sir John Fastolf, was spotted returning with a convoy of fresh supplies for his 1,200 men-strong troop, part of the 5,500 men laying siege to the City of Orléans. It was essential they prevent him from joining the bulk of the English army, stationed in the Bastilles, a group of forts positioned North-West of the town. A seasoned captain, Dunois had taken immediate action.

Now, with the first booming of artillery through her open window, she woke instantly. No one had told her an attack was to be launched. D'Aulon knew it would upset her. Abruptly, she stood up, dressed in the male clothing she typically wore. As a warrior, she considered it the most practical attire to merge within a man's world and always be ready for combat. She was almost as tall as d'Aulon, and of strong build, in a healthy peasant way, yet nothing could conceal the feminine grace of her movements. Her chestnut hair was cut short, the page hairstyle framing her wilful face with its stubborn chin. Everything about her expression and posture showed that she meant business.

Jehanne wanted to be on the battlefield with her men and resented the fact that Dunois had sidelined her. In Dunois' mind, women did not wage war. *One more embarrassment on the battlefield to worry about,* he thought. In addition, being an agnostic who believed only in the power of his intellect and sword, he was suspicious of her claims of having received orders from divine voices. He was more inclined to trust his own strategies rather than those of Sainte-Catherine and Sainte-Marguerite, or even Saint-Michel, the Archangel.

He would soon get to know the real Jehanne.

She summoned one of her pages and requested her arms. He brought them, running. Her spirit storming in wrath, she hastily donned full battle armour, with d'Aulon's help. She went out and mounted her black steed, which the other page had harnessed and brought to the door. Again, d'Aulon assisted her, weighed down by her armour, to mount the nervous animal. While she impatiently spurred the charger away, showering sparks onto the pavement, another attendant handed her across the window, the white Standard inscribed with the words *Jhesus Maria* in flaming gold letters. With a clatter of hooves, she flew through the streets of Orléans. She crossed the town like a raging wind, passed the cathedral, and burst forth through the Burgundy Gate into the fields like a silver flame.

By the time he himself was ready, despite his best efforts, Jean d'Aulon could not catch up with her. He was in charge of her personal safety, appointed by the Dauphin in person! Cursing aloud, he galloped towards the fray.

The battle had shifted to the ditches of the bastilles Saint Loup, half a league eastwards, where Fastolfe had taken refuge. Having grown used to the powerlessness of the French entrenched behind the city walls for many months, the strike had taken him by surprise. The few raids attempted outside the walls had all turned into defeats for the French. It seemed impossible to breach the blockade of the English siege. As a result, the situation was dire in Orléans, with the population near starvation.

When d'Aulon at last caught up, Jehanne had already dismounted and was climbing the embankment of the small fort on foot, reviving the efforts of the French troops, who had been faltering. Looking strong yet strangely vulnerable in her bright armour sparkling under the sun, with her Standard floating high above the fray like a herald of the Divine, she revealed her formidable energy, courage and faith. The unexpected, ethereal sight of the girl who would become known as the Maid of Orléans, was enough to inspire renewed hope in the French. As for the enemy, it puzzled them at first, even as they revelled in widespread jeering and vulgar comments. But, as the fighting continued, this initial perception by the English turned into concern and fear.

D'Aulon had rushed to Jehanne's side. Having rallied a group of shield-bearing soldiers, he instructed them to stay close around her. He thus hoped to protect her from the projectiles hurled from the bastille's walls. And once they had breached the walls, he would ensure the same team shielded her back.

It was the first time Jehanne had engaged in earnest battle. All those who saw her that day were filled with awe, and then energised with renewed combative enthusiasm. She carried her armour and weapons with ease, radiating a charisma that spread to all on the field.

"We do the fighting! God will give the victory!" she exhorted her troops.

Her galvanising effect was such that every single man around her, whether simple soldier or seasoned Captain, would have readily given his life for this hallowed assault. The French rallied around her under the name of Jehanne la Pucelle, Joan the Maid, while the English, fearing her, branded her Joan the Sorceress.

At the end of the day, the three hundred English force within the fort of Saint-Loup were either slain or captured, and the supplies seized.

On returning within the city walls, "In five days' time, you shall be free of the enemy!" Jehanne told the people.

Although Orléans was not yet liberated, la Pucelle's first appearance on the battlefield was already changing the course of a war that had devastated France for nearly a hundred years. During long decades, the country had been plundered and bled by the English. Violence and coertion were the norm; the burning of entire villages, common place, accompanied by the usual atrocities such as murder, rape and torture. The destituted realm of France had turned into a playground for the English soldiers and a major source of income for the Crown of England. The English royals, once used to these stolen luxuries, would not give them up easily. Lacking adequate leadership, the French nobility were drowning in a quagmire of internal conflicts and rivalries; treacherous alliances were forged with the English, and the population had lost all hope in their Lords, trying desperately to survive on the meagre resources left for them. Within this political context of desperation, Jehanne, a seventeen-year-old peasant girl, believed to be guided by voices from heaven, was seen as a divine messenger sent to shatter the existing stalemate and reverse the course of the war.

Because of its strategic position on the river Loire, a natural East-West border defining English-occupied territory,

Orléans was key to the future of France. That evening, after dusk, for the first time following months of hardship, the giant bells of the cathedral rang out in joy. They rang through the night.

When the news of this first victory reached the royal court at Blois, the Dauphin Charles, legitimate heir to the throne of France, knew he had placed his trust in a fitting warrior. Perhaps, she was indeed an envoy of God, and perhaps the promise she had made that he would be anointed King in the sacred cathedral of Reims, would come true after all. After decades of defeat and bloodshed, a renewed wind of hope blew through France.

16
STORMING THE WALL

1429, FRANCE, ORLÉANS

Les Tourelles

The English had received a severe blow, but they still held the town of Orléans under the tremendous pressure of siege. Jehanne was overcome with anguish at the sight of the town's people struggling for survival in the intensifying state of famine. Fortunately, she had been able to provide some relief with the convoy of supplies she had brought from Tours at the time of her arrival. This, they had smuggled with ease into the city, thanks to the casual, overconfident attitude of the English. In addition, there were also the supplies seized from Fastolfe.

But Jehanne could see that the only way to bring permanent relief to Orléans was to take back control of the bridge across the river Loire, and thus reconnect Orléans with the southern free half of France. To achieve this, the reputedly impregnable bastille of Les Tourelles, erected at the opposite end of the bridge and controlling its access, had to be reclaimed from the English. But first, the adjacent bastille of Les Augustins, shelter to an important garrison, had to be taken.

The English Commander in charge of this section of the siege, a sour man named Glasdale, was acutely aware that Les Tourelles was the key to the city. It could not be allowed to fall into French hands, and he had prepared his men to defend the twin-towered fortress at all cost. More than anyone else, he despised and slandered the Maid.

Refusing to waste time, Jehanne worked hard to convince the Commanders of her army over the next few days. They were reluctant to accept her bold strategic moves, favouring the more prudent option of waiting for the reinforcements expected from the Dauphin. Relentlessly, she pressed on and made it happen in two successive acts.

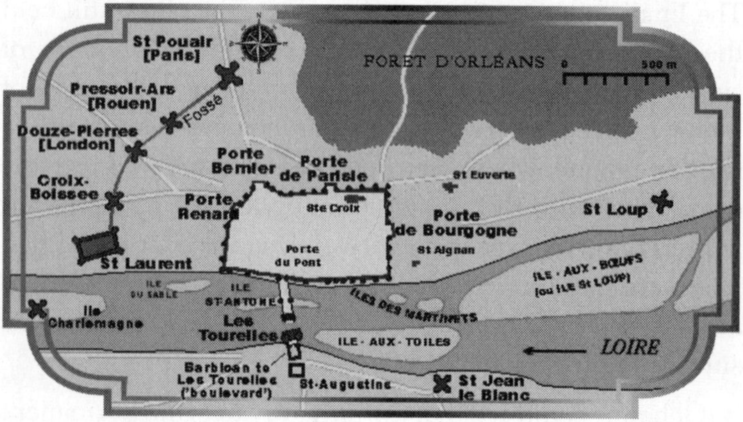

For a start, the French army crossed the river at a narrow point, using a bridge made of boats lashed together. They found the fortress of Saint Jean Le Blanc deserted. Glasdale had moved all his troops to concentrate on the defense of the two bastilles of Les Augustins and Les Tourelles. The French warlords regrouped to the south of the river and assessed the situation. They agreed it was going to be a tough fight. Nevertheless, Jehanne ordered the attack. By now the men were eager to follow her, looking up to her as a true Messenger of God.

Again, her bold plan of action resulted in a crushing defeat for the English. That day, Les Augustins fell to the French. Six hundred English soldiers were taken prisoner and two hundred French prisoners freed. Some English survivors took refuge in Les Tourelles. But by then night had fallen and the assault on Les Tourelles was deferred to the next day.

Although the soldiers followed Jehanne unconditionally, the Commanders were still reluctant to draw plans based on what they perceived to be her mystic fervour. Again, they argued that waiting for the troop reinforcements promised by the Dauphin was a more prudent strategy. But Jehanne retorted that none knew when they would arrive, or if they had been dispatched at all. The English were in a defensive position and fairly disorganised; they had lost many men. Waiting meant surrendering this exceptional advantage.

Now was the moment.

At dawn the next day, Dunois was still raising objections to her plan. Referring to the voices of her patron saints, she countered him with the words: "You have taken your counsel, and I have received mine."

She ordered the Burgundy Gate opened, and she burst out, with d'Aulon at her side carrying her banner, followed by her troops. This enraged Dunois. Like La Hire, Gilles de Rais and the other Captains, he was left with no choice but to catch up with her. The fiery Gilles de Rais, always willing to taunt Death, laughed loudly in admiration of the Maid. With a devilish burst of laughter, he was the first to react. He mounted his horse and lead his veteran guard across the Loire on her heels. To Dunois, he yelled, "I like this gal! From this day on, wherever she goes, I go!" And he spurred on his charger, a wide grin across the face.

Jehanne, Jean d'Aulon, and her most devoted followers merged with the soldiers left on guard duty for the night at Les Augustins. At once they proceeded with preparations to storm the wall of Les Tourelles.

The whole area looked like a scene from Hell. The frantic trampling of hooves, the movements of carriages and men had destroyed the vegetation, including the scattered attempts at growing crops. Ruined buildings, burned houses, blackened trees and bushes were everywhere; thick trodden mud restricted mobility. But worst of all was the all-pervading stench of the dead. Corpses lay everywhere, heaped together or scattered in lonely profusion. Neither the English nor the French had had the time or energy to attend to their dead.

Jehanne wept at the ghastly sight: her beloved countrymen bleeding and dying stabbed her to the soul. D'Aulon, who remained with her at all times, reportedly said: "She could not see French blood without her hair rising in horror at the sight."

The men moved into position, ladders were brought, siege-towers moved forward, catapults anchored. The entire area became a scene of frenzied activity, with the clatter of arms, men shouting, and the whinnying of horses.

On the wall, the English were swept by a wave of feverish effort, preparing for what they perceived to be a fateful battle. At the end of this day, whoever held Les Tourelles would be the victor, for years to come. They worked frantically and tirelessly, hauling up all kinds of projectiles and boiling enormous cauldrons of pitch. On the parapet walk, the famous and dreaded English archers formed a disciplined, compact line of defence.

By then the bulk of the French army had caught up, engulfed with the furious fever of war. Differences were forgotten. The divine wind of wrath raised by La Pucelle inspired every man on the field, from simple foot-soldier to noble knight. When she spurred her charger to lead the assault, with d'Aulon at her side brandishing high her Standard, the French rushed forward as a single unified body, bristling with spikes, sparkling with white shining metal. Glasdale, standing on the wall, heard the deafening clamour. In that moment he felt his blood run cold. Something in him knew that, sorceress or not, he was standing at the receiving end of divine justice and that his doom had come upon him. Nevertheless, for all his shortcomings, he was a proud warrior, and he made his stand fiercely.

> *There are moments when the Spirit moves among men and the breath of the Lord is abroad upon the waters of our being; there are others when it retires and men are left to act in the strength or the weakness of their own egoism. The first are periods when even a little effort produces great results and changes destiny; the second are spaces of time when much labour goes to the making of a little result. It is true that the latter may prepare the former, may be the little smoke of sacrifice going up to heaven which calls down the rain of God's bounty.*
>
> *Unhappy is the man or the nation which, when the divine moment arrives, is found sleeping or unprepared to use it, because the lamp has not been kept trimmed for the welcome and the ears are sealed to the call. But thrice woe to them who are strong and ready, yet waste the force or misuse the moment; for them is irreparable loss or a great destruction.*
>
> Sri Aurobindo, *The Hour of God*

The ensuing French onslaught was so violent that it was difficult to contain. The English troops fought bravely, pinned against the walls, attempting to repel the flood of foot-soldiers and horsemen, but were remorselessly pushed back, step by step. By mid-afternoon, most of the English soldiers had retreated within the walls, and the first French ladders were raised against the walls. Jehanne had dismounted and seeing victory within reach, grabbed her standard from d'Aulon. She climbed a ladder's lower rungs, waving her high-flying *Fleur-de-Lys*.

At that moment, following a sound of violent impact, in a sickeningly slow movement, she fell backwards with a short cry, like a wounded bird. She landed in d'Aulon's arms, while he cursed himself for having allowed her to move away from his sphere of protection. She had been struck by a bolt in the chink of her armour, between her left shoulder and neck.

Glasdale knew that if the sorceress fell, the morale of his troops would rise, adversely affecting the French. He had thus summoned his best cross-bow archers and given the command to target the witch. Cheers erupted on the wall, as d'Aulon and de Rais, having ordered a shield of soldiers around them, dragged Jehanne back to safety.

In the centre of a circle of warriors, Jehanne lay on the muddy grass behind the front line. But, to everyone's surprise, she regained control of herself. Against all advice to wait for the surgeon, she ordered d'Aulon to break off the tipped shaft of the bolt protruding from her back. In a feat of unbelievable courage, she pulled the bolt out with her right hand. She began to bleed profusely and on the verge of losing consciousness, she summoned her chaplain, Jean Pasquerel, to hear her confession. Meanwhile, d'Aulon applied a compress of oil to the wound and wrapped a crude bandage around her shoulder. The bleeding slowly subsided.

In the meantime, without the Maid, the assault had lost its momentum. The fighting had already gone on for six long hours. The casualties were high, and the English still held Les Tourelles. Dusk was setting in, and the Commanders considered recalling the troops for the day.

Undaunted, Jehanne could not endure the thought. She knew victory was still possible. Overcoming her weakness, she ordered Jean to fetch her charger and help her mount it. They galloped to Dunois on the front line, where she begged him not to give up, insisting that victory was now or never. She assured him the English could not hold on for much longer. They had lost many men and depleted most of their ammunition on the wall.

Carrying her heavy banner herself, despite her injury, she cried to the men surrounding her: "Watch my Standard! When the *Fleur-de-Lys* reaches the walls, Les Tourelles will be ours!"

And once more she led them into the assault.

The English had resisted with admirable tenacity, but on seeing the Maid seemingly returning from the dead, leading her men with unabated courage, panic spread through their ranks. When she and her *Fleur-de-Lys* reached the wall, poorly defended, now, the end of Les Tourelles was near.

"Victory is ours!" Jehanne cried.

In an ultimate effort, the fortress was at last conquered.

On seeing the battle was lost, chaos ensued among the remaining English troops, who attempted to flee by swimming across the river. Most succumbed in this endeavour. Glasdale himself, who had jeered and spat the worse insults at the Maid just a few days earlier, was among those who drowned in the Loire. Five hundred English soldiers perished in Les Tourelles or drowned in attempting to escape; the rest were taken prisoners.

The English would never recover from the lost battle at Les Tourelles, which marked the beginning of their slow retreat towards the channel, losing terrain and allies year after year, till the French finally forced them back to the island of Britain forever.

As night at last fell, Jehanne, after twelve hours on the battlefield, rode across the bridge that had been hastily repaired. She entered the city of Orléans in triumph. In the light of torches, the people of the town offered her a delirious welcome, and the ensuing festivities continued the entire night.

At last she reached the simple house of her hosts. There, d'Aulon helped her dismount and disarm. Finally, she sat and ate some bread dipped in wine.

Before he retired for the night, Jean d'Aulon made sure Jehanne's wound was cleaned and attended to by a competent physician. He had some food and wine too, then in need of silence, walked to the nearby city wall, where sentries were pacing. From this vantage point, he could see the campfires flickering behind the English lines, eerily silent compared to the sounds of festivity rising from within the town walls.

Yet, regardless of his faith in Jehanne, he found it hard to believe that the seven-month long siege of Orléans had been lifted by the Maid in just seven days. Even more disturbing in the scale of his own beliefs, was the strange and unsettling experience that had shaken him to the depths at the peak moment of the battle. When Jehanne had led her second assault, he had witnessed an eerie golden light flickering around her, and for a brief instant he had had a mind-shattering vision of a Goddess, as vast as the Universe itself.

Much later, he came to know that the English soldiers too, had said that *when attacked by the terrible Maiden, they had seen what appeared to be flights of golden butterflies sparkling all around her form.*

Until that day, d'Aulon had never fully realised WHO or WHAT, in truth, she was.

He returned to the house and settled in the small basement room he shared with Jehanne's pages. Outside, in the streets of Orléans, a multitude of joyful voices were chanting, *Noël! Noël! Noël!* Worn out at the end of an exhausting, victorious day, on a simple bed of straw, he fell asleep instantly to the sound of the cathedral bells, ceaselessly ringing their powerful anthem of triumph.

17
END OF THE ROAD

1971, SOUTH INDIA

La Ville Blanche, Part 1

Just before dawn, Lionel had slipped into a deep sleep. Part of his consciousness drifted in and out of a familiar ancient world resounding with the clash of warfare. In this strange state of awareness, he could hear the heavy bells of a cathedral ringing persistently. He tried to wake up, but could not. He felt emprisoned by a timeless glue. The sound of the bells kept him pinned in another slice of time he could not comprehend.

At last he opened his eyes, but was in such a disoriented state that he could not figure where or when he was. The bells kept on ringing, but at a higher pitch than in his dream. Was it a memory? He could not tell. He raised himself on one elbow and looked around: it all came back. He had been lying on the pavement under the porch of the Ganesha temple. The sun had risen. A priest, dark-skinned, dressed in a white dhoti and sporting the sacred Brahmin thread across chest and shoulder, hair tied in a bun and a red vertical mark on the forehead, was vigorously sounding the large bell at the temple gate.

It surprised Lionel that he had not been unceremoniously requested to move away. The previous evening, he had been roaming around town in search of shelter, when a friendly tailor in the market, who spoke excellent French, as was still common then, invited him for a simple South-Indian meal.

The kind man had urged him to sleep at the temple, where he would be safe and undisturbed, at least until dawn.

Lionel rose, rolled up his sleeping bag and walked to a nearby public fountain, that was already being used by some rickshaw-wallas for their morning ablutions. He waited his turn and then scrubbed from head to feet all the dirt accumulated during the trip from Madras (his last shower had been at the railway station's public restroom the day before).

Finally as clean and decent as possible, he asked for directions and headed towards his final destination, the Ashram, which happened to be close by.

On his arrival at *la Ville Blanche*, the White Town, he did not own so much as a shirt or the luxury of pants. No shoes or sandals either. He walked barefoot. His chest was uncovered and the lungi he wore was not long enough to cover the ankles, as tradition demanded. It was cut short at the knees. At some point he had split it into two, and kept one half to use as a towel, or headgear when the sun was too harsh. To be honest, he did not even have any underwear either. As usual, his little cloth hand-bag hung from one shoulder, while his battered sleeping bag dangled from the other.

In this attractive attire he showed up at the main gate of the Ashram and entered. In those days, there were always four or five elderly *sadhaks* (disciples), sitting on the verandah, facing the gate, each impeccably dressed in white kurtas and dhotis (more Bengali than South-Indian), looking like impressive pashas. They were, he discovered, equivalent to what one would call bouncers in a night club – a crude comparison. Aware that he had reached another crossroad of destiny, Lionel was tense, but got himself under control and walked in boldly, his naïve lines in rudimentary English, which was all he knew at the time, ready on the tongue: "Excuse me, I would like to meet the Mother. When can I see her please?"

To his heart-wrenching surprise, he did not get the chance to utter one word for, at his sudden appearance, all five sadhaks jumped up as if they were spring-loaded, and promptly formed a wall, akin to defence players' facing a penalty shot in a soccer game. The white pashas morphed into fierce piranhas. 'Halt! Not a step further! How dare you? This is no place for you. Get out! Right away! Now!' were their unambiguous words. He was not welcome.

His heart sank all the way down to his feet, while his thoughts ran wild: *What was wrong with these people? Were they not supposed to be spiritually developed? Were they not supposed to read his thoughts and understand him without words?* This was what he had imagined in his idealistic expectations of the moment. Instead, they displayed the aggressiveness of a pack of bulldogs. Till then his shattered, run-down self had harboured the hopeful vision of being close to his cure, and perhaps his resurrection. Now, such childlike hopes had been smashed to smithereens: he was thrown out like a mangy dog, or worse. He was back in the street. In truth, he was devastated.

IT - WAS - THE - END...

And so he walked away, wandering aimlessly amongst the hot streets of the White Town, then along the ocean, past the old lighthouse, not knowing what to do, where to go, where not to go. He walked for a long time. Lost in his world of despair, he stepped on a shard of broken glass, and his right foot began to bleed profusely. Physically and mentally exhausted, spent to the core, he sat down on the steps of a shaded verandah.

Slumped there, on the verge of tears, with hunger tearing at an empty stomach, desperate and just wishing it would all end quickly, he noticed some movement and looked up. He saw a man walking along the opposite pavement, and perhaps perceived a faint glimmer of light. With no better hope to cling to, Lionel got up and crossed the street. As he approached the man, he felt a strange kind of resonating kinship.

Later, he came to know the man was an artist, a gifted painter of European origin, who had lived a long time in India, in the Himalayas, going by the Tibetan name of Thupten. He was indeed dressed like a Tibetan monk. At first sight, he reminded Lionel of the Khyber Pass monk, but no, in comparison Thupten bore obvious class and nobility; he was the genuine article. Thupten stopped and smiled, signalling he was listening.

Almost incoherently Lionel blurted out all his misery in one single, long, desperate shot: "I found a book in Rome, *l'Aventure de la Conscience,* then crossed half the world and came all the way here, hoping to find out what this is all about. I walked into the ashram to see the Mother and these bouncers just threw me out like a filthy dog, and yes, there is more – I am crazy in my head. Totally crazy. What should I do?"

Feeling like a complete idiot, Lionel thought in despair that he had ruined his chance.

Thupten remained silent for a while, looking him up and down. Then he spoke: "Not surprising, considering the way you look. Some ashramites are pretty conservative in their ways, and for them you must have appeared nothing more than a misdirected beggar."

"But shouldn't we expect these disciples to be spiritually evolved? Shouldn't they have shown compassion, or some understanding?" Lionel asked.

Thupten smiled, ignoring the remark. "Don't worry about all this. I think you should meet Satprem himself, the author of your book, in person. You will find him every evening at the Ashram's sports ground, behind the tennis courts by the ocean. You can't miss him; he always wears faded blue shorts and sits there on the wall, contemplating the surf and relaxing."

In a strange way, Thupten's description abruptly triggered an ancient, faint memory of a man sitting on a wall, facing a lake, but Lionel could not place it in the actual world and it faded as fast as it had come. However, Thupten's words had a profound, soothing effect on Lionel. They talked for a while, and Lionel's hopes rose a notch: here was the first person ready to listen to him with some interest and compassion; a person who had provided him with useful information; a thin thread to hold to and follow.

So he took Thupten's advice, and that same evening, at five, when the heat of the day had considerably abated, having bandaged his injured foot, he went to the recommended place on the sea-shore. He entered the tennis grounds; no one asked questions; he walked around the courts to the low wall facing the immense bluish-green expanse of the Indian Ocean. Lionel recognised the man at once, sitting on the sea-facing wall. Blue shorts or not, there wasn't a shadow of a doubt. A rather thin man, he fitted Thupten's description;

his eagle gaze fixed on a far-away spot on the ocean. Lionel knew this was *the one person* he had to meet.

He also knew that the steps he was taking at that moment were of utmost importance. That feeling, in tandem with his inner prayer not to trigger another bouncer-effect, helped him find the right way to speak, politely and respectfully, in a more controlled fashion than when he had addressed Thupten. He approached, stood beside the man and said: *"Excusez-moi, Monsieur, êtes vous bien Satprem? (*Excuse me, Sir, are you Satprem?)"

The man turned slowly to face him. Lionel got the impression that he was being gently but accurately X-rayed in that single, sun-like, long gaze. Finally, a simple "Yes?" came the reply, pronounced in a soft voice.

Lionel forgot all his carefully prepared sentences. To express his predicament, he spilled his story in telegram style: "I came across *l'Aventure de la Conscience* in Rome, and I read it. I have this absurd perception that this book brought me here. I am crazy in my head and I have lost complete control of my mind, which has become the prey of ceaseless attacks of anguish. I have this distinct feeling though, that the person you describe in your book as the Mother, is the only being who can understand what's happening to me. Then, when at last I arrived at the Ashram's gate, these men threw me out like a dirty dog! I have no idea what to do next, or how to come out of this pit of darkness into which I slip deeper day by day. Thupten thought you could help, and he sent me to you."

His abrupt and rather silly tirade took a few seconds to sink in, and Satprem remained silent for a while. He asked no questions, only his name.

"I am Lionel."

Satprem turned his face back towards the ocean, staring into the distance as if he was in fact gazing far beyond. There was the rhythmic sound of the surf tumbling on the beach and the cries of the seagulls. Lionel could hear the *plop, plop* sound of the tennis balls behind him, the occasional shout of the players and the comments of a handful of watchers, all of it dulled in a soft haze, like in a daydream. For a brief moment, time remained suspended. He stood petrified in this extraordinary interlude of destiny.

When at last Satprem spoke, to Lionel's surprise, he was amazingly direct, sharp and clear. He declared: "You must see the Mother at once. I will arrange that. She will know what your next move should be."

Then he turned and looked at him with a smile and piercing eyes. "But please, do me a favour, Lionel: cut that hair! And do it 'consciously', like an offering to the Mother. Come back tomorrow at the same time."

And that was all. Lionel was a little dazed by an answer that was cryptic, yet reached far beyond his expectations. It was a miracle! But he had to cut his hair. He knew he must. He reflected on this. He was not particularly attached to his long hair; not anymore. It had just grown, as was customary in the tribes he had been roaming among, and of course, it had been a symbol of his rebellion against the Establishment. But he was cast away in an alien land and the said Establishment had been left far behind, having lost all substance. What was there to prove here? Nothing. There were so many sadhus with longer hair than his, matted at that. Who gave them a second glance? Besides, he was in such a state of despair, that cutting his hair was a small price to pay. Such was the depth of his psychological misery that he would readily have given the thumb of his right hand as *Guru Dakshina,* like a modern-day Ekalavya.

At the first opportunity, he borrowed a pair of scissors, and sitting crossed-legged on the floor, without a mirror, he undertook the job himself since he could not afford the barber shop, leaving only a minimal short crop. He soon realised that in the hot and humid climate, cutting off his hair provided unexpected relief. Once done with this chore, along with his hair, for good measure, he also threw his notebook into a street trash bin. And with them perished the last remnants of his turbulent past.

Truly, he had become nobody.

At last, his fortunes took a better turn. That evening, he had a place to sleep, and a bathroom to wash in. Moments after his meeting with the writer at the tennis court, he had encountered two young, smart-looking European girls, about his own age. They had been crossing the playground to go to the beach that stretched beyond. The contrast in their respective conditions was extreme. On one hand were these beautiful girls, tanned and elegant, quietly strolling the waterfront with a little bag dangling on the shoulder, containing towels and bikinis, as if they were on the French Riviera, and then there was him, a half-naked, mind-deranged white-skinned vagabond, lost on the Coromandel coast. Like two antipodal worlds meeting. Despite the cardinal differences, an instant kinship bound them together. It was as if he was meeting family members at the corner of the street, never seen before, but somehow intimately known.

They sat together and talked. Predictably, Lionel couldn't help telling them he was crazy in his head. It didn't seem to alarm them much, and instead of running away, they casually gave him the key to their apartment nearby, with these words: "Any time you need a shower, Lionel, you can come and use our bathroom."

They also told him they were working as assistants to the Chief Architect of a new township project – the City of Dawn – which was just beginning, some ten kilometres north, on a deserted plateau. At the time, he of course had not the foggiest idea about this project.

Later, another encounter resulted in him having a bed for the night, in a small room, part of a secluded, peaceful beach house. This was a luxury he had not experienced in a long, long time.

It looked like his guardian angel, after having beaten him mercilessly and forced him to reach *La Ville Blanche,* was at last giving him a break.

The next day, at five, he was on the tennis court again. Satprem was sitting on the wall, expecting him.

"You look better without the burden of your hair, Lionel. Tomorrow, you will see the Mother at 11 in the morning. Show yourself at the main gate of the *Samadhi* at 10.30 and ask for Suchitra. She will take care of you."

This was unexpected. Things were suddenly happening at a fast pace. A short conversation ensued. Satprem asked how he was faring. Lionel explained his marooned state and described his penniless situation. He also told Satprem that his psychological condition had much improved in the last twenty-four hours. He felt less under attack, more positive, and infinitely grateful for the intervention.

Like father and son, they sat in silence on the wall, enjoying the cool ocean breeze, till the sun had set and the fast falling tropical dusk had settled. Only then did they part, with a smile but not a word.

That night at the beach house, for the first time in weeks, Lionel slept in peace. Once again, just before dawn, he was visited by a faint, distant vision that felt like an ancient memory. When the sun rose on the ocean, he woke. He remained immobile on the bed, keeping his eyes shut, slowly, delicately, pulling the thin thread of recollection.

18
THE KNIGHT AND THE WIZARD

539, ISLAND OF BRITAIN

Beyond the Wall

The forest was thick, dark and throbbing in ominous silence. Bors kept riding undaunted, his charger following the narrow trail, occasionally snorting while brushing through the thick foliage. Often, Bors bent flat over the horse's powerful neck, under the impeding low branches. The day was young and he was not unduly worried, thinking to clear the forest by noon. He could have taken the old Roman road used by the regular travellers, but then it would have taken him the better part of another riding day to reach the abbey. He didn't want that.

Ever since he had received the cryptic message from his brother, he had been eager to meet him. Bors was not alarmed by the loneliness of the woods, though the forest was known to be the refuge of renegades and bandits of all kinds. The past decades had seen him involved in many perilous situations, brought on either by the Quest or the subsequent war which had torn the kingdom apart. As one of the few surviving knights, he had a blasé attitude, a mix of detachment and indifference to danger.

Bors and his elder brother Lionel, were the sons of King Bors of Gaunnes, himself the brother of King Ban of Benoic, father of Lamhcalad, also known as Lancelot. Along with Ector de Maris, bastard son of King Ban, they formed the clan from Armorica – a lineage that, because of their overseas origin, made them stand apart from the rest of the Round Table Brotherhood.

Bors was stout and sturdily built. He possessed a naive quality akin to purity. He was slow to react, but once his mind was made up, he was as powerful as a charging ox. He was completely loyal to his brother.

The lost Battle of Camlann had seen the demise of their King, two years earlier, leaving the kingdom in a state of profound disintegration. The sons of Mordred had poor understanding of State affairs and showed no interest in governing Britain as a unified nation capable of withstanding Saxon invasion. And so, turning away from the brilliant spear-heading civilisation based on honour and individual value that had flourished under the reign and leadership of Arthur Pendragon – a spectacular bright light in the long, dark, post Pax Romana period – Britain had returned to a state of chaos, plundered and decimated by scores of petty warlords with no unifying allegiance. Meanwhile, the Saxon invaders were gaining more control over the land day by day.

As for Lionel, he was torn by indecision. Brought up with the high ethical values that had led him to a place at the Round Table, when confronted with this wreck of a kingdom, he could not figure out where his duty lay. He often wondered why fate had spared him and his brother, while so many more valuable knights had lost their lives in this fratricidal war.

He wanted to meet the soothsayer who had foreseen it all, a long time ago, even before the birth of Arthur, to seek his advice. But the man had mysteriously vanished decades ago, and it was not even known if he was still alive. Thus, Lionel had undertaken this solitary quest. For two months now, travelling north, he had been riding and questioning people throughout the land: peasants in the fields, traders on the road or in hamlets, landlords and noblemen in their crude castles.

Riding alone, without the help of a squire, his armour was down to a bare minimum, to the few pieces he could don without assistance – chain-mail for the torso, legs and arm protection, and a light Sarmatian style helmet. He had only his valour to count on and defend himself with if he crossed paths with brigands. Of course, he would never part with the sword gifted to him by the King himself, in better days, nor the shield featuring his arms – a roaring lion, known throughout Britain. An entire life in the knighthood was bound to attract some fame, whether he liked it or not.

As an itinerant Knight of the Table, he was well respected and he and his horse were always looked after wherever he went. Usually, he was given free shelter and food, unless he was in the wild, when he would simply lie under a tree for the night, wrapped in a woollen blanket.

Twelve days ago, he had crossed Hadrian's Wall. The Roman conquerors had built this seventy-five-mile-long fortification, which ran across Britain from ocean to ocean, almost four centuries earlier, to prevent barbarian invasions from the north, and protect the Empire.

The next day, Lionel had finally stumbled upon valuable and apparently reliable information as to the whereabouts of the elusive soul he had so long sought. Immediately, he sent word to Bors, through a monk travelling south.

Bors emerged from the forest much later than he had expected, in the late afternoon. The change was abrupt. One minute he was still struggling through the underbrush, the next he was sitting on his horse atop a hill, the forest behind him. Before him, a magnificent panoramic vista revealed itself. A chain of mountains barred the horizon; closer, low hills rolled, alternating with scattered woods and barren moor; and just below, lay a large lake with ink-black water, reflecting the mountains. Slightly away from the lake-shore, a massive stone edifice stood, built like a fortress. At one end of the building, a turret rose higher than the rest, enclosing a bronze bell that was tolling for vespers, its crystal-clear sound carrying for many miles in the calm evening air. Bors had reached the abbey.

A furlong beyond, facing the lake, was a three-feet-high stone wall, erected to mark the boundary between fields, or serve as cattle pen. He could just distinguish a far-off silhouette, sitting on the wall. Closer to the abbey, he recognised his brother's charger, left to graze in the rich clover. Another silhouette was walking towards the wall, that looked like his brother. The whole scene was infused with a deep sense of peace. In joy, Bors took his time to leisurely ride down the hill.

Lionel had dismounted. He followed the directions given by the two nuns dressed in maroon and black, whom he had met near the gate of the abbey, and walked towards the lake. He felt intimidated and anxious, wondering if this was the Enchanter he was looking for. But there was no reason to doubt, for he could see the subtle sparkling that enhanced the scene, and feel the soft wave of warmth caressing his pounding heart.

A very old, unassuming man sat on the low stone wall, facing the lake, dressed in sheepskin held together with a wide leather belt at the waist. A brown woollen cap with flaps covered his ears. His face and legs were so thickly covered with hair that it was difficult to decide whether the creature was man or beast.

Undaunted by appearances, Lionel spoke: "Greetings! I am Lionel, son of King Bors of Gaunnes, who rules across the Southern Sea."

The man slowly turned his gaze away from the infinite depths of the lake's waters and looked at him, with an intensity akin to that of the sun.

"You took your own time, Lionel. We have work to do," said Myrddin Wilt, frowning. Merlin – the Wild Man of the Woods, Wizard and former Counsellor to the King.

19
STAIRWAY TO HEAVEN

1971, SOUTH-INDIA

La Ville Blanche, Part 2

That same morning, clean shaved, sporting his new one centimetre long, military-style haircut, and dressed in the same minimalistic but neat outfit, Lionel arrived at the Ashram gate. Behold! Worse than *déjà vu*, the spring-loaded, white-clad sadhaks jumped at him. But this time, he had news for them.

"Excuse me, I have an appointment. Suchitra is expecting me, and she will take me to the Mother. Please allow me to pass."

To his surprise, they relented quietly, even amicably, as if nothing had happened just two days ago. There came forward to greet him, an amiable Indian lady, petite, with long, single-plaited black hair. She took him in her charge. She wore the typical khaki shorts and white blouse that was donned by ashramites, male or female, when they expected to participate in sporting activities. The lady was friendly in an almost maternal way, and to his surprise, he felt like he had a family again.

She made him wash his feet and hands, and that done, looked him up and down and asked in a rather sweet tone, "Is that all you have? Why don't you wear a shirt?"

"I'm sorry Ma'am, I have no shirt, and yes, this is all I own."

She looked rather surprised, but understood instantly. "Wait a minute..." she said and went into a room.

When she returned, she carried a long scarf of white cloth, rimmed with a thin golden band of *zari*, which she arranged over his shoulders and chest, in typical South-Indian style. Then she accompanied him to the foot of the staircase that led to the Mother's room and left him there. A wooden, white-painted, open-air staircase led up to an aerial landing, and her room, which looked like a cabin floating in mid-air. Lionel climbed two dozen steps and looked around. The scene would remain engraved in his memory forever. He stood on the staircase among a short queue of devotees, all dressed in impeccable white kurtas, dhotis or sarees, holding a single flower in their hands – all very much reminiscent of some age-old Indian tradition. He too, held a light pink rose, given to him by Suchitra, with instructions that, when the time came, he should give his flower to the Mother. It seemed to be a strange, well-orchestrated ritual, and he wondered what good all this could bring. Once again he was sticking out, at the receiving end of people's stares: *What is this hmm...beggar doing here, on the way up to the Mother's abode?*

But such thoughts flickered only in his confused mind, the result of a paranoia that had developed over time. The people in the queue showed no such disdain. They smiled at him in a brotherly manner. At least he did not have long hair all the way to his bum, he thought; this was a definite plus point. He was still wearing nothing under his minimal lungi, but he was not even conscious of this. It was the natural result of the heavy battering he had endured during the preceding weeks and months. Some ruthless god (or goddess) had mercilessly hammered and purified him, forcing him into a state of mental naught and physical nudity close to that of a newborn. The fresh removal of his generous mane contributed even more to his feeling of vulnerable nakedness.

As it would turn out later, the Mother was not bothered with such profane matters, as long as her visitor was sincere and genuine in his aspiration. All considered, from the perspective of millennia-old Indian tradition, he was just another *sannyasi* or sadhu. Some of whom, such as the Naga Sadhus, cultivate abnegation to such an extreme that they walk the world stark naked, smeared with ash.

He had reached the White Town just in time. There would be only a few more weeks when these meetings with the Mother would be allowed for newcomers. Then the doors would be closed to all but her direct attendees and the few blessed individuals she was working with. It would have been impossible to meet her at a later date. And had he found a closed door, Lionel would never have recovered his psychological balance. The probability is high that he would have died a slow death, like many less fortunate seekers, in some squalid drug den 'on the way to Kathmandu', to use a cliché phrase of the time.

The status quo remained till September 1973, when the strong hand of her entourage, in an aggressive move to assert dominion, closed her doors for good, to all but themselves.

She withdrew from her body on 17th November of the same year.

Till that precise moment on the staircase, with all his reading, questioning and guessing, Lionel had not come close to realising WHO or WHAT, in truth, she was. Only now did he become conscious that something rare and remarkable was unfolding. All around him he could perceive a brooding immensity in the atmosphere.

But he had yet to be thunderstruck.

20
THE MOTHER

She is the golden bridge, the wonderful fire... [III-2]

1971, SOUTH INDIA

La Ville Blanche, Part 3

Lionel stood in the queue and waited. At the end of what felt like an eternity, but in truth was a short wait, the line began to move forward. It was bizarre in that the Ashram attendants, with extreme precision, controlled the movements of the group. They gave the impression they had served in the army and something had rubbed off. Strategically positioned, they barked instructions in low voices: 'Now go!' 'Stop!' 'Wait... wait...' 'Go!'

He was like a leaf in the wind, sent hither and thither. He was completely disoriented; he did not know if any of this made sense. Void of expectation, he had no idea how the Mother looked in real life (he had only read about her), whether she was middle-aged or older. All he knew for sure was that she would not be a seventeen-year-old maid.

Lady Suchitra had warned him, in French (the language was taught at the Ashram school), that this was to be *une entrevue silencieuse* (a silent meeting); there would be no talking. He was to just sit in front of the Mother and remain silent. It all sounded very mysterious. How on earth was he to convey his problems in silence? His panicked, grinding mind tried to formulate its absurd little speech: *I am crazy in my head, Ma'am, you know, and...* But after a while he gave himself up to the unknown, and surrendered. He became silent and watched, like a naked bird perched as his own witness on this aerial staircase.

In this stop-go, stop-go movement of the queue, Lionel at last reached a suspended catwalk, which appeared to be the access to the Mother's room. *Where am I? How did I get here?* His inner compass was spinning in a frenzy. He felt like a patient being prepped for surgery. As if he had received a light dose of anaesthetics, he floated in and out of reality. He had reached the apex of not being in control of anything regarding himself and his world.

Suddenly, he was propelled into her room.

In that first split-second instant, Lionel froze, mouth agape in a silent 'Awww!', like a child... Possibly, it appeared disrespectful to some, but it didn't matter. In that moment nothing mattered anymore; nothing at all. For no apparent reason, he was TERRIFIED. When he saw WHO was inside the room, or more explicitly, WHAT was inside, and around, and far beyond, as an extension of HER – *Something* indescribable, undefinable – he stood in shock, petrified, face-to-face with the Whole Universe in its unimaginable Divine form. The room had disappeared, and in the centre of this Cosmic Infinity was the fragile shell of a very small, elderly woman.

For a brief moment, shaken to the depths, he stood trembling like an aspen leaf.

Seeing Thy great form of many mouths and eyes, O Mighty-armed, of many arms, thighs and feet and bellies, terrible with many teeth, the world and its nations are shaken and in anguish, as also am I.

This eternal moment lasted no more than the blink of an eye. Like the shutter of a camera opening and closing, *cla-clac.*

Done, finished, move on... It would not have been possible to bear for one more second the rush of that Niagara of cosmic immensity without literally exploding. At the same time, so much had been poured into him as a vessel during that brief instant, that his consciousness was saturated.

It would take months, years, no, his whole life, to assess and assimilate the magnitude of that tsunami.

Lionel had read the *Bhagavad Gita* during his time in Geneva and Rome. When hours later he returned to the realm of normal life, the memory of that ancient poem resurfaced. He recognised the vision and knew that no description would ever convey the experience better than the narration given by Sanjaya to the blind King Dhritarashtra. In a stasis of suspended time between the two armies, many of whom were kin ready to annihilate each other on the battlefield of Kurukshetra, an immortal dialogue took place: Krishna, for the love of Arjuna, the Commander of the Pandavas, revealed to him his Universal Form.

> *The Vision of the World-Spirit*
>
> *Arjuna: If Thou thinkest that it can be seen by me, O Lord, O Master of Yoga, then show me Thy imperishable Self.*
>
> *Krishna: What thou hast to see, this thy human eye cannot grasp; but there is a divine eye (an inmost seeing) and that eye I now give to thee. Behold Me in My divine Yoga.*
>
> *Sanjaya: Having thus spoken, O King, the Master of the great Yoga, Hari, showed to Partha His supreme Form. Arjuna sees him and overcome with marvel and joy and fear, he bows down and adores with words of awe and with clasped hands the tremendous vision.*

Arjuna: I see all the gods in Thy body, O God, and different companies of beings, Brahma the creating Lord seated in the Lotus, and the Rishis and the race of the divine Serpents.

I see numberless arms and bellies and eyes and faces, I see Thy infinite forms on every side, but I see not Thy end nor Thy middle nor Thy beginning, O Lord of the universe, O Form universal.

I see Thee crowned and with Thy mace and Thy discus, hard to discern because Thou art a luminous mass of energy on all sides of me, an encompassing blaze, a sun-bright fire-bright Immeasurable.

Thou art the supreme Immutable whom we have to know, Thou art the high foundation and abode of the universe, Thou art the imperishable guardian of the eternal laws, Thou art the sempiternal soul of existence.

I behold Thee without end or middle or beginning, of infinite force, of numberless arms, Thy eyes are suns and moons, Thou hast a face of blazing fire and Thou art ever burning up the whole universe with the flame of Thy energy.

The whole space between earth and heaven is occupied by Thee alone, when is seen this, Thy fierce and astounding form, the three worlds are all in pain and suffer, O Thou mighty Spirit.

Seeing Thy great form of many mouths and eyes, O Mighty-armed, of many arms, thighs and feet and bellies, terrible with many teeth, the world and its nations are shaken and in anguish, as also am I.

I see Thee, touching heaven, blazing, of many hues, with opened mouths and enormous burning eyes, troubled and in pain is the soul within me and I find no peace or gladness.

As I look upon Thy mouths terrible with many tusks of destruction, Thy faces like the fires of Death and Time, I lose sense of the directions and find no peace. Turn Thy heart to grace, O God of gods! Refuge of all the worlds!"

Krishna: I am the Time-Spirit, destroyer of the world, arisen huge-statured for the destruction of the nations. Even without thee all these warriors shall be not, who are ranked in the opposing armies.

Sanjaya: Having heard these words of Keshava, Kiriti, with clasped hands and trembling, saluted again and spoke to Krishna in a faltering voice very much terrified and bowing down.

Arjuna: Salutation to Thee a thousand times over and again and yet again salutation, in front and behind and from every side, for Thou art each and all that is. Infinite in might and immeasurable in strength of action Thou pervadest all and art everyone.

I have seen what never was seen before and I rejoice, but my mind is troubled with fear. O Godhead, show me that other form of Thine; turn Thy heart to grace, O Thou Lord of the gods, O Thou abode of this universe.

Krishna: This that thou now seest by my favour, O Arjuna, is my supreme shape, my form of luminous energy, the universal, the infinite, the original which none but thou amongst men has yet seen.

Sanjaya: Vasudeva, having thus spoken to Arjuna, again manifested his normal image as Narayana.

Bhagavad Gita , selected excerpts Chapter 11,
translated by Sri Aurobindo

So much compressed substance went into that single second of intense stupefaction.

Regaining composure, Lionel walked into the room. On his left a very old lady sat in an armchair. He went in like an automaton, devoid of volition or feeling, and sat crossed-legged on the carpeted floor, in front of the Mother. He looked into her eyes. She looked into his. He sat there a few minutes in silence, as prescribed. The flower exchange took place. He received a bright red rose.

But in the limited view of his questioning mind, nothing was happening. *Something* was supposed to *happen*, wasn't it? Or was he too thick-skinned to perceive what was going on behind the veil, now that it had morphed into a more subtle tone?

Towards the end of the encounter, Lionel was overcome with distress. Some faint premonition told him he would never meet the Mother again in this physical world: this was a unique, non-replicable moment in his existence. Gently, he moved his head from left to right, as if trying to say with desperate intent, but no words: *...but then, what should I do with my life?*

It was his soul's burning question.

As abruptly as he had been launched into the room, he was flushed out by an aide, while an impeccably dressed-in-white devotee was shot in, in his place.

The silent meeting was over. The last thing Lionel saw as he rose to leave, was a large, sparkling crystal vase, placed on a low *gueridon* to her right. It contained a magnificent bouquet of beautiful, vibrant *Fleur-de-Lys*. Superimposed, Lionel envisioned a white and gold Standard flying in the wind to the resounding clash of arms in the background.

When he became aware of the world around him again, Lionel was back down in the Ashram courtyard, standing in front of Sri Aurobindo's *Samadhi,* the Master's final resting place, surrounded by devotees paying their respects in silence. No one paid him any attention; as if it had all been a dream and nothing of this had taken place; the same old him in the same emaciated body, all alone and lost in this world. After a while, he walked out, back into the busy street.

All that he had experienced since he had stepped into the Samadhi that morning was so alien that the mind was a poor, inadequate instrument to grasp the magnitude and meaning of this lightning-brief foray into the realm of the Mother. Had he been less distressed, he would have realised that everything that had to *happen* already had during that formidable first second when he had entered the room; an astounding experience few human beings have had the grace to receive. And that he might get the answer to his burning question when he met Satprem the next day.

He didn't know it then, nor could he foresee, how inconceivable and mind-shattering the answer would be.

21
THE ANSWER TO THE QUESTION

1971, SOUTH INDIA

La Ville Blanche, Part 4

Thirty hours had passed. Lionel and Satprem sat on the same wall between the infinite sea and the tennis grounds. They remained silent for a while, caressed by the gusts of the cool breeze coming from the Bay of Bengal.

Lionel had the intention of conveying his dispirited impression that *nothing had happened,* and to ask Satprem what he suggests he do next to *get fixed properly.* Was there some miraculous mantra he should recite one lakh times or something? Anything?

But before his first pre-words were ready to pass through his lips, Satprem smiled and silenced him with a swift movement of his hand. He had news.

"I have a message from the Mother for you," he said.

Lionel froze, listening.

"She told me you have to go to the Himalayas."

Long silence. It sounded like a thunderclap and took a few seconds to sink in.

"The Himalayas?" Lionel repeated, suddenly alarmed.

"Now. You must go to the Himalayas now."

This time Lionel's heart skipped a few beats. "But... I have just come from there... from North India! I travelled 3,000 kilometres south, riding trucks, trains and buses like a beggar, and you are telling me to go back?"

He was in a state of absolute panic. "I have no money, my visa has expired, and my physical condition is far from healthy; you can see that."

Satprem shrugged off all his whining, and after a while, made it evaporate, totally. But it took some hard work. Lionel was so very reluctant to hit the madness of the road again; understandably so. During the past few days there had been a cease-fire in his war; he had found something here in this strange town on the Coromandel Coast, some kinship, some beings capable of understanding him; something which, after a long, long time, felt like true family. Thupten, Satprem, the two friendly French girls, the lady Suchitra, a few others – however briefly met here and there, had listened to him, understood his predicament, and were trying to help. In their own way they had been where he had been. All his life he had been the oddity, the weird one, the unfitting. Here, he realised, there were other people like him!

But Satprem went on. "Listen most carefully now, Lionel. She added these very important words." He paused, to make sure it would properly register in Lionel's mind.

"This is the possibility of his life, she said."

Another thunderclap. What was the meaning of this? Lionel was dumbfounded.

Satprem patiently explained that the Mother had *seen* the 'possible' future for him: "*Seen,* not imagined. Do you understand the difference? Do you realise what *that* means? The Mother, she is not bound by Time or Space. She is free. She *sees.*"

Lionel tried to grapple with the concept in his mind. He had always refused to give way to any form of religion, magic, or superstition. But in this case, there was no hint of any of these, and as Satprem conveyed his message, he recollected WHO and WHAT he had seen in that room, just a day before. It had been anything but an illusion. He still shook when musing on that vision that had encompassed not only universal Space, but Time too.

Satprem continued: "Do not fear! If she has seen this for you, be certain of one thing – it IS possible and you CAN make it! If not, she would never have uttered the words. And do not worry about your visa or any other petty limitation. You have seen by yourself that there is another player here, another power at work."

Lionel made a serious effort to assimilate and process all this; to visualise the implications.

Satprem went on: "But you must learn to read the signs. There WILL be signs. As you have come to understand, she brought you here without your active participation. Can you imagine how things will change now that you are consciously aware of WHO is your guide? I know and realise your predicament, believe me. I have been a sannyasi myself *, a long time ago..." While speaking these words, his eyes twinkled as though he might re-live his own past through Lionel's adventure.

"Here, I got these books for you, which I hope will help you in your enterprise." He handed over a copy of *The Basis of Yoga* (a compilation of letters from Sri Aurobindo to his disciples), and *The Mother,* a concise booklet written by Sri Aurobindo, which Satprem knew would be an eye-opener, throwing light on the four aspects of the Universal Mother and the vision Lionel had experienced. It was important for Lionel to gain some education on these subjects. He also gave him his own latest book, *La Genèse du Surhomme — On the way to Supermanhood*.

As a last piece of advice, Satprem advised Lionel to stay away from the popular pilgrimage sites; that was nothing more than 'spiritual tourism', he said. If Lionel was to meet someone, it would not likely happen in such places.

Meet someone? Lionel stirred at these words. How or why on earth would he meet anyone of importance?

Satprem continued undisturbed, leaving the mystery unsolved. "Again, have no fear. You will be guided and you will *recognise* him. Look into his eyes, and you will see the sun."

Lionel listened transfixed, knowing better than to interrupt. It felt like an initiation.

With these last words, they parted.

Strangely enough, though fully aware that Lionel did not possess the financial means to travel, Satprem did not offer him money or any other kind of practical help. It seemed that non-interference was a tough but necessary prerequisite for the path of the sannyasi.

However difficult it was to heed the admonition, putting aside his rising apprehension and the fear gripping his guts, Lionel willingly submitted himself to the new ordeal, for he now knew who his guardian angel was.

And in truth, he didn't have a choice.

The following morning, like pilgrims of old, with a heavy heart, he heaved his cross onto his shoulder again and set off. No sooner had he reached the highway to Madras, a Tata truck, loudly blaring music, stopped and picked him up, before rushing on full throttle towards the new unknown.

[* *Par le Corps de la Terre, ou Le Sannyasin*, by Satprem]

22
INTERLUDE IN TIME

1971, SOUTH INDIA

La Ville Blanche, the Mother's Room

A few days earlier, Satprem had walked at his usual brisk pace across the Samadhi, on his way to his twice-weekly meeting with the Mother. In a corner of his mind he had made a note to check about the young man, Lionel.

It was one of those rare moments of tranquillity in the Mother's day, well after the ushered *tohubohu* of visitors had died away. Satprem entered her room without a sound; wearing the half-smile he always had on his face when he came to visit her. He sat crossed-legged on the soft-carpeted floor, in front of her. First things first, he carefully laid down his cassette-recorder on the carpet, to his right, and set the microphone between himself and the Mother's chair, slightly to his right as well. He pressed down the red recording button, along with the start button, making sure the tape was rolling. Then he relaxed. His sacrosanct recording routine invariably drew an amused smile from the Mother.

She remained silent, and so did he. One could hear the muffled sounds of the street below – the distant honking of a car, the *clank-clank* sound of a cycle-rickshaw in search of a customer, the occasional exclamation of a lone street vendor, and crows quarrelling in the Service Tree at the Samadhi. The old-fashioned clock on the wall painstakingly counted each second of a diluted Time.

Without preamble, the Mother spoke: "I have met this young man who came to see you twice… (she makes a tenuous gesture with two fingers). Very thin. I don't think he has much strength left, but… I was to decide whether he would return to France, or go to the Himalayas… The Himalayas are slightly beyond his strength, but if he goes to France, he will sink."

"Absolutely," agreed Satprem.

"So I believe I should give him a chance to try. But if he doesn't hold on, he will be crushed."

"Better to be crushed while searching rather than be crushed falling." Typical Satprem.

"*That* is our opinion. But among ordinary beings… there is not two out of a hundred who would choose this. You have no idea, oh!... However, he has shown good will, so we will give him his chance.

I wanted to tell you. I said I would give him a reply this evening.

Between both possibilities, let him go to the Himalayas."

"I will tell him," Satprem assured her.

The Mother again: "Tell him also that this is his highest possibility we are giving him here… He would have accomplished his maximum in his life if he goes there."

They both remained silent for a long time. At last, the clock valiantly chimed each stroke of the hour.

23
ON THE ROAD, AGAIN

1971, SOUTH INDIA, MADRAS

Lionel's minimalistic bag had suddenly become heavier: the books! But then, for nothing on earth would he have parted with them. They were the only physical, tangible testimony that the incidents of the past few days had been real, not an elaborate illusion, a trick played by his ruined mind. He had once again returned to his world of suffering, his own private Golgotha, about which no gospel would ever be written.

For the past twenty-four hours, he had been roaming endlessly in the suburbs of Madras, unable to leave the city. All he knew was he had to head north. The problem was the Himalayan range is 3,000 kilometres long; how the hell was he to get to the right place? Could not Satprem have given him an address at least? A State? The name of a town? Something? No, the only vague address he got was this gigantic chain of mountains stretching all the way from China in the East, to Tajikistan in the West. It was truly crazy.

He had reached Madras in a flash, riding the musical Tata truck. Both driver and cleaner sang continuously to the tunes emanating from a dreadful cassette player cranked to maximum volume; the first of its kind Lionel had ever seen in an Indian lorry. The loud Bollywood music, combined with the rattle of the dilapidated truck and the roar of the diesel engine, created an assaulting racket that almost shattered his eardrums. He was in no position to complain though, for he was a guest in this surreal vehicle, and the driver was proud to share with his guest this new technological marvel. Almost stone-deaf, Lionel finally got dropped off south of town, and continued on foot. In his simple logic, the next step was to proceed northward. Thus, he walked towards the northern exit of the city.

That's when the trouble started. Something was wrong.

He was stuck. Despite his best efforts, he could not leave the city. He had tried the railway station. He had boarded a Calcutta-bound train, just to be thrown out by the conductor at the second stop, at an absurdly tiny station in the middle of nowhere. He had tried the next train, to no avail; no one wanted him on board. One conductor even threatened to turn violent. Finally, Lionel left the station and trekked to the highway. He waited, hungry and tired. No truck would stop. He walked to a petrol pump, requesting a lift from several truckers, among them a couple of Sikh drivers, who were usually accommodating. Nope, his plea was ignored again and again. He could have cried in frustration. At this rate he would reach the Himalayas past the next blue moon.

By then, night was falling, so he walked back to the small railway station to find shelter. At that precise moment, a train pulled in, going in the opposite direction, towards Madras, and stopped. The conductor, like a shimmery cardboard cut-out in the open carriage door, smiled at him. Without thinking, Lionel boarded the train and sat down in the open doorway. The conductor offered to share a few *murukus* (those crispy, spiral shaped, fried snacks) with him. Lionel thanked him and slowly munched the muruku with the appreciation of the famished, while watching the passing landscapes of the busy city suburbs. In a jiffy he was back at Madras Central. He spent the night there on an isolated bench at the end of a platform.

When morning came, he realised that not only was he back to square one, but also to banging his head on a wall again and again, while stubbornly attempting to head north towards Calcutta, where he had come from. He got into thinking. The Himalayan range stretched in a wide arc from East to far in the West. What if trying to get to Calcutta was just a silly attempt to retrace his own steps and follow a known route that would somehow feel within his comfort zone? Then it slowly dawned on him that to go North, he might have to go West first!

So, westwards he turned. And lo! In no time he was happily cruising National Highway 48 in a truck, heading towards a far-off city on the Deccan plateau, located at an elevation of about 1000 metres. And not just in any ordinary truck. No, no, he was blessed! That truck was the latest, luxurious Ashok-Leyland model, in which, thanks to the kindness of the driver, Lionel was invited to stretch full length on the vast bunk at the back of the cabin.

And thus, relaxing like a prince on his couch, Lionel interrogated himself, for the first time investigating lines of thought he would never have dared to before. Could it be that there was a modus operandi behind all this, some subtle language he still could not comprehend? Perhaps he was not that crazy after all. Only uneducated to the ways of communication of a ruthless *force* going straight to its goal (and doing its best to carry him along in the process); following the most efficient route as per its own far-seeing vision. The trouble however, rose from the fact that this route would not necessarily be the most obvious one endorsed by his short-sighted human vision. More so when he didn't even know what the destination was! Besides, its course might inter-connect pre-set markers in space-time, unknown to him, but inescapable in the grand scheme. Just like Piazza Campo de' Fiori, the Pink House, the ghats in Kashi, and the Mother's room, could there be more of these mileposts to come? And hence the friction between two simultaneously functioning modes: one of ignorance, the other of insight.

At least that was one burgeoning theory.

By dusk the second day, under the crimson cast of sunset, the Ashok-Leyland truck slowly entered the crowded, dusty suburbs of the post-independence-declared capital of the bygone but nevertheless prestigious Mysore State, Bangalore.

24
THE CIRCUS

All stumbled on behind a stumbling Guide,
Yet every stumble is a needed pace
On unknown routes to an unknowable goal.
All blundered and straggled towards the One Divine. [X-3]

1971, SOUTH INDIA, BANGALORE

Having thanked both the driver and his helper-cleaner for the long, uninterrupted ride, Lionel jumped off the high cabin of the Ashok-Leyland. He was feeling refreshed, having spent most of the Madras-Bangalore journey dozing on the upper berth. Thankfully, the truck was brand new, and no one had fitted a sound system yet. On top of this, he had not suffered from hunger pangs either. At every stop, usually in one of those roadside trucker's *dhabas,* where one would sit crossed-legged on *charpoys* arranged around a low table, the generous driver had offered him food at par with what he ordered for himself – two *rotis* with *rajma,* and some *dahi*. And the mandatory *chai,* sweet and milky. Mid-journey, they had comfortably slept on charpoys for a few hours, at one of these stopovers.

Now that he was in an unknown part of India, Lionel was disoriented. So he squatted on a pavement, pulled his map out of the bag and unfolded it to check out his options, considering he still had to get to the Himalayas. At this stage he had not gained one iota in latitude when compared to Madras.

At that moment, he felt on top of his head a gentle tingling that drew his attention towards the blaring, distorted sound of a loudspeaker, overpowering the cacophony of street noises. Looking up, he saw a military-green Willis Jeep, with one of those large trumpet-shaped speakers mounted on its roof, flanked by two large panels on both sides, featuring the huge image of a roaring lion. The lion seemed to sparkle in the semi-darkness of twilight, giving the impression that it was alive. Across the lion's mane, in big colourful capital letters, he read, flashing: BOMBAY CIRCUS. A man holding a microphone sat beside the driver, haranguing passers-by in Kannada, the local language, to attend the evening show of the circus. When the Jeep passed at a slow pace in front of Lionel, the man waved at him with a big smile across his face. And then, in an instant, it had gone. There remained only the noise of traffic, the concert of honking, and the general bustle of an Indian city.

Lionel shrugged off the incident as a mere distraction and shifted his attention back to the map. He would have to head to Hyderabad next. But first, he had to find a decent spot to spend the night. As a fair substitute for a bedroom, he chose a bus shelter, which he shared with several homeless beggars, including a family of north-Karnataka labourers who had come to the city to seek employment – a young man and his wife, and their two little children. They all wore the pretty, colourful clothes typical of the *Lambadi* nomadic tribes. The man sported earrings, and the woman had a large silver ring pierced through her left nostril. They did not speak to him, though the children occasionally smiled. For the parents, he was too alien to approach.

At first light there was still a chill in the air. He rose, rolled up his sleeping bag, and left the shelter. Moving on, he walked northwards. But as the day passed, a sense of *déjà vu* reminded him of the recent Madras scenario. Only now, he seemed stuck in Bangalore. Similar attempts to head north, be it by road or by rail, towards Hyderabad this time, turned into exhausting disappointments. He tried to hop onto trucks on National Highway 7, and climb aboard trains at two minor railway stations – Cantonment and Yeshwantpur. Everywhere, he was ruthlessly evicted. It was infuriating, but more than that, it was physically taxing and psychologically distressing. He was torn between despair and rebellion. Now and then he would stand in the middle of the road, throw a blasphemous stare at the skies and shout like a madman at the top of his voice: *Hell and damnation! What the fuck am I doing here?*

Passers-by barely noticed him, and that made him even more frustrated. His mood shifted from revolt to despair, and he walked aimlessly, like a zombie, along endless crowded streets. Passing a small airfield called Jakkur, seat of the local aero club, on the road out to Hyderabad, he even considered the far-fetched idea of hitch-hiking a ride on a plane. But he was driven away from the gate by an angry *Gurkha* watchman armed with a stick, and intent on using it.

Late afternoon that same day, in a different part of town, once again the circus Jeep came cruising along the boulevard, its loudspeaker screaming Bollywood music. Lionel felt attracted and annoyed by it at the same time.

He tried to get to the main railway station. He had been famished for a while. On the way, a shopkeeper called to him and offered him some food. The meal looked odd, with lots of onions (he hated onions), but he was so hungry that he ate the stuff precipitously, onions and all. Shortly after, he felt uneasy in his stomach. He hopped on a bus and back-tracked to spend the night in a *Gurdwara* he had noticed earlier, near a small lake surrounded by a park. There, sick and desperate, he vomited in the middle of the night. Bangalore was turning into a place of nightmare.

Similar circumstances in life may repeat themselves again and again, insisting on the lesson one has to learn, until one eventually gives in and accepts the change within.

He awoke in terrible shape, as if suffering from a deep hangover. He could not remain at the Gurdwara, so he walked towards the central railway station. Lo-and-behold, the circus Jeep popped out from a small lane like a Jack-in-the-Box, turned onto the main street and went off, speakers blaring. This time, the image on the Jeep had changed; the lion had been replaced with a clown face, featuring green hair under a tiny black hat, and a red bowtie. Lionel failed to find the clown funny and decided that he would not pay any more attention to the irritating vehicle that kept finding him again and again. If there was any kind of message attached to it, to hell with it. It wasn't helping.

It was close to mid-day and getting hot. Lionel was walking through a busy commercial area called Majestic. Plenty of small shops and a multitude of mini-malls crammed into building basements: the Burma Market. A place where all possible smuggled goods could be found and purchased for a handful of rupees. Great for those in need of a cassette player or a fake Rolex watch, but Lionel could not have cared less; he didn't have any money, and he had no interest in a Rolex anyway. He just wanted to get to the Himalayas, still a good 2,000 kilometres away. On the positive side, he estimated he was drawing close to the Bangalore City railway station. He plodded on.

He had crossed the Majestic area and reached a point where, abruptly, the dense concentration of buildings thinned, and every street ended in a broad dusty road, almost empty of traffic. He walked across the road and stopped dead in his tracks, staggered.

In front of him, lay a vast expanse of wasteland, spreading from the foot of a short cliff; a drop of maybe thirty metres. The view from his vantage point overlooked a sweep of flat land the size of several football fields, and beyond, the dense city resumed itself. A few cows and goats grazed on occasional blades of grass, and rare passers-by walked across the barren ground. But this was not what had caught his attention.

Down below, in the middle of this no-man's-land, scintillating under the mid-day sun, stood a huge multi-coloured circus tent! Lionel froze, stunned. It was marvellous, beautiful, ethereal, yet real at the same time. The sight was like an oasis turning up in the heart of a desert. The golden aura surrounding it was not of the sun, but the more subtle love-light of a *Million d'Oiseaux d'Or* (Myriads of Golden Birds), as written by the poet Arthur Rimbaud. It hit him in the heart like a burning thunderbolt. In a moment of instant recognition, a silent voice in him screamed: *This is it! This is what you have been looking for!*

The pure, divine beauty of such moments swiftly wipe away the debt of extreme miseries accumulated along one's journey. All prior sufferings, regardless of their intensity, dissolve in that instant. If only one could retain a newborn's innocence and understand the divine language, there would be no need for pain along the way. One could walk the sunlit path at all times…

Yes, there are happy ways near to God's sun;
But few are they who tread the sunlit path;
Only the pure in soul can walk in light. [VI-2]

It was now crystal clear that *this* was what he had been searching for without knowing it, wandering aimlessly through this city for the past two days.

Lionel caught his breath and looked around. There were steps going down. He used them to reach the bottom of the cliff. Everything suddenly seemed very peaceful around him. The sounds of the city reached him, but in a muffled manner. He walked towards the circus. Many vehicles, trailers, cages, and smaller ancillary tents surrounded it – the usual circus scene. On most of the trailers he could read, printed on their sides in bold calligraphic letters: BOMBAY CIRCUS. As he got closer he could smell the odour of wild animals – felines, elephants, horses and camels. He heard the occasional roar or trumpeting.

It was an idle time for the circus; the shows were later in the day. All was quiet. Next to the main circus tent there was a large open canopy without side-walls, sheltering a group of three elephants, peacefully chewing on a bale of hay. A little apart, a man sat crossed-legged on a mat, having just started his lunch, brought on a large brass plate by an aide. He had a clean-shaved head, and was simply dressed in work pants and *kurta*. He looked up and waved at Lionel to come and join him. Lionel's gaze met the man's sun-like burning brown eyes, and he sat down on the mat in front of him. The aide returned with another *thali* for Lionel. There were two chapattis, rice, dal, a small cup of curd, and some mango pickle. It was simple but well prepared and very tasty.

Not a word was said.

The man did not speak till the meal was over. Lionel felt close to him, and had no desire to converse either, merely grateful for such an enjoyable meal. He felt so good in that exceptional moment under the circus tent, in the company of this unknown-known man, near the powerful elephants, that he did not wish for it to end. He had been very thirsty. When he drank the plain water in a brass mug, it tasted like nectar. The aide returned and took away the plates.

At this point, the man asked Lionel in Hindi, *"Aap kahaan ja rahe ho? (*Where are you going?)"

Lionel did not know what to say, so he pulled out his map, intending to use it to explain that he was going to the Himalayas for a retreat as a sannyasi. He unfolded the map and went on spreading it out between them on the mat. But before he could turn the map and orient it so that South was on the man's side and North on his, while it was still upside-down to him, the man put his right index finger on a specific point on the map; a map about six square feet in area.

Keeping it there, he looked straight into Lionel's eyes, with fiery intensity. *"Vahaan! Aap vahaan ja rahe ho.* (There! You are going there.)" He paused.

Lionel leaned forward to look at the map. The man's finger was pointing at the most North-Western state of India. More precisely, his finger was set right in the middle of the crown-jewel of the Indian Himalayas: Kashmir. When the man finally lifted his finger, Lionel read the name of the town he had been pointing to: Anantnag.

Seconds went by. Speaking now in remarkably clear English, the man said the cryptic words: "He is waiting for you."

"Waiting? Who is waiting?" asked Lionel, shocked.

But the man would say no more on the subject. After another moment of silence, he continued in a quiet voice, expressing what he perceived as a natural truth: "I can see doubt in your mind; you think you are weak, feeble, sick, and in a way you are right. But never forget this: you, I, and him as well, are all valiant *vibhutis*, powers incarnate, emanations of larger beings unbound by time and space. And these beings have chosen to send a small portion of themselves to play seemingly insignificant, yet powerful roles, now and many times through history. You too, have chosen your part in this undertaking."

After another pause, he said: "Have faith; your strength matches your challenge."

Under the impact of this revelation, Lionel's mind was in turmoil, but before he could ask any questions, the man spoke one last time: "Now you must go. You have a long journey ahead. Do not waste time. The railway station is just a few furlongs that way." He pointed towards the buildings at the opposite end of the wasteland.

They both stood up. Lionel thanked him for the meal and then took his leave. Still puzzled on his way out, he turned back and saw a last image of the man casually tending to the elephants.

Shortly thereafter, Lionel reached Bangalore City railway station. On platform number 2, an express train was ready to depart, engine steaming, bound for Hyderabad. He climbed into one of the crowded third class carriages and sat down at the wide open door. The conductor, standing on the platform, whistled vigorously several times, and within seconds the train noisily set itself in motion. As the train gathered speed, the conductor expertly grabbed the handhold beside the carriage door and jumped in, hopping past Lionel with a smile.

25
KURUKSHETRA

Dust, only Dust, and Men Gone to Dust.

1971, NORTH INDIA, HARYANA-PUNJAB

There was an enormous building on the right side of the road, surrounded by high walls painted bright red. Lionel walked along this never-ending wall. Finally, he came to a tall double-gate of thick metal, like that of a fortress, painted red too. This monstrosity could have been a tropical Alcatraz, but it was, in fact, a factory of a scale one saw only in India. His long forgotten family-owned mills in Lorraine seemed like miniatures in comparison. And on top of the gate, an immense metal arch bore the name: HERO CYCLES LTD. In his quest for *he-had-no-idea-what,* he had reached Ludhiana, Punjab.

His days were blurred in a downcast fog of sameness. He had lost track of time since he had met the circus man. Was it days, weeks, months? He had passed through Hyderabad at the peak of a heat wave, with temperatures soaring up to 44 degrees Celsius, and had been stricken with severe diarrhoea, probably from the absurdly unhygienic onion dish he had ingested in Bangalore. At first, he had not paid much attention to it, thinking it would subside. It wasn't his first *Delhi belly* and wouldn't be the last. But the ailment had aggravated to the point of being debilitating; he had to defecate several times a day. He could feel his diminished strength leeching away further day by day.

Painstakingly, he was dragging himself through Punjab. His entire life's horizon had shrunk into a burning inferno of dusty roads baked under the searing sun. He travelled the straight roads, always straight, dusty and monotonous roads; past an endless succession of ugly towns erected along the highway – a perpetual, never-ending semi-urban corridor. Trucks were everywhere; on the road, parked haphazardly on the road-side, in the dust. And there were shops and more shops of truck parts, car parts, motorbike parts, tractor parts. It seemed that the entire district thrived on mechanical parts of all kinds, and the whole landscape was the blazing forge in which they were cast.

He went through them all, those dusty towns from Delhi to Ludhiana – a succession of almost identical, nondescript entities, aligned along National Highway 1: Sonipat, Panipat, Kurukshetra, Ambala... By some absurd adverse fate, ever since he had crossed Delhi, he never got picked by a long-haul truck. Call it bad luck, or the work of a nameless god assigned to shape him on his anvil... into what? A wreck of a man? A newborn? He didn't know. Sometimes he felt he would burst with overwhelming rebellion. And frequently, regardless of the people who stared at him in shock, he would turn his face to the sky and yell at the top of his voice, not once, but again and again, till his voice turned into a pathetic croak: *POU-RRI-TURE! (Fuck this!* A loose translation that cannot possibly capture its unique connotation). For pure venting, nothing could replace a good old curse, pronounced in the French language. Given the circumstances, such blasphemy could hardly make his fate any worse. He was viewed as a madman anyway. Who really cared?

Truckers offered him short hops in rattling lorries, from one town to the next, or one village to the next – an exhausting progression under the searing heat. Every day he begged for food, every night he sought shelter in some temple or *gurdwara,* or simply in some recess in the pavement. He walked and walked... he could not stop. Rest was rare. Not that he did not wish to collapse somewhere, but then, where?

There was always someone harassing him for being in the wrong place or passing remarks about his white skin; they would not leave him in peace. But he had by then understood that the 'way of the sannyasi' was to walk, and walk more. To walk ceaselessly during the day, beg for food in the evening, extending his brass bowl to households and shopkeepers, and sleep at night, when possible. And the same thing began again the next day. And the next. If only he did not have to punctuate this sad routine with finding a place to shit, more and more often.

Among the faceless towns, Kurukshetra stood out — by its negative. The very name resounded with the clash of arms, the creak of chariot wheels, war cries, shrieks of pain, horses whinnying, the trumpeting of war elephants... The name was packed with the memories and glories of one of the most consequential battles that took place in the history of mankind. Kurukshetra, the place where the Pandava and Kaurava armies had faced each other in silence, while between them, in a stasis of suspended time, Krishna had initiated Arjuna, finally revealing his Universal Form.

Where had all this gone? Lionel looked all around and could find nothing. Absolutely nothing but an endless, overheated plain of grey dust, stretching to infinity, except for a few phony, kitsch monuments in town, raised to the glory of a long-forgotten past. Nothing of this held any substance. It could as well have happened elsewhere or never have happened at all. All that was left was dust.

Lionel's spirit was broken, his feet bleeding, and the hunger pangs that tortured him were never appeased.

But he went on through more faceless towns – Jalandhar, Pathankot, Jammu. He went on and on, heading North, towards a town called Udhampur.

He came to realise that for this insane enterprise into which someone (or *something*) had thrown him head first, despite himself, the essential quality required was not courage. Courage was worthless when all else had collapsed and one was just being continuously ground by fate, like *atta* in a millstone. Courage did nothing to help. In reality, the very concept of courage did not exist anymore for Lionel. For one being tortured on the rack, what was courage? He just passed through the millstone, being ground down further and further till, at the end, he is suddenly spat out into freedom – either a dead man or a survivor. The outcome depended purely on destiny. No amount of courage could make a difference.

What was really needed, Lionel understood, was something else altogether, another quality, rarely spoken of. It could be called *obstinate resilience*. He felt this truth at work in each cell of his body and in the depths of his soul. Only obstinate resilience could carry a human being through an ordeal so extreme. And if such was his destiny, he would stand alive at the end... or not.

If he did emerge alive, he would barely remember that he had a name.

Then one afternoon, rattling along in a truck carrying a load of bricks and cement bags, sitting wedged between the driver and the cleaner, barely conscious, he felt just a tiny wisp of cooler air pass briefly through the open window. And with it a strange new smell. Then it was gone. But it was alien enough to attract his attention.

After days and days of travelling through this infinite, monotonous, burning, hellish plain, his glazed gaze had been lost on an invisible spot behind the truck's dashboard, when through the dusty windscreen, a part of his mind tried to decipher the image forming in the background. He attempted to concentrate and focus, raising his tottering head straight to look ahead.

In the hot, fuzzy, shimmering air, he could distinguish something in the far distance; something that had slowly materialised and replaced the horizon – a line of cumulus clouds, white and mushrooming.

After a while, rather abruptly, a scene took shape under the line of clouds, and there it was, without doubt, massive and formidable in contrast to the flatlands of the past weeks. A miraculous, towering range of mountains stood in front of him, stretching to infinity on both sides. It was still hazy and half-real, but yes, there it was. It was not a dream.

The Himalayas.

26
TUNNEL OF HOPE

1971, HIMALAYAS

Kashmir Valley, Part 1

The Jawahar Tunnel in the early '70s was the umbilical cord linking Kashmir to the rest of India; the only connection providing access to the remote, disputed areas along the border with Pakistan. Guarded vigilantly by the military, it burrowed through the Pir Panjal Range, the first line of mountains in the western Himalayas, at an elevation of 2,200 metres. The two-and-half-kilometre long tunnel was the first important road work to create easier access to the Kashmir Valley. Prior to its commissioning in the mid-fifties, the road wound higher to the Banihal Pass at 2,800 metres, and was vulnerable to landslides and avalanches. Frequent road blocks often rendered the pass unusable, particularly in winter. The tunnel was thus a determinant factor that relieved the Kashmir Valley from its isolation, linking the towns of Banihal and Qazigund. It reduced the driving time by many hours and provided uninterrupted access throughout the year.

Sitting on a stone block in front of a tea-shop, Lionel felt grateful. The shop owner had offered him a cup of steaming hot tea, along with three *Marie* biscuits. It was early morning, and chilly. Lionel lauded himself for not having parted with his sleeping bag throughout his journey in the South, because from now on he would badly need it at night; his own private little luxury in life. It certainly looked battered, stained and discoloured, having travelled and been used and abused all the way from Europe to Banihal, via Afghanistan and South India. Other sadhus he had met on the hill road were content with a thin blanket. A few did not use any covering at all but a thin cloth sheet, and he wondered what fire within kept them warm and cheerful. They smiled in appreciation on seeing his bag, but none ever showed envy or jealousy.

He had reached the hamlet at the tunnel's entrance late in the evening, and spent the night protected from the nocturnal drizzle, under the corrugated iron awning that extended from the tea shack. The black gaping mouth of the tunnel was 100 metres further up the road. A group of armed Jawans stood there, near a barrier, checking every incoming vehicle before lifting the barrier and allowing it through. A few armoured vehicles were parked on both sides of the road, and machine-gun nests dotted the entire area, built of piled-up sandbags and protected from rain and snow by a square of rough corrugated iron, supported on a light metal structure. A pair of alert Jawans manned each of these weaponised rabbit-holes.

A military barracks cluster was located on the left, to shelter the small army contingent stationed there, dedicated to protecting the tunnel. It gave one the feeling of crossing a border into another country, reminiscent of the Khyber Pass. A lengthy queue of trucks snaked along the road, waiting their turn to proceed into the tunnel. The sky was overcast, and a chilling drizzle came and went intermittently. The monsoon had started, and long trails of fog crept along the steep forested slopes. Lionel shivered.

Though increasingly plagued by the persistent dysentery contracted in Hyderabad, which was getting worse, his present geographic position, right at the gateway to Kashmir and the High Himalaya, provided him some solace and hope. Chances were his ordeal would soon end, he thought.

But first he had to find a truck willing to take him across. The Jawans did not allow anyone through the tunnel on foot. If you wished to go on foot, you would have to climb the high pass, and that made little sense. After a while and enquiries among the (mostly) Sikh drivers, he got his ride: a good-looking Tata truck with the usual lush paintings, and pompons hanging all around. It had a nice spacious cabin. No heater though, and regardless of the chilly weather, the jolly driver insisted on keeping the windows wide open all the time. The cleaner didn't seem to mind.

Lionel was anxious what the reaction of the Jawans at the barrier would be to the uncommon white sannyasi in a truck. Uneasily he remembered that his Indian visa had expired several months ago. Besides, he had heard rumours of acts of war between India and Pakistan; Kashmir, by its geographic and political situation, was an ultra-sensitive area. The truck moved forward in the queue, reached the barrier attended by two Jawans, automatic weapons hanging loosely on their sides, and paused. The cleaner jumped down, ran to the duty officer's shack with the vehicle's documents, bill of lading and the last weighbridge certificate. In the meantime, the Jawans performed a thorough search of the cabin, throwing a brief suspicious look at Lionel, but nothing more. Once dismissed by the officer, the cleaner grabbed his stack of documents and hopped back into the truck.

One of the guards waved them on calling: *"Challo! Challo!*

Go ahead!", while the other lifted the barrier. The truck moved forward and entered the tunnel.

It took a while to traverse the black, water-dripping rocky vault at a tentative fifteen kilometres per hour, but then, a white oval appeared far ahead, and little by little grew into the tunnel's exit. Abruptly, they emerged into bright blinding sunlight, under a vivid blue sky. There was a plain below and tall peaks all around, some shimmering with pristine snow. Lionel squinted, his heart beating wildly. He was in Kashmir!

Anantnag was the next stop.

The truckers' destination was Srinagar, the state capital, some fifty kilometres further north-west. They dropped Lionel on the roadside, at the crossroads past Qazigund, about five kilometres short of Anantnag. Alone at this spot, he watched the truck disappear behind a bend. Taking his bearings, he started walking at a brisk pace towards Anantnag.

By the time he reached the town, it was late afternoon. Even in his pitiable state of mind, he couldn't help but admire the beauty of the place, with its small wooden houses built on foundations of stone, the flowering fields, the lush orchards. No wonder Kashmir had earned the epithet of 'Switzerland of India'.

However, there was an urgent matter to take care of. He had been shivering ever since the sun had dipped low behind the mountains, and had to find something warm to wear. From the moment he had reached the foothills he had known he would have to tackle the problem of the cold. So, in anticipation, he had saved a few rupees from his evening collections. In a small market at the periphery of Anantnag, he got himself a pair of typical white Kashmiri cotton pyjamas, tied with string at the waist. He used his lungi to cover his chest, and he still had the precious scarf given him by the lady Suchitra. His condition, though still precarious, had improved.

Lionel realised the human landscape too, had changed dramatically. The whole scene was now Islamic, with an underlying Sufi influence. The way people dressed, their beards, the women with their heads wrapped in a shawl, but surprisingly not shy. In some ways it reminded him of Afghanistan: there was a sense of pride and nobility reflected in the people. Even more so with the shepherd tribes who came down from the mountains – men with black hair and reddish beards, moving their herds of tall mountain-goats with their distinctive whistling (blown through the teeth, not the lips). They barely looked at him as they passed with graceful strides, at a swift pace.

Just as he had in Afghanistan, Lionel felt close to these people, and had a strange, unexplained kinship with the land too. Here again, hospitality felt warm and natural. On occasion meeting a group of shepherds taking a break on the roadside, he squatted among them. They smiled at him, without a word, as if he were a member of their tribe. Sometimes food was shared. It was something paltry, but in his miserable condition, lost, sick and desperate, such little acts of warmth were enough to give him the heart to get up and move on.

Five days had gone by and Lionel still wandered aimlessly up and down through Anantnag and its neighbouring hamlets. The more time that passed, the more he felt like a piece of iron being ceaselessly hammered on an anvil. He suffered from recurrent bouts of fever, perhaps due to the dysentery, or maybe because of the cold he had contracted due to inadequate clothing; he didn't know.

One bright moment had occurred though, at the end of the second day, when one man noticed he was poorly apparelled and asked Lionel why on earth a 'civilised', educated young man from 'abroad' would wander around randomly (it was the third time the man had spotted him in the area). Lionel, as usual in such conversations, could not provide a satisfactory answer. Anyhow, the man called his daughter and gave her some instructions in Kashmiri. The little girl rushed into the house and returned after a while, carrying a brown woollen sweater. She handed it over to Lionel. It wasn't new, but in good shape, except for a small hole in the side. Altogether a wonderful gift. Lionel gladly accepted with gratitude. Slowly sipping a cup of hot *chai,* also brought by the little girl, he noticed she had light-blue eyes. Finally, he got up, offered his thanks and took his leave. They exchanged the traditional *as-salaam alaikum* and *wa alaikum as-salam* while touching the forehead with the right hand, and Lionel moved on.

He was still plagued with the urge to defecate many times a day, and the condition was not improving. Every small town had a free Government Health Centre, but the care provided at such centres was basic and dated. To get rid of his debilitating dysentery, he had visited many such establishments along the way, from Jammu onwards. But most of them did not have a resident doctor, only a few nurses, who giggled as soon as he went in. The hospital facilities were primitive, the medicines administered were free but few and antiquated. The ubiquitous treatment offered in his case was pathetically inefficient – a white semi-liquid fluid to swallow, which looked and tasted like plaster of Paris. It brought no relief whatsoever.

By then, he knew all the public latrines in town. At any moment, he knew which one was the nearest to rush to! Those latrines were dreadful places. Built as a long alignment of contiguous wooden cabins, slightly elevated over a trench dug in the ground. Two wooden steps led to a rough, planked floor, with a circular hole in the centre, about twenty-five centimetres in diameter. Knowing how to use these *defecatoriums* had turned into an art for Lionel. First, since many previous customers had somehow missed the hole, he had to check which cabin had been the least contaminated by misfire. It was important since he didn't have the luxury of shoes or slippers. Second, he had to pick a cabin with a working lock, to avoid the disagreeable surprise of a tall bearded man suddenly popping into his cabin (the man usually apologised profusely). Third, it was essential to shut his mind to the smells, and sounds of neighbours in action. Last but not least, he had to remember to fill his little brass bowl for the final clean-up. Fortunately, there was (almost) always a large barrel of water available nearby, which could also be used to wash one's feet at the end of the chore.

Afterwards, he usually felt better for at least a few hours, allowing him to carry on.

He didn't have a choice, really. The inescapable 'way of the sannyasi' imposed by the ruthless Force that had attached itself to him, urged him to walk, and walk, and walk. No amount of rebellion or despair influenced It in the slightest. It knew what It was doing; with or without his collaboration.

Finally It would bring him to a crossroad of destiny, where all the influences in him met in one cataclysmic moment.

There, he would be compelled to make a tremendous soul-choice.

27
GHOSTS OF THE PAST

PART I: OBLITERATED GHOST OF THE PAST

1973, KASHMIR, ANANTNAG

One and half years had passed.

Buried in his new down-jacket, hastily purchased at the Roissy Airport in Paris a few days earlier, collar pulled up, Lionel shivered in a green-coloured Jammu & Kashmir Government bus, one of those ubiquitous models that sport absurd accordion type window panes, most kept half open because they are opaque. Winter was at its peak. It had snowed heavily and continuously for several days. Then a sudden bout of warmer weather had set in, causing sleet and rain to soak the mountain.

At a deserted crossroad they had left behind the board that read: ANANTNAG 27 KMS. On the tortuous, narrow road, the bus painstakingly worked its way uphill, past the modest village of Verinag. An unfathomable precipice lay on the left, several hundred metres deep, ending in the river below. Anyone looking down with attention would have distinguished at irregular intervals, the wrecks of mangled vehicles – trucks, jeeps, buses – decorating the foaming white waters.

What a comforting view, Lionel thought, even as the left rear wheel of the short-bodied bus swayed in the slush, narrowly missing the abyss by a few inches.

He had completed his time in the Alpine troops a few months earlier. Like a moth irresistibly attracted to the light, even at the risk of being burnt to cinders, as soon as it had become financially possible, he had boarded a direct Air India flight from Paris to New-Delhi, followed by a non-stop, long-haul sleeper bus to Srinagar. Back in the '70s, the Sheikh Ul-Alam International Airport was an exclusive military airfield, with no civilian enclave; the traveller had no other choice. The very next day, without a pause, he burrowed deep into the Kashmir valley again.

Lionel soon realised the absurdity of his enterprise, considering the prevailing weather – snowfall, bitter cold, sleet, fog, and the threat of landslides everywhere in this steep terrain. But he had already proved he could be a perfectly stubborn imbecile when the times called for it! Regardless of consequences, and haunted by a vision of the past, he headed towards a small, insignificant road-side *mandir,* a Hindu shrine in the mountains, nested on a protruding rock formation adorned with orange flags.

Nothing could have stopped his mad momentum.

The better part of an hour had passed and the refrigerator-like bus was approaching Lionel's destination – this nondescript mandir – as one may encounter now and then on any Himalayan roadside, in the middle of nowhere, at a detour or curve, where truck drivers pause for a brief moment of prayer. But instead of getting excited, Lionel had developed a bad feeling about this. For the last few kilometres he had perceived that something was very wrong with the landscape. As if the panorama revealing itself a little at a time with each curve of the road, in some odd way did not match his pictorial memory of the topography. When the bus finally negotiated a last hairpin and approached the expected location, an impossible sight met his eyes.

The entire mountain was gone!

A sinking sensation developed in his stomach. Everything had been erased – forest, road, mandir and all... One of those violent landslides, so common in the Himalayas, had swept away the mountain flank, with all it held – forest, road, and whatever man-made structures had been standing there. In its aftermath, it had left a chaos of rocks and mud, mixed with tree trunks and rubble, through which a freshly bulldozed pathway, precarious and scary, served as a makeshift road for the queue of vehicles inching forward. A rumour began circulating among the bus passengers that the landslide had struck at night, and there had been no casualty.

Strangely enough, the mainstream of the avalanche seemed to have targeted the exact spot where the little mandir had stood. A small group of military Jawans were controlling the alternate uphill-downhill traffic system they had enforced for the perilous crossing. A pair of olive-green JCB excavators, operated by the BRO (Border Roads Organisation), were still at work, with a team of Kashmiri labourers.

Lionel sat up straight in his seat, aghast. Through the bus window he questioned one of the road workers: *"Yeh khab huah? (*When did this happen?)"

"Kal, Sahab! (Yesterday, Sir!)" the man replied.

Flushed away, the mandir! Gone... as if it had never existed, except in his dreams.

That day Lionel should have understood that when one's

destined hour has passed, *it has passed*. Unfortunately, he did not. Thus, he would have to pay tribute once again.

GHOSTS OF THE PAST

PART 2: ENDURING GHOST OF THE PAST

2005, KASHMIR, ANANTNAG

Three swift decades had gone by.

Perched on the pillion seat of the motorcycle, Priyadarshini stared ahead, over Lionel's shoulder. She could see the oncoming signboard that read: ANANTNAG - 5 KMS. She looked away towards the incoming town, still unable to figure what had suddenly gone wrong with her man.

They had left Srinagar early that morning, heading towards this part of the Valley. The night before, she had noticed Lionel's odd behaviour: absent-minded, preoccupied, irritable. This was not like him; even more so since they had embarked on this long-awaited motorcycle journey through the heart of the Himalayas.

They had left behind Manali and the Kulu Valley, explored the unique and magnificent Manali-Leh road to Ladakh, crossed countless arid mountain passes, one after another, to nearly 5,000 metres elevation. They had alternately ridden and trekked, criss-crossing Ladakh for several weeks, and reached the northernmost part of India – the remote Nubra Valley along the Chinese border. On the way, the world's highest motorable road, culminating at Khardung La, 5,360 metres above sea level, treated them to a regal view of the Himalayan range.

For more than a month they had cruised along those mountain roads. At last, they had crossed the last pass leading to the Kashmir Valley, Zoji La, and taken a break at Sonamarg. There, for a while, they switched from the motorbike to a pair of mules, and rode to the blue ice of the Kolahoi Glacier. Finally, they had reached Srinagar, two days earlier. Throughout this expedition, Lionel had always been enthusiastic, cheerful, and caring – in pleasant and difficult times alike.

But now, something was frightfully amiss. It seemed that he was obsessed with some ghost from the past he wouldn't talk about. She knew Lionel had been to Kashmir a long time ago, long before they had met, but she possessed no details; he had always been very secretive about that period of his life, and she respected his reticence, knowing better than to question him.

It was Priyadarshini's first time in Kashmir, and she too, had fallen in love with the land and its people. They had chosen as their temporary home a charming house-boat on Dal Lake. It was as close as one could get to the slogan on every Kashmir Department of Tourism brochure: *Welcome to Paradise on Earth!*

Priyadarshini had wanted to visit Gulmarg that day, the well-known winter-summer resort, boasting the highest golf course in the world. But Lionel, set in his sour mood, had insisted on heading east instead. He said there was a beautiful Sikh Surya temple in Mattan, with a surprise waiting there, that she would love. She had not wished to pick a fight over such a petty matter, so they had agreed they would ride to Gulmarg the next day. However, a strange feeling of foreboding rose within her. A nagging knot of anguish mysteriously lodged itself in her heart.

But, once on the road, Priyadarshini forgot her uneasiness. Lionel had been so right about her surprise: she had fallen in love with the sacred fish in the Surya temple pond. Thousands and thousands of them! Each about thirty centimetres long, they looked like trout. Leaning over the pond, she could touch them with her hand; they teemed in such great numbers that the surface of the water vibrated with sparkling ripples created by the carpet of shiny fish backs reflecting the sun. It was beautiful. She fed them and watched them rush to the bread crumbs in thick waves of golden backs.

And when they had finished, they would turn towards her, throw their head out of the water with their big open fish-mouths and ask for more. One could almost hear them say: *"Priya, Priya…we are hungry! More food, more please!"* They teased her with intelligence, like little water-puppies. For her, it had been a sacred moment. These little water creatures were fearless and friendly, simply because no one had ever hurt them, or fished and eaten them. This knowledge had been transmitted into their genes, generation after generation, gradually replacing their innate predator-wary instincts.

It looked like fish could evolve quicker than humans.

On their way back from the temple the mood had changed. Priyadarshini noticed the signboard, and soon they entered the city of Anantnag. The traffic was dense and Lionel slowed down. They came to a crossroad in the centre of town. Another signboard pointed right, towards Srinagar.

Without warning, Lionel abruptly turned left. *Where on earth is he going now?* wondered Priyadarshini. *What has gotten into him again?* Attempting to be heard above the cacophony of traffic and engine sounds, she questioned, "Change of plan?"

"Not really," he replied. "Just scouting for a place I think I have been to in the past. Give me ten minutes exploration outside the town. I'm looking for something… someone maybe..."

Yeah, ten minutes, you bet, she thought. *Some…one?* She didn't understand what he had meant. All she knew was that it was getting late, and soon it would be impossible to get back to Srinagar before dark.

Suddenly, she was on high alert. Lionel was not riding in his usual calm, smooth manner; he was rash, aggressive, and edgy. She felt as if a black curtain thrown by invisible hostile forces had fallen upon them. Her ears were buzzing; something blurred her vision. She wanted to scream, *"Turn back! Turn back! Forget this! Whatever it is, forget it!"* She was on the verge of panic, and paralysed at the same time. It felt as if a thick layer of cotton wool had enveloped her and she could not utter a word.

Lionel zoomed madly through the thick traffic, along a busy street that looked like it led south-eastwards, out of town. She could have cried out "Stop!", and he would have stopped. But she did not. Thus, headlong into the darkness they plunged.

They had reached the edge of town and the road opened out; the houses became more and more sparse. Lionel shifted gears and sped up to full throttle. The big 1000 cc flat-four engine roared to life, and the powerful motorcycle propelled them out of town in a tremendous bout of acceleration, like a lioness leaping towards her prey.

Meanwhile, on the same road, a middle-aged lady, dressed in traditional Kashmiri attire and a beautiful shawl wrapping her hair, was travelling in an auto-rickshaw, to visit her son. The rickshaw driver stopped on the left behind a parked truck, opposite the house. The lady paid him and got down. She rushed across the road in happy anticipation of meeting her son. Halfway, she suddenly noticed an enormous motorcycle rushing towards her. She froze, then panicked and ran on.

At the same moment, Lionel saw the woman shoot out from behind the truck and veered to his right in a bid to avoid hitting her. But he had not taken into account the perverse scheme of those unseen partners of fate, working with precision from behind a dark veil. When the woman began to run, the collision became inevitable.

The impact was formidable. Half a ton of metal and riders, at high speed carries a fearful amount of kinetic energy. The front left side of the sleek Honda Goldwing hit the woman with full force and she was thrown off like a rag doll. The shock caused the motorcycle to veer to the right and plunge into the one-foot deep ditch on the side of the road. By then Lionel had lost all control over the vehicle. Under its own momentum, the motorbike carried on at high velocity, trapped in the ditch, for another ten metres, till it hit head on a small cement bridge that stood across the ditch perpendicularly. The motorbike took off violently and somersaulted, while both riders were hurled high into the air. All three landed at three different spots along the road, several metres from each other.

The road had turned into a battlefield. Priyadarshini and the woman lay motionless, far apart. The motorcycle was a distorted wreck resembling a dead horse. Lionel, perhaps more seasoned in handling disasters, had rolled over on hitting the ground, and was the first one back on his feet, though bleeding from several injuries. There was a dirty mix of oil, petrol and blood spreading over the road, and a sickening smell. Horrified, Lionel instinctively ran towards his wife, who lay immobile on the tarmac. Taking her in his arms, he saw that her helmet was cracked on the left side.

"Priya! Priya! Say something, my love!"

He carefully removed the helmet and examined her cranium, then checked her limbs for movement, and noticed there was no trace of blood on her; only a few drops from his own split forehead had fallen onto her leather jacket.

As he held her, she slowly returned to consciousness. Considering the damage to her helmet, she must have received a violent blow to the head, but she appeared physically intact, though mentally in shock. It was a miracle. He helped her up and guided her to a grassy patch on the roadside where, with great care, he made her lie down to recover.

In the meantime, some passers-by had taken care of the still unconscious woman and rushed her to the nearby Anantnag General Hospital in an auto-rickshaw. Perhaps the same one that had brought her to this fateful spot.

The following fortnight was spent recovering from physical and psychological wounds. Every alternate day, they shuttled between a nursing home in Srinagar, to fix Lionel's injuries, and the Court of Anantnag, to attend the hearings on the case that had been lodged against Lionel by the Anantnag police. 'Reckless driving' was the charge, and he was out on bail. Whenever possible, Priyadarshini, who as it turned out was the least incapacitated of the trio, visited the Srinagar Government Hospital, where the lady had been transferred, anxiously following-up on her slow recovery after the first two critical days in the ICU.

Spending so much time at the court, they gradually got to know every lawyer, clerk and judge, for two reasons. First, Lionel was a *firangi* (foreigner), and thus regarded with a certain curious respect as a guest in Kashmir. Second, Priyadarshini had an exceptional easy-going, warm-hearted attitude to people; she also spoke the local language perfectly. In this way they became the special mascots of the Anantnag Court, among an all-embracing assortment of criminals, ranging from petty thieves to chained, dreaded terrorists.

Then, on the eighteenth day after the accident, the hospital discharged the injured lady.

On the twentieth day, in an unexpected move that touched Lionel and Priyadarshini's hearts deeply, the lady, still weak on her legs and assisted by her son, went to seek an interview with the judge in charge of the case.

"I never wished to file a case against these people," she told the judge firmly. "The police proceeded without my consent or knowledge. This accident was the will of Allah. Please let them return to their family!"

Such was the natural generosity and compassion of these beautiful mountain people.

On the twenty-first day, the judge declared Priyadarshini and Lionel free to go home.

Indian courts are notorious for the lengthy process needed to close a case. But in the Court of Anantnag that day, there was great joy and celebration. Among the local lawyers, none could remember a road accident case having been resolved in a mere 21 days. What had begun as an act of doom, ended as the starting point in weaving cross-cultural threads of understanding and love.

It had required a great deal of bludgeoning, but at last Lionel had received the message.

A man cannot reverse the wheel of his fate.

28
MILLION D'OISEAUX D'OR

1971, HIMALAYAS

Kashmir Valley, Part 2

Many days had come and gone. Lionel was a wreck. Among a long succession of criss-crossed Indian States, Kashmir was becoming as bad as the rest, or worse. A major contribution to his breakdown was his aggravating, feverish, sick condition. He was not even capable of revolt anymore, walking ahead zombie-like, without thought, without reason, without aim. He was spent to the core. He didn't know where he was, or why he was where he was. Sometimes, he travelled by short-bodied bus, sometimes he walked, for long exhausting hours. He did not care where he was heading: he was the hapless subject of a thrust of destiny or whatever entity governed his fate; as helpless as a leaf in a wild wind.

He had left Anantnag behind and wandered along country roads leading to secluded villages in the mountains, reaching locations bearing exotic names such as Pahalgam, Kokernag and Verinag. But nothing 'happened'. No sign, no manifestation of anything or anybody; only persistent nothingness and suffering.

Weeks had passed since he had crossed the tunnel.

He was in a remote village embedded in a pine forest, named Daksum. The location was beautiful, and under other circumstances, he would have deemed the place idyllic, but he was famished, sick, and the road ended there. Relentless hunger had made him light-headed, and he was feeling a strange inner pressure, an urgency to do something, but he didn't know what. Without thinking, he boarded a bus, returning towards the flatlands of Kashmir. Strangely, he was the only passenger, alone except for the driver and conductor, who had not bothered about the fact that he was a ticketless traveller; he merely smiled knowingly. Lionel sat in the middle of the empty bus, on the right, against the window. All accordions pulled-up, he had a magnificent view of the mountains. His private, personal bus. It had never happened before. It was mid-morning; the sun was bright and he had a wonderful feeling of freshness, with the cool air rushing onto his face.

They arrived at a crossroad. Atop a bent metallic post he saw a battered green road sign that read: ANANTNAG - 36 KMS. Without warning, the bus veered sharply to the right and left the Anantnag road to venture deep into another valley, heading north, destination unknown.

Lionel was about to get up and yell above the loud rattling sounds: *"Hey wait! I am going to Anantnag!"* But then, he realised that he had this elated, fresh feeling in the bus, and it was just easier to let go. He wasn't even troubled by his tummy, having relieved himself in Daksum, just before leaving. The bus went on for another ten kilometres of winding roads, till they reached a wider valley with paddy fields and a lazy river flowing to his left. It looked fertile and prosperous. They arrived at a tiny village, stopped a few minutes, but no one boarded the bus, and it moved on, venturing deeper into the mountains.

The empty bus thundered away; perhaps the driver was

impatient to reach his final destination. They had barely covered a kilometre, and Lionel, madly jolted in his seat, was idly watching a small group of women working in the paddy fields to his left, when suddenly he felt an insistent tingling sensation at the top of his cranium, so imperative that it forced him to turn his head to the right and upwards, towards the mountainside.

And 'Awww!' There it was – a stunning, unworldly vision!

On a steep barren slope, there was a long winding flight of steps going up the mountain, perhaps five hundred feet, made of ancient stone and lined with a few scrawny trees here and there. At the top of the steps, the slope abated to shoulder level before resuming an even steeper incline, covered in pine forest. On the shoulder, a small Sufi shrine stood, painted white and green, adorned with green flags that floated in the breeze, and crescent moons. The shrine sparkled with an unearthly light. A Light that felt like power, love and light all at the same time – the fabled *Million d'Oiseaux d'Or* he had seen, what seemed like aeons ago, hovering over the Bombay Circus, but infinitely more intense this time – powerful and pure golden!

A voice screamed within him: *This IS the place! This is the moment! Get down! Now!*

Lionel got out of his seat, grabbed his stuff and navigated his way down the aisle of the scrambling bus, holding onto the top railing for dear life, to avoid crashing against the empty seats, all the way to the driver.

"Krupiya bus ruk dijiye! (Please stop the bus!)" he shouted.

Amid the racket of the engine and rattle of the bus, the driver did not get the message and forged ahead, merely glancing at him with a vacant eye.

"Krupiya bus ruk dijiye, abhi! (Please stop the bus, now!)"

At last, the driver got the gist and hit the brakes, but by then the vehicle had covered almost a kilometre. Lionel thanked the conductor, got down and walked back towards the village, no longer visible since it now laid behind several bends of the road.

It took a while. By the time he reached the base of the steps, everything looked normal again – an ordinary Sufi shrine on top of a hill. He had come across similar ones before. It appeared higher than he had initially thought, and he was weary, thirsty and hungry. Instead of starting the ascent, he walked to the village, a few furlongs downhill, and at the tea shop, requested a glass of water, and respectfully, a free cup of tea. The owner reluctantly complied. Sitting on a bench, Lionel sipped the hot beverage slowly, considering to climb the hill immediately thereafter.

He got up, and suddenly found himself assailed by an almost uncontrollable urge to defecate. By now, these urgencies came to him every few hours, accompanied by violent spasms in his tummy. He *had* to find a place. So he rushed into the paddy fields on the opposite deserted side, where no one seemed to work, and relieved himself beside a small stream of clear water, which he planned to use to clean up. He squatted there for quite a while, waiting in distress till the spasms passed, while he realised with growing urgency that *he should imperatively be somewhere else.*

WHACK! WHACK! Without warning, a barrage of vicious blows descended on his back with such violence that he fell half-conscious in the sandy creek, his body twisted in pain. When he was finally able to raise himself on an elbow, he saw through the mist of his agony a strong irate man standing above him, threateningly brandishing a stick, and hissing: *"Jao yahan se, bekaar saala, mera khet koi hugne ka jagah hai kya?* (Get out of here, miserable beggar. Do you think my field is for shitting?)"

The guy had popped up out of nowhere and sneaked up from behind. Lionel, so involved in his predicament, had failed to see or hear him approaching.

Heaven that had been so close, had suddenly given way to Hell. From being on the verge of a pure miracle, he had plunged into absolute catastrophe.

The thrust of destiny, when it comes in full swing, is ruthless and shows no pity.

He was back on the road, back-broken and barely able to walk. It seemed that an infinite length of time had elapsed since the moment he had stepped out of the bus. Something was crying in his heart too, as if his most hidden soul was in deep throes of pain. He began climbing the steps slowly, in a pathetic re-enactment of a Christian Calvary, painted in Kashmiri shades; missing from the scene, only a crowd spitting at him and three brigands.

All the way to the top he had an odd feeling that it was a futile effort, but he continued nevertheless. He reached the landing. There was a vast rectangular terrace, dominating the valley, with a low stone wall on two sides to guard against the steep drop. On the mountainside, a building crowned by a typical onion-shaped, green-painted dome, housed a prayer hall. It was empty. A few small annexes were attached to the principal building.

In the centre of the courtyard stood a small mandir, which looked neither Mahomedan nor Hindu, perhaps a mixed creation of both faiths. Strange things happen in these mountains, and orthodoxy sometimes gives way to a faith free from the shackles of organised religion. The mandir was square, less than four metres wide. A needle-sharp pinnacle topped the roof. There was one tiny window on each of the three sides of the building, all covered from within with very thick green, perfectly opaque curtains, so there was no way anyone could look in. The fourth side, facing the prayer hall, had a thick wooden door, painted green; so undersized that it seemed to have been designed for a dwarf. The door was locked from outside with a heavy padlock, and above the lock, there was a narrow opening with a wooden shutter, which oddly seemed bolted from within.

The entire place was silent and empty; not a soul around. The atmosphere was eerie. Lionel's heart beat like crazy – from the arduous climb and the despair of his own soul screaming to escape.

Finally, after looking around, he found a man who appeared to be the caretaker of the premises. The man explained in rough English-Hindi that the mandir was the home of a hermit, a saint who had forever renounced the world. A long time ago, this holy man had taken a vow. The villagers built the mandir as per his instructions; he entered it, never to be seen again.

For decades he had lived within. No one remembered exactly how long; the caretaker's father had attended to the place before him. An absolute recluse by choice, the holy man had survived in this tiny cell with almost no sustenance. Through the small opening in the locked door, devotees brought him buttermilk, fruit and water once a week, and that was all.

Upon further questioning, the caretaker confirmed that yes, another man had come there that day, before Lionel turned up; a rare visitor, one he had never seen before. The man had stood before the mandir for a while, praying. After which he sat on the little wall, musing, facing the stunning view of the valley. He sat for a long time, as if expecting someone. Then, abruptly, he rose and left.

By not being the impeccable warrior he should have been when the Hour came, Lionel had shamefully wasted the precious, gifted moment of his blessed encounter. In this unprepared world, where imperfection is still the norm, there are but a few rare cracks, through which the Divine can slip in and reach us. Those are narrow in space and short-lived in time. One cannot afford the luxuries of nonchalance or apathy, and miss the point of confluence where space, time, and protagonists converge and meet – for the moment won't wait for us.

The next morning, Lionel went early to the fields with his little bowl of water, only to discover he was shitting blood.

When the bull charges at you,
You may leap on its back, and it carries you away;
Or you cringe, and it crushes you.

Satprem

29
THE GORDIAN KNOT

1971, HIMALAYAS

Kashmir Valley, Part 3

A week passed by. At first, Lionel thought it was all over, that he was doomed till the End of Days; that God himself had conspired with the Devil to design this special, personalised torture for him. Perhaps he was truly guilty of some terrible crime? Perhaps he deserved the punishment? Perhaps, in the grand scheme of things, Ignorance *is* the crime?

He had ventured into Srinagar, the state capital, hoping to find a decent hospital, and cure his rapidly deteriorating intestinal condition. It was only 50 kilometres away. Filled with self-pity and anguish, he now considered death as the possible outcome of this misadventure. In moments of pure distress, he would imagine his dead body lying abandoned in a roadside ditch, with a pack of wild dogs coming to feast on his corpse at night. Such unattended human bodies, part devoured, he had seen more than once in Afghanistan.

Nobody would give a shit.

Between Anantnag and Kokernag, in a village called Achabal, there was a dog – an ordinary, typical Indian village dog, small in size, brownish in colour. But this dog was special. Lionel had walked through the area so many times that he had had plenty of opportunity to observe it. This dog had lost its hind legs. They were gone, completely.

Was it a birth defect? Had it been run over by a vehicle and maimed?

Whatever the cause, this dog was a recurrent source of anguish for Lionel, who was deeply affected by its misery. The legless dog dragged itself through the village in search of food in the garbage piles. 'Dragging' was the word. Since it had no legs, its damaged rear body was dragged on the road, forever leaving a thin trail of blood behind, from a permanent, never-healing wound, caused by constant abrasion. The immense effort this dog had to exert just to survive in its miserable life, was unthinkable; lifting itself and pushing forward with its forelegs, overcoming its own weight and the friction produced by the rear end of its body scraping the ground. And yet it moved forward, going somewhere.

When Lionel saw it for the first time, he thought: *This dog will be dead tomorrow.* But no, day after day, week after week, each time he passed through the village of Achabal, merciful death seemed to abscond and the dog was still there, alive, enduring the torture of its mutilated body.

As it attracted flies and vermin, the villagers, even children, threw sticks and stones at it. So it crawled away, eating whatever it could find. Lionel reminisced that in the Western world the dog would have been sedated and euthanized, as an act of grace. Not so in India. The villagers considered it okay to throw stones and shoo it away, but it was not okay to help this creature to die. *That* was a karmic matter between the dog and its Creator. Out of the two cultures, Lionel was no longer sure which one had the right approach.

The dog gave Lionel food for thought. There were moments when he fell into a deep-black pit inside himself, rotting in hopelessness, still defecating every hour, losing weight, getting more skeletal day by day. But then, seeing this dog, he would think: *This world can be cruel, yes, but understand, compared to that dog, your ordeal amounts to nothing; nothing at all! What the hell are you complaining about?*

And thus, just like the dog, he kept moving on, surviving on scraps of food, dragging his bleeding feet day after day.

Srinagar brought nothing good. No cure, no incoming surge of well-being provided by the Jammu & Kashmir State capital. No hospital would give him anything but the absurd plaster of Paris. For more sophisticated treatment, one needed money. 'Go to Delhi,' he was told.

Wherever he went, he was looked on as a pariah.

Then, to add to his misery, as if all this was not enough, there was a CBI officer, tenacious as a bulldog, who took a grudge against him and tormented him. Pakistan and India were at war, and the preposterous idea had crept into the zealous mind of the man that Lionel could be a Pakistani spy.

"*Aap kahaan ja rahe ho? Aap yahaan kyon ho?* (Where are you going? Why are you here?)" he kept asking aggressively each time they met, as he patrolled the street. On several occasions he was taken to the local branch of the Intelligence Bureau, for interrogation, before being unceremoniously released. Lionel was never able to answer the questions to the officer's satisfaction, since he himself did not understand why he was roaming about, or where he was going. He could not tell the cops he was on a quest for something he didn't know; for a place he had no clue about. It would have only infuriated them more. He began to fear the harassment could take a dangerous turn; a consideration that finally drove him away from Srinagar.

He was soon back in Anantnag district, and Achabal, and to the dog. Just like the village idiot and the beggar-woman dressed in a tattered jute bag, he had become part of the local scene – the mad white man. The inescapable scene that had been set for him to confront an ageless nemesis.

Twice more – thrice in all – did the golden miracle come to him, setting into place all the elements for the fateful encounter. Each time, circumstances aligned themselves in a stunning act of cosmic precision, and each time he rebelled and floundered. The fathomless black NO lurking inside him took over repeatedly, and he simply did not volunteer to plunge into the new dimension offered him. *No, no, and NO! Fuck everything! I won't have any more of this bullshit!*

Such was the destroying power, the force of negative revolt lodged within him. And with each encounter, the negation grew stronger.

The second time, strangely, everything was erased from his memory. Later, he could only remember that the setting for the fateful meeting had been another mandir somewhere; that's all there was, the rest a blank. This total lack of memory was clearly indicative of his dislocated state of mind.

Lionel was experiencing the ultimate *NIHIL* in the deepest, darkest core of his being. A black filthy NO that makes one choose to die rather than get up, stand straight, and say or even scream YES! to life, YES! to love! Physically and psychologically, he was an absolute wreck. He could feel the antagonising powers at war within himself, and this was not just a figurative image but a true physical sensation. He knew he had become a prized, coveted object of possession, in the power struggle of titanic occult entities.

This Gordian Knot, coiled and rooted in the subconscious depths of his being, impossible to untangle, held him captive in a vice. There was no merciful Alexander in sight to save him by severing the ugly nexus with a single stroke of his sword.

No, it was solely up to him.

This was the convergence of truths to which his destiny had brought him. Decades of existence, centuries perhaps, were now mercilessly focused on this single, hideous knot.

There was no escape.

In the rare moments when he had enough clarity of mind to stand back and observe the unfolding of each of these proceedings, he could discern a threefold pattern to the events:

Scene 1: He would be dragging his carcass along some non-descript road, drowning in abject self-pity; he would climb aboard a truck or bus.

Scene 2: Some casual event would trigger a refreshing wave of well-being and lightness, of which he became aware, both in body and mind. It felt like going through some strange process of purification, like a shower of Ganga water cleansing him.

Scene 3: Without warning or further ado, the flashing of the *Million d'Oiseaux d'Or* would explode, while some subtle hand seized his head almost physically, making him turn and look straight into the deluge of gold.

There was no time to consider, think, ponder. It called for a spontaneous, immediate choice: to plunge into the Unknown right then – or not.

The third and final attempt by this infinitely patient Grace remained etched in his mind with total clarity, for this life, and perhaps others to come.

He was in a truck, in the front cabin between the driver and his cleaner, somewhere past the village of Verinag, on the way up towards Banihal. On the right flank of the hill road appeared a small waterfall. The driver stopped and parked the truck in a narrow layby. The three of them stepped out of the cabin and went on to enjoy a rejuvenating bath under the cascade, with soap and shampoo – a long forgotten luxury. After a while they hopped back, refreshed, into the truck and moved on. Lionel felt a profound sense of alert lightness, as if he was floating in the truck cabin instead of stagnating in his usual state of gloomy despair.

And then, abruptly popping out from behind a bend in the road, the miracle struck. Another small mandir sprang into view, all flaming in the sparkling supernatural light, and the man was standing there, praying in front of the shrine, bathed in the same light. Lionel could see him in such close proximity this time that he noticed he was wearing a turban and Western-style clothing, such as modern Indians prefer. Something in him screamed: *"Yes! This is it! This is HIM! Stop the truck, you fool. Get down, here and now!"*

But Lionel sat frozen in the truck, paralysed by the gigantic NO rising from the depths of his being like a black Hydra. He sat petrified while a loud rumbling sound invaded his mind like the sound of an incoming avalanche, blocking out every other thought process. His whole physical being had become the stage set to host a titanic conflict of Cosmic Forces; between Good and Evil, Creation and Destruction, Love and Hate. His smothered soul yearned to run towards the sunlit path, but it could not. For he was just a block of stubborn, crass negation, denser than granite.

Meanwhile, the truck kept moving, and moving, till at last it all faded away slowly. What remained in his seat was the void shell of himself, dry like a fruit pressed of its last drop of juice; dry and dead.

> *... it is a noose that,*
> *once you put it round your neck,*
> *turns into a Gordian knot, which,*
> *if the scythe of Death does not cut it,*
> *there is no untying.*
>
> *Cervantes*

PART III

THE BLACK CLIFF

30
THE DARKEST DEED

1431, FRANCE, ROUEN, THE OLD MARKET

Over two years had passed since the Battle of Orléans.

And twelve months before, Jehanne La Pucelle had been captured. She had been leading a small army, about 400 strong, of her most faithful knights and soldiers. With precious little support from the now King of France (the Dauphin she had fought for; who had been crowned at Reims shortly after Orléans' victory), she was assisting the city of Compiègne, under siege by the Burgundians.

Early in the invasion, Burgundy, a powerful eastern province of France, had contracted a political alliance with the English, thus escalating the conflict into a civil war. Jehanne, by her efforts alone, had raised funds and recruited men for her campaign; from among the people under English oppression. Despite being situated well within Burgundian-controlled territory, Compiègne, a well-fortified town, had valiantly resisted, remaining loyal to the legitimate throne through the war.

It was dangerous territory, but this was not the cause of her capture. The irrefutable reason was dark and shameful. The Duke of Burgundy, a shady politician, was notorious for having adopted the English-favoured methods of war and politics: bribe, deceit, treason. He had secret allies within the court of France and thought the time was ripe to put them to use.

Jehanne, the Maid of Orléans, had indeed been betrayed.

Jean d'Aulon, who had shared her fate, reviewed for the hundredth time in his mind the circumstances that had led to their capture. Though guilt-ridden, there was nothing he could have done to prevent the Compiègne disaster. Behind the veil, the trap had been set. *Or could he have?* Though she had shared with him a premonition of her upcoming misfortune, Jehanne could be stubborn when she thought she was doing the right thing for the good of the realm of France; no amount of convincing would change her mind. When she believed in a mission, she threw herself body and soul into it, with no regard for her own safety. That made d'Aulon's task of protecting her all the more challenging.

Still, deep within himself *he knew* that had he been more alert and responsive, *he could have saved the Maid*. He had had a fleeting vision of a bridge closing, a presentiment, a word spoken by a little voice deep within; unassuming, soft, but vibrant with a note of truth, beckoning him towards the city walls. He could have listened, heeded the signs, and hastened the Maid's withdrawal with ease. But no, *he had not*. When in a situation conducive to a strategic retreat, instead of falling back with the rest of the army, he had kept on fighting, caught in the folly of pride, gore and violence, till it was too late. The traitors, seizing the opportunity, had played their hand.

Sometimes, when a convergence of circumstances triggers a twist of fate, a minor act, or the lack of it, can become the seed of unfathomable consequences; a two-way avenue.

Thus, he had failed to fulfil his primary duty – Jehanne's safety. For precisely one year and seven days (he had been counting them), this silent, intimate knowledge had slowly eroded his sanity. Guilt never ceased to grip his heart like a vice, day and night.

Yet the ambush had been master-minded with great care and accuracy; the intelligence detailed. By one of those adverse twists of fate, the small group accompanying the Maid got cut off from the bulk of the French army while it retreated. The Garrison Commander, a shady character by the name of Flavy, lackey of her fiercest opponent at Court, the ambitious La Tremoïlle, saw his opportunity and gave the order to raise the bridge.

A few brief minutes would have made the difference. Jehanne and a small group of her men found themselves stranded in the field, cut off from the safety of the city walls. In an instant the enemy surrounded them. They turned up in such overwhelming numbers that there had been no way to resist. The fight was over before it began. The Maid was pulled down from her charger and seized.

Not once, but an infinite number of times, had the Maid been betrayed. The ugly truth was she had become an embarrassment to all. To the English, who had been shamefully routed by a woman; to the Church that felt it could not control her; to influential Commanders in the King's army, who were choking on their own jealousy. Even the anointed King himself, Charles VII, did not know what to do with her, with all her fire and spirit, while he was preparing, weak and ill-advised as always, to compromise with the implacable enemy of France.

As a result, she was jailed in Rouen, struggling and absolutely alone, facing a rigged trial of the Inquisition. Following her capture, she had been detained in premises belonging to Jean de Luxembourg, a Burgundian collaborator, till he sold her for a hefty sum to the English. The process took a long time and several rounds of negotiation. The English immediately transferred her to the city of Rouen in Normandy, deep within English-controlled territory, intent on keeping her out of French reach and possible rescue attempts. Freedom for ransom was denied. From the start, the English were intent on washing away their defeat in her blood. They also knew that if freed, she would relentlessly come after them again. Owing to her incomparable charisma, they considered her infinitely dangerous as a warlord.

As for her companions-in-arms, each faced a different fate. After a few months in the custody of Luxembourg, Jean d'Aulon escaped, while the English were transferring him to London as a piece of high value on the chessboard of war. A few others, regarded as regular pawns, were freed against moderate ransoms, while the least valuable soldiers of her party were summarily executed. She was deeply distressed by this, but knew it to be part of a well-established feudal system of war, peace, and settlement.

Captured Kings were routinely freed against ransom, but not Jehanne. Her power was so legendary, her influence on the people so great, that even the Throne of England feared her. The Regent's humiliation was such that he would have no peace of mind till they burned her at the stake as a witch, with specific instructions that nothing be left of her, but fine ashes dispersed into the wind.

D'Aulon had spent several months as a captive in the fortress of Clairoix, near Compiègne. But as soon as he escaped the grip of Luxembourg, his first move was to seek the French King Charles' intervention and gain his support to attempt a rescue. The King's enthusiasm for the mission was lukewarm, entangled as he was in a complex political situation. But there were Jehanne's loyal and faithful captains, who had been contemplating a similar course of action. They were the hard-core lot who had once been murderers, arsonists and rapists by profession or inclination, but had been subdued by the Maid while under her command. They had developed a respect for her akin to worship and were prepared to fight for her to the death. They would dare attempt any operation to free her, provided there was a chance of success, however slim. Among them were the Comte Dunois, La Hire, and Gilles de Rais. They were seasoned Commanders, afraid of nothing, as well as excellent strategists.

Under pressure, despite a depleted treasury, Charles reluctantly sanctioned and partly financed a rescue attempt. However, for obvious political reasons, he insisted they keep the operation low profile, to be carried out in the most discrete manner. If discovered, it could not be traced back to him. Despite the fact that he owed the crown on his head to the Maid's valiant efforts, Charles did not wish to be officially involved.

Nearly a year into her capture, despite the high courage and risk-taking of Jehanne's friends, it soon became ominously clear that it was a case of too little, too late: the rescue operation had turned into a logistical nightmare. The locale of Rouen itself was an issue, the limited means another, and the absurd clause of secrecy from the Burgundians, a third. La Hire and his troops had taken possession of the small town of Louvais. As a base of operation, the position was strategically sound, located just seven leagues from Rouen, less than a riding day. However, it soon became plain that Rouen was extremely well defended, with a sizeable garrison attached to it. The English retaliated and La Hire's forces, trapped in Louvais, found themselves under siege, with almost no room left to manoeuvre. The conditions were not favourable, and the rescue attempt had to be postponed again and again.

As for Jean D'Aulon, he had been shuttling anonymously between Rouen and Louvais, gathering information and helping to figure out a workable plan of action. It was a risky affair. If recognised, he would be arrested on the spot. And the news was not good. His heart was torn as he heard whispered reports of how the Maid was treated, a combination of physical ill-treatment and mental torture. The conditions of her imprisonment were appalling, always chained to a heavy log, sometimes she was even kept in a small metal cage. Sick from malnutrition, lack of hygiene, and food poisoning (possibly an intentional ploy by her captors), she was compelled to fend off constant threats of rape from her jailers. She had to attend lengthy interrogations and exhausting cross-examinations, forced to stand chained before a horde of sixty inquisitors. Aggressive and ruthless in their questioning, they were headed by the remorseless Bishop Cauchon – himself on the payroll of the English.

Her torment went on for five long months. The records of the trial, seemingly ordinate and civilised, by no means reflect the reality of her atrocious ordeal. D'Aulon was filled with rage and revolt at the stories filtering out from the prison and the court room; his anger further fuelled when confronted by the apathy and disinterest of the people of

Rouen, who, broken by decades of English violence and oppression, were incapable of rebellion. Through relentless propaganda, the English had induced a fair share of the population into believing that she was indeed a witch and a heretic. Throughout this war, division, deliberately nurtured by the English, was the trademark of the French; a permanent feature of weakness.

Jean felt frustrated and helpless. He had never heard of anyone guarded with such extreme measures and with such cruel zeal; captive kings, perhaps. The daily news that filtered out was unreliable for the most part. The latest rumour was that Jehanne had recanted and would be condemned to life imprisonment. D'Aulon found this hard to believe, and considered it likely to be a ruse; he knew first-hand how vehemently, and with what persistence, the English wanted her death.

Jean d'Aulon was right. A few days later, early in the morning, a fresh rumour began to spread like wildfire through the streets of Rouen. An elevated pyre was being erected in the *Place du Vieux Marché,* the Old Market Square, flanked by two tribunes for high-ranking dignitaries to preside. Shortly thereafter it was officially announced that Jehanne would be dispatched to the flames the next day.

When Jean d'Aulon heard the news, his heart turned icy cold. The helplessness of the situation was maddening, and he found it difficult to maintain clarity of mind, filled as he was with rage and frustration. He at once sent a galloping courier to inform la Hire.

But la Hire was pinned down in Louvais, equally helpless. The same day, a large number of English foot soldiers were brought in from neighbouring garrisons, to guarantee crowd control. Eight hundred soldiers were to line the short distance from the prison to the site of execution, and fall behind Jehanne's tumbril as it moved forward. The English were taking no chance: the Maid would meet her fate.

The next day, a Wednesday, as the sun rose, d'Aulon knew that all hope of rescue was lost. He was a helpless wreck, an unwilling participant in a living nightmare. He walked to the dungeon where Jehanne was detained (all horses had been banned from the streets for the day), and merged into the crowd that had already gathered, praying and kneeling before the tower where Jehanne was held – the sinister Castle Philip Augustus. Many wept. By then the entire population had realised the magnitude of the tragedy that was to unfold. In one of the most barbaric acts in the history of mankind, an unspeakable crime would be perpetrated before their eyes. A pure, beautiful, untainted sun-eyed child, the pride of France at a time of extreme suffering, would be executed in the most horrific manner: Jehanne, nineteen years old, daughter of Jacques and Isabeau d'Arc, was to be burned alive in public, in the market square.

And there was nothing, absolutely nothing d'Aulon could do about it. Tears rolled down his cheeks, and he did not know if they were from sorrow or rage. Perhaps both.

Shortly after nine o'clock, the gates of the castle opened wide. A clamour rose from the assembled crowd, and a cart appeared on the bridge with Jehanne. She stood beside the two priests who had been designated to assist her in her final moments. She wore a long white shirt, and on her head, a mitre-shaped cap, which had stencilled in black ink the words *heretic, relapsed, apostate, idolatress.*

Having crossed the length of the bridge, the cart came to the mud road, guarded by two lines of English soldiers, restraining the crowd. Suddenly, d'Aulon saw her, quite close by, beyond a sea of shoulders, heads and spikes. A cataclysmic shock engulfed his entire being. The last time he had seen Jehanne was when they had been captured and detained at Luxembourg's castle of Beaulieu. She had been decently treated then, as a political prisoner. Only now, when he saw her, did he realise the magnitude of the ordeal she had been subjected to. Gone was the strong, flamboyant warrior. In her place, chained to the cart, barely able to stand, was an emaciated child-woman. Her head was shaved under the grotesque hat, her eyes sunken deep in their sockets, their flaming light extinguished; her cheeks hollow. She had deep raw wounds round her ankles, where the chains had rubbed for months; sores were visible on her naked arms.

What have they done? What have they done in one year of captivity, including five months of trial? Paralysed with horror, he stood agape. Then, like the people of France present that day, under the hood he wore to avoid recognition, Jean d'Aulon, a forty-one-year-old hardened soldier, wept like a child, his mind and soul shattered.

The grim procession reached the *Place du Vieux-Marché* – the largest paved plaza in town, surrounded by tall high-roofed houses. Abruptly, the high pyre came into view. Jehanne, seeing it, let out a slight cry of dread through her lips, as if she had seen Death itself standing on it. The cart stopped in front of the main tribune.

What followed was a farce, a macabre pretence at justice; a series of sermons read aloud, proclaiming to the crowd, the endless list of her crimes, errors, sins and evil deeds, followed by another list of noble justifications on the part of her tormentors. Finally there was a statement from the Inquisition: '*We declare you to be heretical and relapsed; and we declare that you, as a decayed member, to prevent the contagion from spreading to others, are cast from the unity of the Church, and given over to the secular power. We reject, cast you off, and abandon you, praying that, beyond death and the mutilation of your limbs, the Church treats you with moderation.*'

As it did with those words, never had the Holy Church stooped so low into demonic worlds.

Thought sat, a priestess of Perversity,
On her black tripod of the triune Snake
Reading by opposite signs the eternal script,
A sorceress reversing life's God-frame.
In darkling aisles with evil eyes for lamps
And fatal voices chanting from the apse,
In strange infernal dim basilicas
Intoning the magic of the unholy Word,
The ominous profound Initiate
Performed the ritual of her mysteries.
There, suffering was Nature's daily food
Alluring to the anguished heart and flesh,
And torture was the formula of delight,
Pain mimicked the celestial ecstasy.
There Good, a faithless gardener of God,
Watered with virtue the world's upas-tree
And, careful of the outward word and act,
Engrafted his hypocrite blooms on native ill.
All high things served their nether opposite:

The forms of Gods sustained a demon cult;
Heaven's face became a mask and snare of Hell. [II-8]

Oblivious to the perverted words, Jehanne prayed with fervour. At no time did she utter a word of blame about her judges, the English, or the Church that had abandoned her. But even with a weak body and a broken spirit, she was no sheep to be taken to slaughter. She demanded a consecrated cross be brought forthwith, and her authority was such that her request was granted. Since there was none on the spot, it was obtained from the nearby church of Saint-Sauveur.

"Keep it raised before my eyes till I die," she said to the priest who carried the cross.

Meanwhile, the English soldiers were growing impatient with the lengthy preparations. Finally, the order was given. Like a vulgar criminal, the English guards brutally forced her from the cart to the pyre, made her climb a ladder and chained her to the stake. A few of her judges, at last moved and horrified by such unwarranted brutality, rose and left the tribune. Perhaps *What have we done?* were the words echoing in their minds. But the cogs of the execution were now in motion and nothing and no one could have stopped it.

The executioners, armed with torches, set fire to the low branches and fagots. The flames began to spread higher. As the acrid smoke rose, Jehanne, her eyes fixed on the Holy Cross, kept praying aloud, calling to Jesus and her patron saints, till she coughed and choked uncontrollably. When the flames reached her, she cried aloud in terrified anguish and pain. The unbearable scream of a sacrificed child. And the terrible high-pitched scream went on and on till at last her head fell onto her chest.

In decades of military campaigning, Jean d'Aulon believed he had seen it all, the horrors of war – the wounded, the dying, the impaled, the raped... He had breathed the stench of the dead, of burning human flesh. He thought he was immune to it all.

Can one ever be immune, as long as one harbours a spark of a soul within?

But THAT? It was too much for him to bear. The sound of that cherished voice screaming in tortured anguish, THAT he could not hear, could not watch, could not endure... He thought he would go mad in that instant. Mad of that madness extreme, the shrieking kind. Mad of the madness that destroys cells in the brain and leaves only an empty shell of a man.

He pressed his hands over his ears and turned away. He pushed through the crowd, his hands still covering his ears. He pushed and pushed through the line of armed English soldiers, who took no notice of him, fascinated by the macabre spectacle taking place before their eyes. Finally breaking free of the crowd, he ran.... He ran along the houses which stood around the Old Market Square, through the streets of Rouen, through the gates of the city. No one paid him heed. Through the countryside he fled, till he could breathe no longer.

But fleeing did not help. He would hear that scream for the rest of his days. And more.

When Jehanne had perished, her lungs scalded and asphyxiated from inhaling the searing hot flames, the executioners were ordered to divert the blaze and exhibit her naked body to the crowd, as public evidence of a thorough execution. Then, twice did the English restock the pyre; twice did they revive the fire, till all that remained of her body was ash.

A strong guard was stationed next to the consumed pyre for the whole day and through the night. When it had cooled the next morning, the ash was gathered, taken to the bridge over the river Seine, and scattered into the wind. Nothing, not even ash, was to be left of the Maid who had dared shame them.

The Regent of England would be satisfied.

31
TAKEN

1431, FRANCE, BETWEEN ROUEN AND LOUVAIS

Crazed, drenched in sweat, exhausted, Jean d'Aulon somehow reached the isolated loyalist farm, less than a league from Rouen, where he had left his horse and arms. Seeing his insane, dishevelled look, his hosts, having gathered in the courtyard, did not dare ask questions. They knew something terrible had happened. There was no wind that day, and they had seen from afar the ominous, black column of smoke rise straight over the western part of the town, drifting slowly away as it turned white. There could be no doubt of its origin. And they could feel it in their bones. A formidable whirl of malefic breath had stricken Rouen, and its ripples would sweep Europe for decades to come.

Jean d'Aulon did not speak a word. Having saddled his mount in silence, he drank some water and went on his way. Bundled in a pack on the horse's back were the arms he could not be bothered to don; only girting on his sword through force of habit. He didn't care about his own safety. Nothing mattered. The horror he had witnessed had extinguished all human feeling in him; he was just a log of wood mounted on a horse, all senses dulled, with no life or emotion. Not even a desire for retribution. What was the point? It would not undo the crime. There was no spirit left in him; he could have died then and there, it would have made no difference.

And so, he somehow let the horse take him back at its own lazy pace along the road towards Louvais.

D'Aulon had been riding several hours, encountering a few odd travellers, mostly pilgrims, on a trail that was shunned by most, for good reason. There was tension in the air. The passing pilgrims threw inquisitive looks at him; he was obviously not an English soldier, nor a merchant or pilgrim. His demeanour and allure, his expensive sword, the ornate pommel, and his sturdy horse, all declared him to be a freedom-fighter knight from the South. To make matters worse, he was ambling along, without any attempt at concealment, oblivious to the fact that he was deep in hostile territory.

By then his tears had dried up, and he had lost touch with the real world. He realised that Jehanne and her mission had been his whole universe, and it had been violently ripped away from him. When the King had appointed him to be her Squire, two years earlier, he had, with or without wilful intent, sealed the fateful bond between them. And from that day, except in prison, Jean had always been at her side, sharing the hardships of all her campaigns, doing his best to protect her, to serve her and ease her burden.

Strangely enough, throughout this close relationship, no ambiguity ever developed in his perception of her. Now that she was gone, he wondered why? Unlike most, soldiers and captains alike, from the day she first appeared at the Dauphin's court, he had felt great respect for her. In time, as he became conscious of her true personality, respect had turned into unconditional devotion. Others cracked salacious jokes about her, at least in the beginning, but never in her hearing, fearing retribution (she was notorious for striking hard at the impious with the flat of her sword). Only Gilles de Rais, who feared neither God nor the Devil, had been brazen enough to utter explicit comments in her presence, while giving vent to a wild loud laugh; but only once. Jehanne had calmly reprimanded him. He never did so again.

D'Aulon himself stated for the record, when he testified some twenty years later at her rehabilitation trial by the Church: '*Although she was a young woman, beautiful and well formed, and when helping to arm her or otherwise I have often seen her breasts, and although sometimes when I was dressing her wounds I have seen her legs quite bare, and I have gone close to her many times, and I was strong, young and vigorous in those days, never, despite any sight or contact I had with the Maid, was my body moved to any carnal desire for her.*'

Self-absorbed and lost in a world of memories and self-pity, Jean did not notice that he had entered a thickly forested area. He was somewhere mid-way between Rouen and Louvais, on a trail he had followed several times. Along both sides of the deserted, muddy road there were tall trees and thick bushes. It was dark and ominous. Foolishly, immersed in his self-destructive state of mind, he let his mount amble along at a lazy pace. He also failed to observe that the horse had become nervous, and was snorting in alarm.

He had entered a narrow ravine and was deep into it when suddenly, with a wild blood-chilling clamour, a band of twelve English foot-soldiers sprang out of the bushes, and in a blink, had him surrounded, his mount immobilised. Two men gripped his horse by the bit, preventing it from bolting. Before he could even move his hand towards his sword and pull it out of its scabbard, he was felled by the violent actions of his assailants; one lot pushing him from the right, while another pulled him from the left. Against such a perfectly coordinated assault, he did not stand a chance. His head hit the ground hard. In a flash, he was sprawled on the ground, stunned.

Through the haze of the brutal shock he could feel a sharp dagger wedged between the ribs on his right side, and warm blood dripping. He did not struggle, did not resist. The dagger could have penetrated deeper and it would still have made no difference to his wasted life. He closed his eyes, opened his hands, and offered his life to the divine Maid. His head hurt and he could taste blood in his mouth as he drifted away into a crimson world.

When he came to, his entire body was in pain. He soon realised he had been bound across a horse's back, with his head dangling down against the animal's flank. Someone had crudely bandaged his chest, and he was shivering with fever. In the background he could hear the soldiers' loud banter about his capture and the hefty price he would fetch when they delivered him to the Bishop.

Awkwardly he tried to turn his head forward. In the distance he saw the upcoming walls of Rouen. He knew then that the London Tower he had once eluded was still waiting for him.

32
TARAS BULBA

1971, NORTH INDIA, NEW DELHI, CONNAUGHT PLACE

"Aap mujhe bataa sakte hai abhi kitna baje hai? (Excuse me sir, could you tell me the time please?)" Lionel asked the solitary passer-by still around at this late hour.

Crude neon lighting flooded the empty shaggy lawn and poorly maintained flower beds, lending an eerie feeling of abandonment to the place. By this time, most of the collection of petty merchants, masseurs, pimps and palm readers who usually crowded the place in the evenings had dwindled to a few lonely scattered silhouettes across the immense plaza.

*"Paune gyaara baje (*Eleven fifteen)," replied the man after a quick glance at his Indian-made HMT watch.

Lionel did a quick mental calculation. The bus stop was just five minutes away. This late at night, it would take less than an hour to reach Palam Airport. He had to report two hours before his flight. That gave him an hour to cater for anything unexpected. *That's fine, I'd better get started now,* he thought.

Lionel had reached Delhi a week earlier. He had painstakingly returned from Kashmir through all the same cities lined up along NH1 – Kurukshetra and the likes – in reverse. There appeared to be no obstruction, no obstacle, no occult activity preventing his shameful retreat. No fire-spitting dragon stood in his way, threatening to turn him to ashes. To his surprise, the journey was smoother than on the way up. It appeared he was floating in the middle of a neutral avenue, where nothing tried to push him this way or that; as if someone was telling him without words: *Okay, so you want to reject what's best for you? Your choice boy, you are on your own now.*

Ultimately, free will is always granted. Not that one would end up abandoned forever. The Divine does not lose itself in retribution or punishment. Such concepts are routinely supported only by blind faiths, religions and sects, in their endeavour to control mankind; always keen to sell a divinity made in man's image, only magnified.

Yet one may certainly feel cruelly alone, although one should at least have the honesty to admit that *we* have abandoned the path, and not the contrary. Meanwhile, in its own subtle world of wise far-sightedness, the guardian spirit takes a step back most pragmatically, and considers the options.

For Lionel, it finally boiled down to a question of inner attitude. From the moment he had hidden himself under a hood of defiance, determined to look to the other side no matter what, a door had been closed and a new line of destiny had begun to draw itself, creeping slowly into the future – hesitant yet teeming with faint intersections of infinite fresh possibilities. But one thing was sure, this new path would have to cross an endless, ugly wasteland of dark ages. He did not know yet how dark and how time-devouring it would be. It might even need a token of death as passage fee.

Having wandered for a few days through the city, famished as usual (and shitting even more than usual), he came across a Frenchman, one of those 'professional' hippies, who knew every trick in the backpacker's bag, any means to make a few bucks, every way to use the cracks in the system to his advantage.

The hippie told him: "Man, what's wrong with you? Don't you see your condition? Given another couple of weeks, we will surely have to cremate this skeleton of yours! You must go immediately to the French Embassy. Don't you know they provide help for guys like you – the junkie, the madman, the sick, the broke? Even for the dead. But you don't want to wait till that stage, right? No questions asked, it's their sacred duty!"

Looking around for an autorickshaw, he continued, "Not that they care about you personally, but you know, they would do anything to avoid the mountains of paperwork and administrative complications resulting from a French national's death on Indian soil." He gave an ironic laugh.

Lionel had never thought he would qualify for such aid and succour; he did not find it funny either.

"Come with me. I'm going there right now to collect my new passport. I know the Consul well and I will introduce you if need be."

This was the precise confluence of moment and location in the circumvolutions of space-time, when and where Lionel's destiny took a drastic new turn. Without giving it a second thought, he climbed into the rickshaw the other guy had just hailed, and off to the Embassy they went.

Just as he had been guided to Kashmir earlier, a new path had apparently been outlined behind the veil and he was kicked into it. A new wormhole had been created to take him across space-time. But in truth, for a while, there would be two parallel lines of destiny floating side by side.

It was still up to him to choose between them.

When Lionel entered the main hall of the Embassy, trailing behind his newly-acquainted friend, a sudden silence fell upon the room. All activity and conversation among staff members ceased as every gaze converged on him. Possibly his looks reminded them of those dreadful pictures of prisoners in the Nazi death camps taken by the Allies when they invaded Germany in 1945, and discovered the ugly truth about *Endlösung,* the Final Solution.

Within minutes he was being interviewed in a private glass partitioned office by an apparently concerned officer, who shot a barrage of questions at him. Lionel found it hard to provide answers that would satisfy the man. Given his more and more puzzled face, it was apparent Lionel had not succeeded.

"Why have you allowed your visa to expire? Where is your return ticket? Why have you got no money? Are you addicted to drugs? Why didn't you come see us earlier, aren't you aware of the seriousness of your physical condition?" And, after listening to a brief, simplified account of his odyssey, came the most impossible question to answer of all: "Why on earth have you lingered for so long in Kashmir; a hot war zone where you could have been summarily shot as a spy?"

The officer went off to meet the Consul. Lionel waited for a while, then predictably went to the bathroom. When he came back, the officer had returned.

"My boy, rest reassured we will arrange for homeland

repatriation as soon as we have sorted out the messy situation concerning your visa and organised a return flight. We will keep your passport till we complete all the formalities." And, with a wince of disgust across his face, "For God's sake, why does this passport resemble an antique papyrus manuscript just excavated from an archaeological site?"

That was his last question. Lionel mused about the *homeland* part for a while, but then took it in his stride. What else was there? He had run out of options for sure.

They gave him a handful of Indian rupees, not a sizeable sum but enough to meet basic requirements, and a visiting card with the name of a doctor at a private clinic, who took care of the Embassy staff's medical requirements.

Lionel took leave of the hippie-master, who had been waiting to see the outcome for his new protégé, left the Embassy and walked down the street a few blocks to where the posh clinic he had been recommended to, stood. It was New Delhi, the Embassies district – clean wide streets lined with trees, few people roaming around, black or olive-green Ambassador cars (the iconic Indian brand) cruising slowly along Panchsheel Marg, sporting some country flag on the bonnet. He was not used to this kind of neat environment; it felt odd.

At the clinic, after a thorough examination (advanced pathological tests weren't routinely done in those days), the doc told him, "Look, the way I see this, you are suffering from an advanced case of dysentery that has aggravated into acute gastroenteritis. You are bleeding internally and frightfully dehydrated. You came to see me just in time before it developed into a generalised infection. I can't understand why this has not already happened. There, take this, drink plenty of fluids; you are young and should be alright. Come and see me for a check-up in two days."

He handed five little innocuous-looking white pills to Lionel. The first one he swallowed on the spot, downed with a glass of water provided by the doc; the others would have to be taken once daily for four more days.

Amazingly, the very next morning, the wretched shitting spree had stopped altogether. The infamous plaster of Paris had been mercilessly put to shame.

Lionel walked along Connaught Place to the bus stop. His appearance had improved greatly. With the money provided by the Embassy, he had purchased decent pyjama-trousers (underwear too, which he found awfully uncomfortable), a smart deep purple kurta with the Nehru style of collar, and a pair of good quality leather chappals. He had also acquired a new shoulder bag, into which he had shoved, besides his precious books, his newly stamped passport with a re-validated exit visa, an Air India ticket from Palam, Delhi to Zurich, Switzerland, and another air ticket to Basel-Mulhouse Airport on the Franco-Swiss border in Alsace. The remaining forty rupees was just enough to pay for the bus, and maybe a coffee or two. He briefly recollected his old pending Swiss issues. Mercifully, he would remain in the international zone at Zurich while changing airplanes.

He was not conscious of this, but he now looked just like a typical European or American tourist — not even a hippie, since his hair was cropped short; just a *pukka* tourist. A careful observer would have noticed though that he was rather too skin and bone for a tourist, and what the hell was that exceedingly filthy sleeping bag hanging from his left shoulder, along with the funny brass bowl?

The truth was, while outwardly looking like a young holidaying American, inside, Lionel was still a sannyasi, with the habits and dispositions of one; he still squatted and slept on the pavement, ate chapatti-rice-and-dal in the cheapest godforsaken tea-shops where no foreigner would consider sitting, urinated in a squatting position against some stinky wall, and shat (rarely since the magic pills had taken effect) in public latrines no foreigner dared enter.

As he walked along the edge of the pavement, he perceived movement to his left; he turned to look. A typical black-and-yellow Fiat Premier Padmini, a Delhi taxi, came alongside, cruising along at his walking pace. The driver flashed him a smile, looking at him through the open window, his right elbow casually resting on the car door.

"Where are you going Sir, at this late hour?" he asked in good English.

"Palam Airport." Lionel replied

"Oh what luck! See my brother there in the back seat? He is going to the airport too, to catch an early flight to Dubai; works as a carpenter in Sharjah. I am dropping him now. Come along, we will be happy to give you a ride!"

"Sure, why not? Thank you very much Sir. I appreciate it," was Lionel's reply. This would be much quicker than the bus and he could save a few rupees.

The taxi stopped and the rear door opened. The brother-carpenter emerged. He turned out to be a towering colossus, about a metre-eighty centimetres tall, with his head shaved clean, and mongoloid features, wearing a tight fitting black *banian*, revealing perfect six-packs underneath. His muscular arms were almost entirely covered with tattoos. If he had to be given a nick-name, 'Taras Bulba' in reference to the Cossack hero, would have been fitting, Lionel thought briefly.

Taras Bulba gave the smile a tiger might have flashed on seeing a fat gazelle within easy reach, and said in heavily accented English, "Please Sir, have a seat!", indicating the open taxi door.

Lionel got in and, surprise, there was another *brother* seated on the far left, whom he had not noticed in the dark. The guy smiled too. Lionel, used to close proximity in buses and trains, squeezed in. Bulky Taras got in too and closed the door. It was a tight squeeze and Lionel began to feel like a sliver of ham stuck between two slices of sandwich bread. The Fiat Premier was a small car and Taras' head brushed the ceiling. The driver, who seemed smart and educated, and spoke good English, started the car while engaging in friendly conversation. And so off they went, amicably chatting, towards Palam. Meanwhile, both brothers in the back remained ominously silent.

Twenty minutes went by. The smart driver still fed the friendly conversation. Taras and brother number two sat immobile – mute, frozen statues. Lionel looked out of the window and got an odd feeling. They were cruising through some eerie suburbs of Delhi, with dwindling residences and much open land, poorly lit. He had not expected the vicinity of Palam Airport to have that kind of appearance. Lionel began to feel uneasy, mixed with a dash of dread.

At that moment, his blood froze in his veins and a brutal anguish seized his heart. Taras Bulba had moved ever so slightly and Lionel felt a sharp pain in his right side. Without looking, he knew. Instantly, he recognised the dreadful, familiar feeling of *déjà vu*. Taras Bulba held a Nepali *kukri*, the dreaded, razor-sharp weapon of the *Gurkha* tribe, pressed hard against Lionel's chest, between two ribs.

The car stopped. The place was deserted, apart from a few thatched huts in the distance, seemingly the edge of some sleepy slum. On both sides of the unpaved road there was a ditch, and beyond that just empty wasteland, merging into the night. Far behind, one or two lonely street-lights glowed in the dark. Brother two opened the left door, stepped down, and Taras, without releasing his firm grip on Lionel, signalled for him to follow out of the vehicle.

In the meantime, Smart brother had stepped out of the driver's seat, walked around the car and was waiting for Lionel on the other side. He was no longer smiling but barked in a most threatening tone, "All your money! Dollars, traveller-cheques, whatever you got. Right now!"

By then, brother two, who had grabbed Lionel's bag, was rummaging through the contents, dumping all his meager belongings in a messy heap on the car's bonnet. He found the few notes carefully kept in one of his books.

"That's all the money I have. I am being repatriated by the French Embassy," Lionel blurted in reply to their confounded stares.

The ridiculously paltry amount, combined with his simplistic answer, further infuriated the trio of *dacoits*. The pressure on the kukri wielded by Taras Bulba became more intense, even as he hamstringed his hostage in an iron grip from behind, his head close. Lionel could smell his fetid breath, reeking of alcohol and *paan*. He could feel too, vibrating in his limbs, the man's anger at having abducted a worthless quarry. Lionel knew the man was capable to kill: while getting out of the car, he had briefly read it in the man's glaring eyes, and a glacial fear had spread its ugly tentacles throughout his entire being. Now, he could feel a trickle of warm blood running under his kurta.

In that moment something snapped in Lionel's consciousness. He knew his end had come; an unworthy end to an unworthy life; here and now in some dark back alley of the Delhi slum-zone. All fear suddenly vanished. He closed his eyes and opened his hands in complete surrender. Then he called, silently, with no spoken words. His prayer was not directed to any deity. He just *called* with burning intensity. In that suspended moment in time, it was as if his being had withdrawn from his body and was floating slightly offset from it, in peaceful silence. The entire world around him, including his assailants, was blurred and unreal. He was ready to go, or stay – either way. He would not even have felt the blow if Taras had stabbed him to death, only slowly drifted away forever.

In those rare moments in life when one truly sinks to the depths of despair, perception becomes widened and one may see direct correlations between events happening in this world, and others hidden behind the veil of reality.

Then came an answer.

A small part of Lionel's awareness, like a detached observer, returned to the scene. It appeared that smart brother was unequivocally the boss. Taras Bulba´s job was to wield the sword and be menacing, to create fear, and to eventually get rid of any embarrassing witnesses if need be. He was hugely successful in his role. At some point, Lionel realised that the kukri was no longer lodged between his ribs and that the three dacoits were having an animated discussion. He thought he perceived an ongoing argument between them.

Then, as if they had settled the matter, Smart brother, the guy with the brains and smooth English vocabulary, turned back to Lionel and, to his great surprise, handing over his bag, spoke these unexpected words, "Okay... so it looks like you truly have no money. I can see that now. I don't know why I am doing this, but look here, I am returning your passport, your sleeping bag, your books, everything except the few rupees you carry. At least it will pay for my petrol."

During Lionel's absence they had frisked him thoroughly and searched every possible cache for a money-bag.

Then, as if he had wasted enough time, the man spat out to his accomplices, "*Challo chalte hain!* (Come on, let's go!)"

The next thing Lionel knew was that the car sped away with a *vroom,* raising a cloud of dust, and was gone. He was left standing alone in the night, in some remote suburb, he had no clue where. His meagre belongings, including his passport and tickets (which carried decent negotiable value on the black market), were in his bag.

Dazed, drenched in a cold sweat, bleeding and psychologically spent, he walked back towards the city. His senses returning, he felt like he had twice crossed the Styx, and returned from the dead.

When all is lost and only the shadow of a man is left, one may wonder what keeps the beaten warrior on his path, or even a new one? What makes him stand up again, though weak, defeated and brain-dead? What makes him grab his sword again for a last stand-alone fight against all odds, if not some irrational faith in a destiny that must inevitably go to its goal, regardless of all the detours and all the falls?

O soul, intruder in Nature's ignorance,
Armed traveller to the unseen supernal heights,
Thy spirit's fate is a battle and ceaseless march
Against invisible opponent Powers,
A passage from Matter into timeless self.
Adventurer through blind unforeseeing Time,
A forced advance through a long line of lives,
It pushes its spearhead through the centuries.
Across the dust and mire of the earthly plain,
On many guarded lines and dangerous fronts,
In dire assaults, in wounded slow retreats,
Holding the ideal's ringed and battered fort
Or fighting against odds in lonely posts,
Or camped in night around the bivouac's fires
Awaiting the tardy trumpets of the dawn
In hunger and in plenty and in pain,
Through peril and through triumph and through fall,
Through life's green lanes and over her desert sands,
Up the bald moor, along the sunlit ridge,
In serried columns with a straggling rear
Led by its nomad vanguard's signal fires,
Marches the army of the waylost god.
Then late the joy ineffable is felt,
Then he remembers his forgotten self;
He has refound the skies from which he fell. [VI-2]

When he showed up at the Embassy mid-morning the next

day, the staff, frozen in their seats, almost fainted. Still in shock and incoherent, he explained what had happened. When they stared at him in disbelief, he showed them the still bleeding wound, where the kukri had sliced his skin. Soon the Consul himself came to take stock of the situation. He was nearly apoplectic. He gave strict orders that Lionel was to be taken in a car to the doc at once. This was quickly done; he got a few stitches artistically embroidered without anaesthesia, and a tetanus shot for good measure (the doc was rather mad at him too, for no reason). Immediately on his return, he was locked in the Embassy attic, where the noisy air-conditioning system hummed constantly... until they could make new travel arrangements.

Lionel had missed his flight the night before, and that got him thinking. The brush with violent death in a dark alley of Delhi, was like the ultimate and most dreadful sign beckoning towards his initial fate: *Don't go away, don't flee! It is still possible! See, your health has been restored; you are not sick anymore; you can still do it! Go back!*

But, by then he was so stubbornly set in his refusal that he would rather have allowed himself to be cut into little pieces by a dozen Taras Bulbas than return to the Kashmir Calvary. Besides, to escape from the grip of the French, would have been another problem. He finally gave up. Thoroughly, ignominiously, he gave up.

Slowly, very slowly, in a subtle world where all possibilities exist, the splendid, elegant line as seen by the Mother, began to fade and disappear, giving way to a newly drawn, unknown future.

The next day, at the scheduled time of departure, the Consul played it safe. Lionel was driven to the airport in an official

Embassy car — a black Citroën with the French flag flying on the bonnet, no less — escorted by a driver and a bodyguard. The officer, the same one who had initially interviewed him, loaded with diplomatic documents and passes, bypassed all the usual formalities and escorted Lionel into the plane, personally putting him in his seat. *Enough of this nonsense* was written all over his face. The man took no chances. Bidding Lionel farewell, he only left just before the flight attendant locked the door of the aircraft.

Shortly thereafter, the Boeing 707 with its red-framed window-portholes, bearing the Centaur logo of Air India on its tail, taxied to the threshold of Palam Airport's single runway. Reluctantly, Lionel fastened his seatbelt, and off he flew...

To another world, another life.

33
THE BLACK CLIFF

1971, FRANCE, ALSACE

Control-Alt-Delete

The French customs officer looked at Lionel from under his dark blue *képi,* set slightly aslant on his head, then at his passport, and at Lionel again.

"Where are you coming from? India, if I am correct?"

"Yes, I am returning from India, Monsieur."

Abruptly, the officer said, "I wonder why anyone would want to go there? It's a land of savages, is it not?"

Shocked, Lionel opened his mouth to reply. But, realising he could not even begin to educate the ignorant man in such a short time, he thought better of it and said nothing.

"Any goods to declare?"

"This is all I have." Lionel indicated his minimalistic luggage.

The officer flinched, looking reluctantly at the sleeping bag, no doubt contaminated with savage Indian bacteria. *There should be a law restricting the import of such filthy objects,* he thought to himself. With professional expertise, he inspected the contents of the shoulder-bag, threw a suspicious look at his sannyasi bowl, turning it upside down as if it might have had a false bottom. He put everything back into the bag and handed it over. Finally, snooty-faced, borrowing one of those ready-made phrases government employees are prompt to use, he announced, "Welcome back. Please proceed!"

Set astride the Franco-Swiss border, Basel-Mulhouse was a low traffic, international airport that provided connectivity to both the Swiss canton of Basel and the French province of Alsace. It featured two sets of immigration posts – Swiss and French. Lionel could see the Swiss officers at the other end of the arrival hall, wearing grey uniforms, in contrast to the dark blue French outfits. He thought he better not go out the wrong gate since the Swiss customs officers would have his name on the wanted list, thanks to his precipitous exit about a year earlier. This odd situation was both alarming and amusing at the same time.

Lionel exited the airport, on the French side, and looked around. It was mid-morning. *Where are the people?* he wondered. *Why is the street deserted except for a few cars? Where are the cows, the dogs, the noisy crowds? Is this a ghost town?* It was all remarkably shocking, especially the *emptiness*. And it was cold too. He was still wearing kurta-pyjamas and chappals. It was Fall and the sky was overcast. Shivering uncontrollably, he hurried to the nearest taxi; there weren't many under the deserted airport awning. It was a Volkswagen K70, bearing a Swiss registration plate; not black-and-yellow but light beige. He paused; he had grown suspicious of taxis. But there was only the driver in the front left seat, who appeared very Swiss and safe (no shaved head either). Reassured, Lionel opened the rear door and stepped in. Thankfully, the car heater was running, and he soon felt better.

He gave the address to the driver who barely threw him

a glance in the rear view mirror, flipped his metre on, started the car, and remained silent. No questions asked, not even why he was so scantily dressed. No argument or bargaining on the rate; the metre was law. *Strange people,* Lionel thought... Though he had been gone only a year, it felt like an eternity. In truth, he now had the impression of a country he had never been to before. Things looked familiar in some ways, but at the same time his perception of the world around him had changed, as if there had been a subtle shift in the fabric of space-time, and he had returned to a *parallel-but-not-quite-the-same* universe.

Lionel sat back in the plush car seat and watched the passing scenery through the window. Due to the combination of jet-lag, lack of sleep, and even more to what he perceived as a time-line shift, he felt light-headed. He had to make a conscious effort to belong to and be part of this new reality, which otherwise masqueraded as a pale, fragile illusion.

It was only a twenty-five kilometre drive to his parents' new apartment in Riedisheim, a modern suburb of the old Alsatian town of Mulhouse. He had visited the place only once, when he had dropped off his motorcycle for safe-keeping, before leaving for Munich. Memories of the past returned to him as if they belonged to someone else. In no time, the K70 pulled alongside the pavement and stopped in front of a posh multi-storied modern apartment building.

He had arrived.

This was the precise moment when, for the first time, Lionel felt something new reaching for him, something foreboding, dark and undefinable, like the vague perception of a shadow. He shook off the feeling and opened the taxi door.

Stepping out, he requested the driver to wait for a while. Of course, he didn't have French currency to pay the fare. He grabbed his stuff, entered the building, got into the lift, and pressed the button to the fifth floor.

Exiting the lift, he turned and walked to the first apartment on the left. He noticed the immaculate walls, no red *paan* spit-marks anywhere. Strangely, he felt nothing. No emotion, no happiness, not even a spark of warmth at the thought of seeing his family again. Just nothing. An absolute blank.

He rang the bell.

A minute later the door opened a crack. He had a glimpse at his mother's face. She threw him a brief glance and *wham!* slammed the door shut. Lionel hesitated, but given a few seconds, understood that she had not recognised her own son; the product of her womb. With his short cropped hair, emaciated face, sunken eyes and flimsy frame, down to a mere 45 kilograms, he looked like a survivor of Natzweiler-Struthof, the notorious death camp brazenly set in Alsace by the Nazis, close to Mulhouse, during World War II.

So he rang again. She opened the door a second time, the expression on her face clearly said: *Don't you dare attempt any more vacuum cleaner sales on me!* Then it dawned on the shocked woman that the man at her door was not an obstinate salesperson, but her own son. She almost fainted. Both his parents had been worried, having had no news of their son for a year; he never fancied sending them letters. Then, all of a sudden, out of the blue, some not-so-encouraging news had surfaced by telex, from a French Embassy in a far-away country, on the edge of the known universe – India. They had gone to the airport to pick him up a few days before, but he had not showed up and his name was not on the flight manifest. It had been another severe blow.

Thus her first reaction was one of anger at not having received any news from him in a year. Next, she burst into tears, having taken stock of his wretched physical condition, and guessing at the psychological distress that showed in his bright feverish eyes.

He asked for money to pay the taxi. Silently, she gave it to him and he went down to pay off the equally silent taxi driver. That done, he reappeared upstairs.

At the table, he ate some food, but spoke little. After a while, when his father turned up, he glanced up from his plate and said lamely, "Hi Dad, I am back." He felt like he was on another planet; like he was a total stranger. Had he ever met these people? He stood up, saying he needed to rest, and walked to the impersonal room he had used only once in the past. He shut the door and pulled the curtains closed. Undressing, he lay down on the soft bed.

He fell asleep in an instant; a sleep so deep it was akin to death. Still, a part of him remained distantly aware, like a witness, even as he sank deeper and deeper into an unfathomable black abyss. He could feel on his skin the touch of the black glue that was swallowing him. It was nothing like a dream, but bore all the attributes of physical reality. His body shook with occasional spasms. There was a strange metallic taste in his mouth. He was aware of every detail of this subconscious realm. There was the strong perception of intimate knowledge and previous experience of this opaque world. As he slowly sank further, he could distinguish, darker than the darkness itself, a wall of black matter, along which he was sailing downwards, ever deeper. It was not smooth or uniform, but resembled the vertical face of a mountain, and pitch black; a tar-coated version of the north face of the Eiger on a moonless, starless night.

After a long time of slow free fall along the black cliff, he finally touched rock bottom. There he lay, in a fetal position, motionless. No vision, no sound, no feel, no fear... Just the Black; and Time suspended.

Death only lasts and the inconscient Void.
I only am eternal and endure.
I am the shapeless formidable Vast,
I am the emptiness that men call Space,
I am a timeless Nothingness carrying all,
I am the Illimitable, the mute Alone.
I, Death, am He; there is no other God.
All from my depths are born, they live by death;
All to my depths return and are no more.
I have made a world by my inconscient Force. [IX-2]

When he woke, it was the middle of the night. He discovered he had discharged all his body fluids – sweat, saliva, urine and semen. It was a mess. *Control-Alt-Delete* had been executed. The soft reboot had taken place in full; the slate was blank. There was only a command prompt blinking on a black screen.

When he had given up the quest up there in Kashmir, he had imagined he would return to his family and a normal, comfortable Western life. He could not have been more wrong. Instead, he had been precipitated into the womb of death, from where he could be born again.

A night and a day went by. The following morning, the doorbell rang. It was the postman. His mother came to his room, where she found him sitting crossed-legged on the bed, immobile, crazed, looking straight ahead into nothingness. She did not dare say a word, but handed over a thick, sealed, manila envelope, bearing on the left corner the colourful French flag – blue-white-red. In the centre, through a wide see-through slot, his full name appeared, type-written, with the address.

He took the envelope and opened it, gazing at the sheet of paper he extracted with blank eyes. It took him a moment to process its contents and bring the information into the real world. But yes, there was no doubt about it: he had just received his marching orders. He was to join the French Armed Forces, the Alpine troops.

PART IV
FORWARD!

34
A PAIR OF SKIS AND A NANA

1971-1972, FRANCE, SOUTHERN ALPS

The Citadel Town

Lionel walked out of his parents' apartment and took the lift down to the basement. There, preserved under a dusty tarp, was his motorcycle. It gave him a pleasant feeling, like reconnecting with an old friend, or a horse, a powerful charger of the chivalric era. In a cupboard, he found his gear too – helmet, boots, armoured leather jacket, gloves. He caressed the helmet and the soft leather of the jacket.

He took a pair of spanners from the rack on the wall, removed the battery from its compartment on the left side of the motorbike, under the saddle, and connected it to a charger he found in the cupboard, and turned it on; a red light blinked. Taking an empty container, Lionel disconnected the fuel line and purged the old residue of petrol from the tank. There was a can of petrol in a corner that his father kept for emergencies, and he used this to refill the tank with fresh gas. He checked the oil level, which read okay on the dip stick, and topped up the engine coolant.

A few hours later, battery charged, the faithful girl coughed a few times at the first touch of the starter switch, then purred like a lioness waking from a long slumber.

Lionel smiled. In a strange way, this inert artefact made of metal, plastic and rubber, this supposedly inanimate object, was the first *alive* entity he felt connected to since he had landed at Basel-Mulhouse.

He had ridden a bit more than five hours when he crossed the Col du Lautaret, a high pass in the arid landscape of the Southern Alps. Although it was early in the season, there was already snow on the road, starting a few kilometres before the highest point in the pass. The snowplough had cleared it, piling it up on the roadsides. Slippery ice covered the road in places and he had to be cautious on the motorbike. It was mid-afternoon and bitterly cold in the mountain-shadowed areas, despite a radiant autumn sun, already half-way down the horizon.

In a broad valley surrounded by lofty peaks, he could see ahead the town he had been expecting – an old citadel town, rich with the history of military tradition, close to the Italian border. He passed an ancient fortification wall and reached his destination – the cantonment. He stopped the motorcycle at the main gate, in front of the guardhouse, where the barrier was down. Several impeccably uniformed Alpine troopers manned the gate. They were easy to categorise thanks to the wide black *tarte* they wore on their heads, something he knew was unique among the Armed Forces. A guard approached him.

"I am here to report for military service," said Lionel. "Where can I park my motorcycle?"

The *Chasseur* looked at him and the bike, surprised at first, then embarrassed. "What are you doing here on a motorbike? You know this is an Alpine Army unit, not a motor-rally training centre! Why didn't you come by train like everyone else? Didn't you get your free train pass, provided by the Government?"

Of course, Lionel had got his pass in the manila envelope, along with his orders, but the prospect of travelling by train brought up some uncomfortable memories. Ever the odd one, he had preferred to ride his motorbike on the 600-kilometre journey from Alsace to the Valley of the Durance (there was a 100-kilometre shorter route via Geneva, but understandably he preferred to avoid Switzerland).

The second guard on duty, a biker himself, understood. "A nice bike you got here!" he said appreciatively. "Wait a moment, I will check with the Lieutenant and see what we can do."

He returned soon enough and pointed to a far-off corner across the immense courtyard, surrounded with multi-storied barracks and several vehicle-sheds.

"Okay, you see that shed over there on the far left? Park your Honda there, behind the line of GBC trucks, against the back wall. It will be safe. But I have to warn you that you cannot use it for the next three months, till you get your first leave."

That was fine with Lionel. He did as he was told.

The first three months were tough. At first, when the medical officer looked at him, all skin and bone, he said in shock: "What the hell are you doing here in a Combat Regiment? You could be discharged if you choose! I can sign this right now..."

But a little voice in Lionel was telling him that despite the anti-militarist beliefs he might have harboured in the past (now he had no beliefs left at all), and despite his condition, or maybe *because* of it, destiny had brought him to the right place. And so he declined the offer.

He would have three harsh months to regret his decision, every single day.

He received his uniforms, his soldier's gear and helmets; he received his skis – a pair of white Aluflex metallics, with Alpine touring bindings, and sealskins for ascending – and his boots; a sleeping bag supposedly rated for extreme low temperatures, his high-altitude white coveralls that would serve as camouflage in the snow, and a cavernous backpack. And though his hair was cropped short, a jeering barber gave him a regular *légionnaire* haircut. He was vaccinated against every disease one could find on the planet, in one single shot that could have killed a horse; twice for good measure within an interval of a month. Most importantly, he received his new girlfriend for the year to come, his deadly *Nana,* the AA-52 light machine gun. He was no longer a pacifist. A far cry from his sannyasi past, he was being turned into a warrior again.

When he walked into the dormitory he was to share with the thirty young men who made up his Combat Section, he chose the top of a 2-tier bunk-bed along a window that faced the white mountains. He sat crossed-legged on the bed, facing the mountain, and never moved. After a while, his roommates shared their concerns in a low voice.

"What's wrong with this guy?" someone asked.

"I heard he has just returned from India," replied another, as if that was explanation enough.

But they left him in peace, and given time, they got used to him and his strange ways. Genuine friendships and respect earned over shared hardships, developed in the following weeks and months. Through endless, forced marches across the mountains, loaded like a mule, pressed by barking adjutants, braving hail storms or bitter cold, compelled to sleep in snow-holes he would dig in the dark on top of polar-blizzard-swept passes, in an intensive process of reconstruction of the body, mind, and will-power, Lionel had to earn his right to life once more.

They say *what doesn't kill you makes you stronger.* At the end of three months of initial combat instruction, Lionel realised he had made serious progress on the long road to self-reconstruction. At about the same time, he was posted to a high-altitude fortified position nested on the Alpine ridges. It was a derelict from the Second World War that had been turned into a military shelter – Fort des Gondrans. On the western side of the ridge lay France, and the citadel town: they could see the cantonment down below when the weather was clear; on the eastern side lay the plains of Italy.

By virtue of the expertise gained from a childhood and adolescence spent on skis every winter since the age of four, he was promoted to Skiing Instructor. Military teaching techniques were crude then, though efficient. The word 'pedagogy', recently coined, had not reached the military outposts. Fresh recruits mostly came from humble families. Some of Lionel's skiing victims originated from the south and had never seen or touched snow. Every day at dawn, in the frigid cold, regardless of the weather, he took his trainees out of the fort, in sun, fog, or snow. He showed them how to attach the boots and skis; he helped them heave heavy rucksacks onto their shoulders and strap a weapon on top of it. He would then show them the valley of Montgenèvre some 1,000 metres below and say, "You okay? Good, we will meet down there. GO!" He then pushed the poor things straight into the slope.

It was a painful process, but they learnt fast. By late afternoon, the last of them had staggered to the rendezvous point, looking like exhausted, glazed-eyed snowmen. They had to make it if they wanted to catch the last ski-lift up the mountain, back home!

What doesn't kill you... Lionel soon learned that this proverb was the cornerstone of the French Army's success.

Winter turned into spring, and spring into summer. By now the white coveralls had been retired, replaced with brown and green camouflage fatigues. Lionel's entire section had been shifted, with all its gear and weaponry, to another high-altitude post – a summer military camp under tents, at the foot of the *Glacier Blanc*, the White Glacier. The camp was set in the heart of Massif des Écrins, a beautiful alpine region; pristine and still devoid of excessive tourism, commanding a magnificent view of Mont Pelvoux and Barre des Écrins. Both mountains ranked among the prime vistas of the southern Alps.

By then, the miracle of body resilience had operated in full, and the 45-kilogram skeleton had turned into a strong, trim, sturdy frame of almost 70 kilos, without a single gram of unnecessary fat. Lionel was physically fitter than he had ever been in his entire life. He had often wondered, when soldiers from other insignias of the army commented about the Alpine commandos, why they were referred to as the 'Animals'. He understood now; only the para-troopers commanded equal respect.

There was appreciable progress on the mind front too. The hard, healthy life had given him undeniable stability. He felt secure; there was no anguish about food or shelter; it was all well-organised and disciplined, even when they were living in camp.

And there was Lionel's romance with the Nana.

Twice a week, invariably, there was weapons' training with live ammunition at the cantonment or in the field, in the mountains. This 'chick' was a monster. A weapon conceived to be handled by a team of two commandos, it was so heavy and temperamental that it needed both men to carry and operate it. On long treks, they would split the weapon into two components; one man transported the barrel, the other the gun section. A third member of the group carried the strips of ammunition, which were bulky and heavy too.

At first, handling the Nana was a terrifying act. The machine gun featured a retractable bipod under the barrel, near the front end. Both commandos would lie flat-bellied on the ground. The gunner stood at the trigger-aiming end, while his less fortunate partner was at the hot end, holding the bipod legs firmly pressed on the ground with both hands to prevent the naughty chick from flying away out of control while shooting in long bursts. The real concern was the fact that the barrel got so damned hot, and the bullets flew out of the barrel mere inches above the partner's helmet. One quickly learned to lay flat as a carpet, nose in the mud, hanging to the gun's legs for dear life while making sure the damn thing wouldn't bite back.

These guns were not accurate, but powerful and very destructive nonetheless. Given the devastating amount of smoke, dust, and debris produced at the receiving end, every tenth round or so came a red tracer, as it was the only way to figure out if one was in effect hitting the target. Now and then the gun stopped without warning. The partner had to insert a fresh strip of ammunition, or sometimes, the 'chick' had jammed, entailing a mess that had to be sorted out while trying not to burn one's fingers. The racket was terrible, tearing through one's eardrums. Since no one had heard of earmuffs back then, plugging two empty cartridges into the ears was the smart way of muffling the sound and avert permanent hearing damage.

Even the second underprivileged pair in the section, those in charge of the *whooshing* anti-tank rocket launcher, were considered better off than Lionel and his partner.

But, like anything in life, it was a matter of getting used to it. After a while, for both of them, the Nana became just a tool of their trade, like an artist's pencil or a carpenter's chisel. Lionel, the retired sannyasi, saw his Nana as a true Daughter of Kali, and treated her with utmost respect. As time passed, his relationship with her evolved from sheer terror to a mix of awe and love. Towards the end, she was his best and only girlfriend.

Then came an evening in June.

The day had been magnificent and rewarding. Lionel had risen well before dawn and in the bitter cold, dressed and equipped himself for a high-altitude climb. For a change, they weren't carrying any weapons, but rappelling rope, crampons and a shoulder strap with carabiners instead. And a light rucksack with water and rations for the day. Lieutenant De Giuli, Lionel's Section Commander, had selected a handful of his best *Chasseurs,* and decided that they would devote this day to just climbing a mountain, for the sole reward of pure joy and beauty.

To their credit, most of the career officers who had chosen a posting in the Alpine Troops, were genuine mountain lovers. Lieutenant De Giuli was rather short and stout, always wore a stern expression on his face, and had an extreme sense of discipline. He was proud of leading the best section in the regiment. To achieve this end, he drove his flock hard, without pity. Despite this, he was well-respected by his men, presumably because he worked as hard as them, and was always just. Lionel liked him for his integrity and righteousness.

Lionel pulled down his *tarte* over the ears, tied his crampons on the rucksack, and grabbed his ice-axe. Under a sky twinkling with a multitude of stars in the black night, he switched on his battery-operated headlight and started to climb the path leading to the Glacier Blanc.

The small group reached the glacier at first light, then stopped and dropped their bags. They attached the crampons under their boots, struggling with fingers rendered stiff by the cold. Once ready, Lionel indulged himself for a moment, contemplating the golden rays of the rising sun, still hidden behind the mountains. There was an extraordinary contrast between the orange-tinted light of the sunrise and the turquoise light radiating from the crevasses in the glacier. The tall standing seracs glowed in a glory of pure blue light that seemed to originate from the ice itself. Whether it be the Alps or the Himalayas, he never tired of the inexpressible beauty of the High Mountains.

In the profound silence experienced at high altitude, only broken by the rhythmic *criss-criss* sound of their crampons on the ice, they resumed their march. The glacier was covered with a layer of fresh snow that could mask hidden crevasses, so they had roped up. Lionel was just behind De Giuli, followed by two of his mates, and Sergeant Grandjean, a consummate climber, closed the march (De Giuli had wisely left Pottier in camp). In front, illuminated by the first emerging rays of the sun, stood the Barre des Écrins, a splendid ridge culminating at 4,100 metres altitude – the highest mountain in the southern Alps.

The climb was not particularly technical; they had faced far more demanding challenges on other occasions. They had to traverse a steep glacier, followed by a rocky ridge leading to the summit. However, it was a high-altitude route and one had to be wary of treacherous crevasses, serac collapses, and weather changes. But it was one of those pleasant Alpine routes, more satisfying for its aesthetics rather than its technical challenge. Truly, the Lieutenant had offered them a treat.

When Lionel reached the summit mid-morning, he stood immobile for a long time near a sturdy iron cross bearing the scars of lightning strike. Apart from the sun, midway to its zenith, a bright star could still be seen straight up, like a diamond set in the deep purple sky. Contemplating the vast world stretching in a 360 degrees panoramic view below his feet, he could feel the strong current of a powerful Life Force running through his blood and every cell of his body.

He knew he was whole again.

The camp was in shadow. Lionel had had a 'bath' in the stream nearby, scaled down to minimal ablutions in the icy waters of the melting glacier. He was refreshed, the fatigue of the day wearing off. As he relaxed on the foldable canvas bed in his tent, he felt solid and well-embedded in his body, with a mind at peace.

Sergeant Grandjean walked past calling, "Guys! Clean and lubricate your weapons immediately! Inspection in 30 minutes."

What's going on now? Lionel wondered. He had heard rumours of military manoeuvres taking place somewhere.

Grandjean continued, "Tomorrow, 5:45 a.m., I want to see you all ready to go in full combat gear. At 6:00 sharp, we move down to the trucks waiting for us at the Pré de Madame Carle. Kalmer, make sure Pottier is on time. Kick his ass if need be."

Lionel knew better than to grumble, but he asked, "Where are we going, Sergeant?"

"All I know is the trucks will take us past the hamlet of La Grave. From the drop point, we will have to cross the Col de la Pucelle. Yeah, it will be hot and tough, I guess..."

35
THE LAST PILLAR

There should be a place on earth which no nation could claim as its own, where all human beings of goodwill who have a sincere aspiration could live freely as citizens of the world...

A Dream, The Mother

1973, SOUTH-INDIA, THE CITY OF DAWN

On that fateful day they had all gathered, crammed together on the narrow space of the scaffold-platform. Lionel and his brother Bors were there, as was Gawain, nephew of the King. Lamhcalad, son of King Ban, stood dashing, tall and slim, but ardent in his work as always. Even Mordred squatted in a corner, sombre and musing. Other knights, queens and damsels of old – Morvydd, Evaine, Blanchefleur – all of them timeless *vibhutis,* had volunteered to converge for another monumental enterprise on Earth.

They crowded the platform, pushing the heavy wheelbarrows of concrete, or forming a human chain to pass along the *chettys,* with the wet mix of cement, sand and blue metal to drop into the plywood shuttering. Some operated the concrete vibrators that sang their distinct high-pitched modulated whine, while others attended to the mixer, thrusting down the sand, stones, and cement into the noisy machine. At regular intervals, the mixer's elevator dumped its load in its own guts with a hard metallic *clank! clank! clank!* This loud clamour of the mixer was the unique signature perceived by all as the beating heart of the concreting.

To the casual visitor, it may have sounded like an

incomprehensible cacophony. But to them, timeless warriors, the rhythmic beat of the mixer, in harmony with the song of the vibrators, composed the divine music of a modern day battle; a music that would remain captured in their soul for eternities to come.

As for Myrddin Wilt, the wizard, though not physically present on the construction site for he was a recluse in his tower of Nandanam, surrounded by ramparts of bougainvillea and gardens of flowers, his underlying presence could be perceived by all. He was the guardian of the Spirit, the unbreakable link between them and Her.

Most of them had little memory of their origins, lost in ancient times and buried behind too many veils of life-cycles. But some occasionally recognised each other. One thing was certain, their renewed gathering as a team of Builders that transcended time and space, had truly established a powerful crew.

And they were joyous! They were building Her temple. Temple? No, that was not the right word. Her House? No, that was inaccurate too. She had wanted a township where the Builders and their descendants would continue Her work, and *that* was the City of Dawn. Equally important, in the town centre, She had envisioned a place where one could learn how to concentrate – an instrument, a tool, a *machine* that would help them call down and embody the new consciousness into themselves, and by extension, into the world. A place through which she could channel Her transforming Force even after departing this world, if it were to happen. She had given a name to this formidable instrument: *Matrimandir,* the Mother's Mandir.

Lionel's latest misadventure in Kashmir had been the last straw. After crossing the dangerous section of road cleared by the JCBs, the green bus had stopped. The curious driver and several passengers got down and swept a look across the landscape, assessing the damage. Lionel, aghast, was among them. The landslide had obliterated all his hopes, hurled into the river below, mixed with the rubble of the tiny road-side mandir. He felt like he had been slapped in the face. *Someone* was forcefully telling him to forget the past and move on.

Thus, in the aftermath of this disappointing winter stint, he had retreated from the frigid Himalayan mountains to the warmer plains.

He did not know what to do; still healing his fragmented mind from the years of mayhem he had been through. Thankfully, his service in the Alpine Troops had taken care of rebuilding his physical body; but the mind is a fragile entity and this takes infinitely more time to mend.

But he had this ancient yet vivid memory of Myrddin, the wizard, sitting on the wall facing the lake near the abbey, and his words: *Together, we have work to do!*

It looked like the moment had come.

Since the whole Himalayan operation had been written off, or at least postponed indefinitely, Lionel figured there was a place where there was no lack of creative work. His inner compass pointed South again, towards a warmer horizon, a barren plateau of red soil bordering the ocean on the Coromandel Coast, a place that did not yet exist – the City of Dawn – a dozen kilometres north of the White Town.

Thus, having travelled south by train (on a sleeper berth, with a valid ticket; circumstances *do* change in life), one beautiful morning Lionel stood at the edge of a deep crater excavated through the red laterite, close to a single lonely banyan tree, in the middle of a vast desert. The banyan, though old, had only one massive trunk, surrounded by an array of two-feet-high circular brick platforms, as one commonly came across in Indian villages. It served as a meeting point, where villagers gathered under its shade, sitting or lying on the platforms to chat and relax. Meanwhile, their goats would eat the hanging sprouts well before they could reach the ground, thus preventing the natural spread of the tree.

It was early February and the morning light was crystal clear, with the sun radiating a soft tint of gold. From the bottom of the fifty-metre-diameter crater, four massive concrete pillars rose towards the brim, laid out in pairs, each sloping inwards in one cardinal direction. They looked strange here, in the middle of the red desert, like alien monoliths emerging from a Martian archeological dig.

The scene below was peaceful. Seemingly lost in deep thought, standing alone on the wide concrete slab at the bottom of the pit, was a man of Western origin, in his late twenties; tall, tanned, and wearing only a pair of scanty red shorts and rubber chappals on his feet. He held a rolled up architectural drawing in his right hand. Focused on a geometrical constellation of white crosses painted on the slab, he was concentrated on solving a technical problem: how to start the scaffolding required to cast the massive concrete slab that was to bond the four pillars together. The local workers hadn't come yet, and he stood alone, considering how to kick off the day's work.

Without thinking, Lionel waved and said, "Hi! Do you need any help? My name is Lionel."

The man turned and looked up with a warm smile. "You are welcome! Come down. I am Lamhcalad."

It felt brotherly and natural, like they had known each other from across the ages. So Lionel climbed down the precarious-looking steps, down to the bottom of the pit. That morning, right then, he began to work, amid the local labourers, under the watchful eye of Lamhcalad, aligning, erecting and connecting the steel pipes that made the scaffold. When evening came, he stayed at the Builder's Camp for the first night, and then the next night, and the next. He never left.

There was no shortage of occupation among the isolated communities of pioneers scattered on the plateau. All the work offered was challenging, from building houses — primitive huts made of bamboo structures covered with woven palm leaves, locally called *keet*, with mud walls — to developing irrigation systems and generating the first embryo of a forest. It was, however, clear to him that the only activity towards which he was irresistibly attracted with a burning aspiration, in which he could involve himself wholeheartedly, was the Mother's Mandir. Nothing else motivated him with the same intensity.

And so, when November came, he had spent nine months devoting himself exclusively to this monumental task.

It was hard work; it was a hard life. The Builders lived in thatched huts without electricity, running water, or any modern amenities. The hot and humid climate was challenging. There were no bathtubs, showers or ceiling fans; as for air-conditioning, no one had ever heard of such a thing. There were plenty of creepy creatures for company, ranging from emerald-coloured snakes scouting the organic roof, to black scorpions invading the cupboards. At night, candles and kerosene lamps were lit. In some ways it was all very poetic and *retour-aux-sources*, very 'new wave'.

The open-air bathroom comprised a two-metre high water tank made of superposed cement rings, featuring a tap at the bottom and one square metre or two of cemented floor, to stand or sit on a tiny wooden bench. A matted fence of woven coconut fronds surrounded the area, providing minimal privacy. There was a metal bucket, a mug, a square piece of brownish soap, and no hot water, even in winter. The waste water fed a line of banana trees. The toilets, a simple trench in the red soil, surrounded by matted palm fronds too, were a good fifty metres away from the huts. The product of one's squatting meditation was covered by throwing handfuls of red mud over it, in the manner of a cat. A battered tin mug was kept there, for this task. Every few months, when the trench was nearly full, it would be topped up with mud, and another parallel trench dug. It was reminiscent of the Anantnag latrines, though far more convivial.

Available funds were meagre. As a result, food was minimal too, restricted to rice, *raagi* or *varagu* (locally grown cereals), dal, and a few vegetables. Two slices of cucumber and half a lime for vitamin C; milk and curd, obtained from the nearby village cows. There was no fridge; meat could not be preserved in the tropical weather. It was vegetarian cuisine by default, and no fancy desserts ever (ice-creams were a long-forgotten fantasy).

The Builders were not paid. They were given accommodation at the Builder's Camp or in nearby huts; they received food and the basic requirements such as soap, mosquito nets, sheets and blankets, or whatever they reasonably required, be it writing materials or a few books to read.

This system, started by the Mother, she had given the name 'Prosperity'. Amazingly, no one suffered from a lack of anything. What more could one want when immersed body and soul in this fabulous adventure? There were no distractions in the desert. The greatest beauty was that the Matrimandir was their life, and their life was the Matrimandir.

Except for the Banyan Tree – living embodiment of the Spirit of the City – next to the construction site, and a few isolated palm trees, there was no natural vegetation on the plateau. There was an unobstructed view of the sea, five kilometres away, across a terrain of hard, red laterite, sloping gently down towards the coast. The eastern horizon bore the curvature of the Earth.

The summer months were searingly hot. The harsh, blinding sun scorched the earth, causing it to crack open like bread baking in an oven. The ground restored the absorbed heat at night, so there was no respite. Boils and infections of all kinds, dysentery and hepatitis, were common ailments among the Builders. Medical facilities were non-existent. Hepatitis in particular, was dreaded because its debilitating effects lasted many months, and could occasionally be fatal if not attended to.

During the land-breeze season, dust storms regularly engulfed the region, covering in five millimetres of red dust everything in one's princely mansion – the floor, bed, tables, chairs if any (a rare commodity, residents mostly used woven-weed floor mats), any uncovered food, provided the brazen crows had not already stolen it.

Besides walking, cycles were the ubiquitous mode of transportation. There was not a single car; just one temperamental Royal Enfield motorcycle at the construction site workshop, and one rattling, sky-blue painted bus that performed connectivity duty every day between the White Town and the Banyan Tree — last stop. The umbilical cord to relative civilisation, the bus was skilfully handled across the canyons by an exuberant local driver, always clad in broad-legged beige shorts and a white T-shirt perforated with large holes. The man sported a generous Lord Ganesha-like tummy, spoke decent French, and answered to the quaint name of Louis-Swamy.

The monsoon was still a perfectly punctual phenomenon in those days, and it exploded with clockwork regularity year after year, before it gradually morphed into an anaemic, whimsical set of rains, with the advent of climate change. For a whole week sometimes, work came to a halt. Cataracts from the sky turned the entire landscape into a one-foot deep lake of brick-red liquid. The air turned thick with humidity. The Builders remained holed up in their (leaking) huts, behind a thick curtain of water pouring from the skies, busy mopping, preventing mushrooms and mildew from growing everywhere, including the nooks of their own bodies. The laterite was essentially a non-absorbent material, and with a lack of vegetation and topsoil to absorb the water, the levels quickly rose. Then, the flood made its way down to the nearby ocean via a complex network of deep, red canyons.

Eight hours a day under the harsh sun was the norm at work; more when concreting took place. The work was physically demanding. Because of the singular, bold architectural concept of the building – a thirty-metre-diameter sphere, slightly flattened at the poles, in the ancient Vedic shape known as 'Vishnu's Egg', supported by four massive pillars, cradled in an opened bud of twelve petals – the construction site was a labyrinth of stairs, steel ladders and scaffoldings where the uninitiated could easily get lost. Working there was akin to being a sailing hand on a ship.

In that initial stage, the skeleton of the structure was being built. Most of the work was about reinforced concrete: positioning and binding the steel rods, which a team of 'bar-benders' had performed in a workshop on the ground, followed by placing and securing the shuttering in position around the steel work. Those, made of thick reinforced plywood, had also been prefabricated in a carpenter's workshop under the supervision of a local *maestri*. When a section of shuttering had been set in place and was ready, concreting would be scheduled, and announced. Additional manpower was required for this labour-intensive phase. On these occasions, volunteers came from the many scattered micro-settlements of the City of Dawn, as well as one or two bus-loads from the White-Town. For the most part, these were *sadhaks* and students from the Ashram, enthusiastically led by their fearless captain, Peredur, the Mother's own personal warrior, whom she had sent into the field.

In the summer, concretings were conducted at night to avoid the scorching heat and glare of the sun. Powerful flood lights illuminated the construction site, which seen from afar, looked like an island of light floating on a black sea. It was a big, joyful event; a feast, a reunion of mankind; a gathering of all creeds, colours, ages, and genders; all poised in a unified effort to embody the Divine on Earth. All came with great enthusiasm to take part in this symphony of sound and light that resounded and shone into the night.

And all of them gave their best to the task.

It was about six in the evening and dusk was slowly invading the sky from the East. They had filled the shuttering to the brim and the concreting abruptly came to a halt. The song of the vibrators stopped, and soon after, the mixer's beat died too. Most of the workers and volunteers had already left the site, eager to have a refreshing bath and wash off the grime of cement and sweat that plastered their skin and hair. Peredur and his busload of aspiring young squires had faded away into the twilight, leaving a thick cloud of red dust behind.

A powerful silence engulfed the construction site.

A handful of Builders remained on the platform. Lionel, his brother Bors, and Lamhcalad, were among them; Gawain too, always the most zealous of the lot. They busied themselves with the collection of concrete samples, cast into small cubic blocks, to be dispatched, once cured, to the lab in Madras, to ascertain the quality and strength of the mix. Blanchefleur lovingly gave them a last finishing touch, as if they were works of art. Having completed the task, the small group sat in silence, allowing the stress of the work to dissolve slowly from their bodies and minds.

They all realised this was a unique symbolic moment. On that day, they had completed the last section of the Mahasaraswati Pillar in the West — the last of the four pillars. The three others, Mahalakshmi in the east, Mahakali in the north and Maheshwari on the south, were ready. The resulting curved structure, an extension of the lenticular slab connecting the pillars, finally emerged from its cradle of earth. It would receive the thirty-metre-diameter, quasi-spherical golden edifice (yet to be built), that would contain the large concentration chamber of the Mother's Mandir: a spacious, subdued do-decagonal hall of white marble, traversed in its centre by a vertical sun ray from above, falling on a two-feet diameter pure crystal orb in the middle of the marble floor, with twelve columns standing around it like a circle of silent sentinels.

Unequivocally, the solid base of the building was set, and they knew it had crossed the point of no return. From this moment onward, regardless of adverse circumstances, nothing could stop, nothing *would* stop, the realisation of what had been envisioned by the Mother.

The Matrimandir would be. As would the City of Dawn.

When they had calmed down from the excitement of the concreting, in the profound wave of silence they shared, suddenly an atmosphere of sadness swept over them. The cool night breeze sent a shiver down their spines and gripped their hearts. Looking at each other, unable to understand what was happening, they tried to shake off the feeling, and slowly rose. One by one, in total silence, they left the platform, the pillar, the island of light. Accompanied by a faint shadow of anguish, they walked away towards their respective huts, melting into the black night.

The next morning, when Lionel woke at dawn, he emerged from his hut. His head was hurting. The night had been difficult; the fatigue of the previous day still clung to him; his entire body was in pain. Concreting had always been physically demanding, but this session had been of relatively short duration – just a few hours. *Why on earth was he feeling so battered?*

He walked towards the kitchen at the Camp for a mug of tea, which he thought might help. On the way, he spotted Morvydd walking at a brisk pace on a converging path. When she came closer, he noticed her tense face and sunken red eyes; she had been crying.

She stopped, and using a very Indian turn of phrase relating to spiritual leaders, she said without preamble, "The Mother has left Her body..."

Lionel stood puzzled, not understanding.

"... last night, about the time we finished the concreting. I just received the news."

Still, Lionel stood numb and speechless, his mind blank. Morvydd cried gently.

At last, Lionel brought himself to consider the impossible, the inconceivable, the unacceptable: *Death? Was that what she had meant? Death?*

Many years later, he was still not entirely sure.

36
THUS IS THE ILLUSION DISPERSED

1972, FRANCE, SOUTHERN ALPS, COL DE LA PUCELLE

"Come on! Don't fool around man. Get up! Sure, blanks can be pretty convincing," the leader of the 'enemy' party said, stretching out a hand to Lionel, still lying on the rocky ground in shock. The rest of his group was already on their feet, moving ahead, chatting with the new arrivals. The section that had masterminded and set up the surprise attack belonged to the 27th *Bataillon de Chasseurs Alpins*, stationed at Cran-Gévrier, further north in the Alps. They too, were active participants in these large-scale manoeuvres which had brought together all the Alpine Troops for a week of extended war games in the mountains. The mood was light and the expanded gathering, in a joyful spirit, clambered the last hairpins towards the Col de la Pucelle summit.

At last, Lionel rose on wobbly legs, wiped the dust off his fatigues, picked up his backpack, lying a few feet away, slung his heavy Nana across the shoulder, and resumed the ascent without a word. His mind and heart were troubled with overwhelming and conflicting thoughts and emotions. There was nothing about this incident that he could share with his companions; they would have merely laughed, not taking him seriously. He was used to keeping these weird experiences to himself. He had trained himself to live with them alone.

He climbed the last steep slope to the pass and was soon

standing on the shoulder, from where he could see the horizon on both sides of the mountain. On the western flank he was leaving behind, a vast expanse of smaller hills gradually rolled down towards the faraway plains, baked by the sun, now low on the horizon. On the eastern side, straight ahead, was a deep valley, partly in shade, and a cool pine forest. Beyond the valley was a far-extending row of snow-covered high summits – the high Alpine range that marked the divide between France and Italy. The late afternoon light painted the mountains a warm tint of gold, and just by looking at the peaks one could feel love expressed in snow.

Before strolling down the path that lead to the road snaking along the river below, and the line of parked olive-green military trucks that would take them back home to the comfort of the cantonment, Lionel stopped for a moment to catch his breath. Keeping his backpack on the shoulders and his Nana across the hip, standing firm, he looked at the world around and mused. Where had the glorious past gone? Where the proud Arthurian knights, Jehanne's fierce captains, the warriors of Kurukshetra, the American boys of Normandy?

He couldn't help but wonder where and when this Great Illusionist show called Life began and ended. How many lives had he left behind in the hazy plains? How many lives waited in the golden light ahead?

Throwing back his head with a laugh, he plunged down towards the valley at the winged pace that only an Alpine Trooper is capable of, towards the waiting trucks, a shower, and a bed.

Death is a stair, a door, a stumbling stride
The soul must take to cross from birth to birth,
A grey defeat pregnant with victory,
A whip to lash us towards our deathless state. [X-1]

EPILOGUE

JEZERO CRATER

2068, (DARIAN YEAR 243), MARS, SYRTIS MAJOR QUADRANGLE

Redemption, off Mangalapura-1

Crawling at low speed, the Russian rover progressed on the uneven surface of Mars. Leonid Volkov had been following the yellow markers for less than an hour. He had counted them and just passed number 360. The vehicle had thus covered exactly 18 kilometres since he had discovered the track. He estimated another 30 minutes till the in-built safety features in the Bravya software would kick in and bring the electric motors to a halt. Under normal circumstances, sufficient power would remain in the back-up batteries to maintain minimal heat and other essential functions for another ten hours. But earlier, he had jury-rigged the circuits to cover the maximum distance. He would be lucky if he lasted three hours before he froze to death in the glacial Martian temperature. Add another four hours of power left in his suit, provided that he set the heater at its lowest setting to save resources. That was it.

When one's life expectancy is down to seven hours at best, panic is one's worst enemy. He took a deep breath and tried to relax. If he wanted to come out of this pickle alive, he had to work out the problem. *Just another live-test; it's not your first. Work it out! In the meantime, keep driving.*

The rover reached a prominent ridge towering to his right, and the markers ran along it.

One Martian day earlier, in the morning of sol 112 into the mission, Leonid had left the habitat dome at MK-2, the *Mars Kosmodrom-2* Russian settlement, for what should have been a simple maintenance run. MK-1, the first Russian base, established twelve years earlier, was at Mawrth Vallis, in the far-off sector of the Oxia Palus quadrangle. This second Russian project, MK-2, had only been operational a few months, manned by its first team of nineteen settlers. Until now, they had spent most of their time laying the foundation of a safe home ground, and still had a lot to learn about the surrounding landscape. Few tracks had been systematically marked out.

Under normal circumstances, they conducted EVAs (Extra Vehicular Activities) with a crew of two settlers. But in this case they had bent the rule. There was no choice. An exceptionally long, though light-weight piece of hardware, a replacement RZ-71 unit, had to be dropped at the site of the primary Communication Station. Located 24 kilometres north-west of MK-2, close to the centre of the 50-kilometre-wide impact crater, the unmanned, automated dish antenna stood 26 kilometres south-east of the neighbouring Indian base, *Mangalapura-1.* The predating Indian settlement was recent too. Commissioned sixteen months earlier, it was part of a joint space program between Russia and India, intent on exploring the Jezero region to assess its resources. Upon positive results, the outposts would be expanded into permanent colonies.

International relationships on Mars, to a large extent, were akin to the management of Antarctica on Earth, and both settlements shared this crucial transmitter facility. The Indian and Russian communities, 35 kilometres apart by the shortest route, equally depended on this antenna site, as their mother lode for Earth communications. Both bases were established along the rim of Jezero Crater. The scientific community had chosen this location on Mars as one of the most promising because of the rich deposits of frozen underground water discovered in the area during the pioneering days of robotic Mars exploration, dating back to the first quarter of the 21st century. The eastern rim of the crater was carved out as a vast river delta, testifying of the abundance of liquid water once having flowed on the planet's surface, eons ago.

Following a brief discussion on the waves the previous sol, they had decided that Russia would provide the device on site, while the Indian team would fix it in place of the former, in the upcoming sols. An automated Russian cargo lander had reached a week earlier, carrying among other supplies, two spare RZ-71s. The original unit had not failed yet, but they had detected an overheating component in one condenser that compromised its long-term reliability. The Russians would collect the old unit at a later stage, for reconditioning or recycling; not a single gram of precious metal or silicon would go to waste.

On Mars, in contrast to Earth, discussions between different nation teams were short, to the point and apolitical, purely committed to solving the problem at hand in the most efficient way. When mankind had taken the bold step to settle in extreme, deadly environments, such as space and neighbouring celestial bodies, there was no room for bickering or conflict. Nationalism and groupism withered in the face of common interest; that of survival and the well-being of the entire Mars community. Mars was the new frontier, the spearhead of mankind's expansion into the Solar System.

It would have been difficult, if not impossible, to fit two people into the rover in addition to the RZ-71, which comprised an extended solar panel, coupled with a pair of large condensers. The darn thing, too long to fit in the airlock, had needed an unorthodox procedure to get loaded on board: depressurisation of the entire rover (a waste of precious air), loading of the panel through both hatches, the airlock kept wide open (the sturdy Bravya vehicle wasn't happy about this; an airlock strictly opens one hatch at a time, some re-programming had been required), and re-pressurisation of the vehicle. This was typical of the occasional, officially unspoken of, non-SOP initiatives that had to be undertaken from time to time, dictated by exceptional circumstances. They had made a note that a discussion should be re-initiated (for the nth time) with the stubborn Earthlings, back there at the other end of the universe, to fit permanent roof-racks on these rovers. Leonid was of the opinion they should just improvise and do it, but the Station Commander was a straight arrow, even more so when it came to her relationship with Earth Command at Kosmodrom Vostochny.

Each Mars settler was highly qualified in his or her area of expertise, be it as a geologist, medic or comm technician, for instance. But in addition, each had to be a jack-of-all-trades to perform and survive in the face of any critical situation. Hence, they were all trained in an array of different fields to be mission-redundant if an emergency called for it. By speciality, Volkov was a mechanical engineer; he had also logged-in maximum EVA time as compared to the rest of the team.

Back in his youth on Earth, he had always been an outdoors person, never missing an opportunity for a mountain trek or electrobike expedition. Born in the small town of Miass, in the Ural Mountains, he had developed at a very early age, an intense fascination and curiosity about outer space and the celestial bodies. Whenever he looked at the star-studded night sky, he had the strange feeling that his most existential questions would find answers there. Being a child of the acknowledged Second Mars Generation, from adolescence he had known that he would become actively involved in the global space exploration effort. He never questioned this or doubted that destiny would one day take him out there.

No wonder then that at age 34, he had been selected as the youngest member of the first team to man MK-2 – the first batch of settlers sent for a shift of nineteen months on the planet. A fresh team would relieve them when the Earth-Mars orbital synchronicity would turn favourable again, allowing to its twenty six months cycle. Considering the transit periods, that would leave the MK-2 base unattended, in sleep mode, for a few months. Meanwhile, a travel of seven months across the blackness of space would take them back home.

Home? Leonid had already spent enough time on Mars to wonder if Earth would still be home for him...

He was a slim and muscular man in his prime, who looked younger than his years. He was of average height, with green, piercing eyes, and sported a short military crop of blond hair. His gait revealed the attributes of an accomplished sportsman. Besides, he had garnered an impressive set of degrees in engineering and physics. It is said that what one reads reveals the person one is, and among the literary volumes of Science Fiction in Leonid's e-book collection, there were the complete works of Fred Hoyle and Isaac Asimov. Even here on distant Mars, a rare hardcover copy of the *Foundation Trilogy* occupied a prominent place in his personal cubicle.

Working in the open atmosphere of Mars was fascinating. It was alien, vast, desolate, and he never tired of the breathtaking beauty of this world. He loved the silence too. Through his pressure suit he could just hear (or rather feel as vibration) the strange faint sounds of his steps or his boot kicking a pebble, and the sound of his breathing and movements. From time to time, someone from base would check his status on the radio. That was all.

It was thus logical that he had volunteered to undertake this exceptional solo mission as the most qualified member of the team. His Station Commander, Natasha Minakova, had agreed, knowing he was their best choice.

There was nothing fancy in this sortie, no room for improvisation. Get to the site, a mere one-hour drive away, put on his suit, depressurise the rover, drop the stuff — it was bulky but light-weight, easily moveable by one man, even more so in the low-gravity of Mars — secure it in the small, non-pressurised geodesic dome that served as a storeroom, next to the large dish-antenna structure, re-pressurise the rover and return to base. Most of the trip would be within line-of-sight, except for the last ten kilometres, which would take him behind a low line of outcrops through more difficult but well-known terrain. The weather forecast was promising, too. According to the met-officer, Dimitri Stanovich, the probabilities of powerful winds or a dust storm in the next 48 hours were next to zero. Leonid would be back at MK-2 well within four hours. With a thirty-hour rover endurance in terms of vital functions, and a certified range of 150 kms available on the power attributed to the electric motor drives, it would be a smooth ride. Besides, they would keep a back-up rover ready for immediate departure with two crew members, just in case he needed help. That part at least complied with SOPs.

It was late morning. All had gone as planned; the tall, reassuring silhouette of the giant Starship parked five kilometres off the habitat site, had slowly disappeared from the field of his rear-view cameras, displayed on the control panel. He had reached the unmanned antenna complex in just fifty minutes. Leonid had depressurised the rover and unloaded the panel; then, he had sealed the airlock. The cabin would refill itself with breathable air at a pressure of one earth atmosphere and restore heat, while he carried the unit to the storeroom in front of which he had parked the vehicle. There, he had spent an unexpected fifteen minutes clearing the accumulated dust that prevented the sliding door from moving freely.

Under Minakova's watchful attention on the videocom, he felt no rush, while he received only positive weather updates. At last, he slid the door open, nothing more than a plain, non-pressurised garage, and carefully laid the replacement RZ-71 unit on a pair of aluminium trestles. The Indian tech team would do the rest. After sliding the dome's gate shut, he hopped back to and boarded the rover, cycling through the airlock. Before removing his pressure suit, he checked the life support parametres. By then, the rover had already restored heat and air quality to normal.

Having checked all systems, he informed MK-2 that he was on his way back, and started the vehicle.

Leonid had been on the move less than thirty minutes, well on his way to passing the outcrops, after which he would be within line-of-sight of MK-2 again, when something unusual attracted his attention. The bright sunlight seemed to have diminished in intensity, and more oddly, there was a strange, unfamiliar sound or vibration that seemed to originate from outside the vehicle. It could be perceived above the humming of the motor drives. Leonid cocked his head slightly, trying to understand the phenomenon that reminded him, as it grew in intensity, of what mountaineers and climbers call the 'bees' – a loud buzzing pulsation in the air announcing the build-up of an electric charge at high altitude, typically preceding a violent discharge of lightning.

Before he could process the correlation in his brain, a deafening thunderclap shook the rover, and everything inside turned an eerie bright blue. A sickening sizzling sound lingered for a few seconds. The vehicle stopped dead in its tracks and an ominous silence took over, disturbed only by a peculiar, unusual howling from the rarefied atmosphere outside and a wind speed that seemed to be picking up. A powerful odour of ozone mixed with that of burned wiring, filled the cabin. For a while Leonid's fingertips tingled. Outside, wisps of Martian dust began to swirl about in a crazy dance.

His attempts to restart the rover were met with dreadful silence: he was stranded in the middle of nowhere, alone, on an alien planet.

So much for the back-up nav and comm systems which should have kicked in instantly. They had stubbornly refused to take over. He spent half an hour cussing, upside-down under the nav console, trying to fix things, with little success. In the process of troubleshooting, he discovered that the aft battery bank had been fried too, thus cutting down by half the rover's range. Although the vehicle was using the latest generation of Goodenough-Braga batteries, reputed for their unsurpassed reliability, this was a serious cause for concern. Even his EVA suit comm unit was dead. When he opened the small compartment on the left side of the helmet, he found a tiny charred PCB, for which he had no replacement.

As for the origin of the phenomenon, he would figure it out later; whether it was the effect of a powerful solar flare or of a sudden local electromagnetic surge. For now, he was more concerned with getting back to the habitat. As he emerged from his dive into the rover's guts, he realised that visibility had dropped drastically. The dust storm compounding his troubles was now so thick that even the closest of the rare track markers had vanished from sight. The total nav instruments failure defied all logic, considering the amount of redundancy built into these rovers. One could conceive, though, that a powerful, never encountered before EMP (Electro Magnetic Pulse) could produce such extensive damage in delicate electronic circuits.

However, it was a fact that little was known about electromagnetic transmissions in a world with a very thin atmosphere, mostly composed of carbon dioxide, such as Mars. As for climatology, so much remained to be understood about Martian weather and other phenomena, that while Stanovich might have appeared wrong, Leonid exonerated him. He knew that some unpredictable factor had caused this event. Perhaps the violent lightning bolt was the fluke that had served as a catalyst; enough to trigger the dust storm?

Day after day, the whole team had been learning the hard way that making Earth-based assumptions on Mars almost always turned out to be a mistake. And on this world, mistakes had deadly consequences.

His thoughts returned to the worrying, inescapable fact that his radio, satellite link, and transponder had been fried beyond recovery. This, combined with the prevailing low visibility, down to a mere five metres, which could last for days or weeks, meant there was not even the slightest chance that anyone would find him before he ran out of vital resources.

Two things worked in his favour though. After replacing three sets of circuit breakers, the motors restarted, and he still had the gyrocompasses working. He could move, while also being able to maintain a straight course. With the absence of any stable magnetic field on Mars, unlike Earth, vehicles were not fitted with a conventional compass, and blind navigation relied purely on satellite triangulation. Thankfully, the gyros gave him some amount of control in running a search pattern to find a known landmark. But he would have to crawl at the speed of a walking man, straining to peer ahead, to avoid getting bogged in one of those treacherous dust pots that typically booby-trapped the plains of Syrtis Major.

By late afternoon, the dust in the atmosphere had become so thick that the dim yellowish light gave way to total darkness. When it became apparent that the headlights were ineffective and would only drain the batteries, Leonid stopped the vehicle and prepared to hibernate for the night. Wishing he had some polar bear ancestry in his genes, he shut down all non-critical systems, reducing the temperature to just a few degrees above zero Celsius. Then he remembered he had bivouacked in snow holes doing his survival training with the Russian Army. 'Can't be worse than that, so let's get on with it,' he mumbled.

Rummaging through the emergency compartment, he found two foam mats which, put one on top of the other, provided appreciable insulation, two high-efficiency honeycombed space blankets, and some dry food rations. There was also plenty of water to drink, but he would have to prevent it from freezing. He prepared himself to last the long night. Sleep would evade him, he knew, but remaining immobile would considerably reduce his oxygen consumption, though O2 was not his primary concern as there were plenty of spare cylinders since they had planned to depressurise the vehicle. Power was the main concern. Power was paramount to provide the minimum warmth for survival on a planet where average temperatures revolved around minus 60 degrees Celsius, plummeting down to minus 125 at night.

Assuming complete power loss, he would soon be no better than a chicken in a freezer, give or take a few hours.

A procession of long hours dragged by. Towards the end of the night, he noticed a few stars showing intermittently in the sky. The dust was apparently clearing. This was good news. In the dim light of pre-dawn, he looked through a porthole and saw the forming shape of a gloomy landscape through the remaining dust haze.

He came out of the cargo compartment where he had curled up on the floor, shivering the entire night. He looked around and became instantly alert. Yes, it was no illusion. At 10 o'clock to his left, less than two hundred metres away, there was a row of fluorescent-yellow markers, each made of a thirty-centimetres-diameter disk standing on top of a two-metre high composite pole. This line of markers, evenly spaced every fifty metres, disappeared into the haze, less than half a kilometre away. The markers were not Russian, but he had seen some of them before; they were Indian.

He had been wise to save the rover's battery power through the night. Predictably, because of the cold, he had not slept a minute, only dozed off just before dawn. He was feeling light headed, but then, there would be plenty of time to sleep when he got out of this mess; provided he did. He opened a panel on the floor, fumbled among the tools in the supplies boxes behind the seats, and dug out a few metres of thick electric wire. In ten minutes he had jury-rigged a power derivation from life support to drive motors. Then he suited up in full, except for the gloves and helmet he would wear and seal just before life support was exhausted. The only thing that mattered now was that the rover had to keep moving along the markers. With grim determination, Leonid intended to make it run, down to the last electron extracted from all the live remaining batteries.

So be it, he thought.

He started the Bravya, listening to the sweet song of the

electric motors humming, and felt the revival of power in the drive. The valiant vehicle surged forward, shaking off the dust that had accumulated during the night. He didn't have a minute to lose; he went straight for the yellow markers; they had become his lifeline.

At first, the rover averaged ten to twelve markers per minute, depending on the terrain. Then the average went down to six. This was the clear sign of depleted battery banks: the system had automatically switched to limping mode to optimise resources.

The visibility had improved, and Leonid discovered unknown features in the surrounding topography. On the track, wheel-indentations appeared in places where the dust had been blown away by the wind. The track ran alongside a rocky ridge, and turned sharply right at the end where the ridge met flat ground in a heap of stray boulders.

Leonid reached the turning point and passed the rocks. Abruptly, a wide, flat plain appeared, and far away, barely visible in the haze but clearly delineated against the background of high mountains making the rim of the crater, a group of domes emerged from the ground. He was saved! There was no doubt: this was *Mangalapura-1.* He would have enough power to take him there for sure, and if not, he would wear his helmet and gloves, and trek the remaining distance on foot if need be.

But then, in that moment, he felt an intense tingling on the crown of his head. A powerful *force* came down the nape of his neck, forcing him to turn and look further to the right.

Then he saw it.

Bathed in a surreal light, was a hillock, about thirty metres at its highest point, irregular and crescent-shaped. A ramp led to a spacious platform that had been levelled on the summit, and in the centre stood a tiny, square building, protruding with an array of sensors and dishes. Leonid had heard of it, but never seen it before. It was the Indian gamma-ray monitoring station.

The whole scene sparkled under a rain of gold; a rain of love. The hill, the station, the dishes, the array of solar panels, all pulsated in the radiance of divine light. At the centre of its source was a man in a white pressure suit, stooped over what might have been a control panel.

Then, as suddenly as it had surged, the golden light faded and vanished.

For a brief moment, Leonid hesitated, attracted by his survival instinct to go towards the group of domes he had spotted in the distance. Salvation, in the form of heat and oxygen, was waiting there for sure. The temptation did not last. In the same instant, coming from planes of consciousness he had no prior awareness of, fleeting images and memories of past defeats crossed his active mind, like flashing warning signs, and he knew with certitude what he had to do.

Leonid veered sharply to the right, towards the hillock that was some hundred metres away. The man had ceased his work, stood up, and seemed to be looking in his direction. Perhaps he was surprised to see a vehicle coming this way, more so a Russian model. Or maybe he had expected it? Leonid couldn't say and didn't care.

At the foothill, he hit the brakes and stopped the rover abruptly besides a small Indian-made Mahindra Mars-Scrambler Mark-3, raising a slight cloud of brownish dust. His dire emergency mattered no more; his heart was beating wildly. With a concentration learned through patient training, he wore, then locked and secured his helmet and gloves. On a touch at his wrist-pad, the suit came live and self-checked itself for leaks. As soon as the green light appeared on his faceplate HUD, he stepped into the small airlock and typed the cycling code on the control pad. The outer hatch opened with a feeble hiss of residual air. He stepped out; the hatch closed behind him. Swiftly, he climbed up the ramp on the shaded side of the hill; it was easy in the low gravity. He emerged into the bright, blinding sunlight.

The man was standing there, facing him, like a glittering statue of a god in a space suit. Enthralled, Leonid fell at his feet and stayed there immobile for a moment, crushed under the impact of the transformation that affected his whole being.

Then he slowly rose again. He saw the badge on the man's right shoulder and the identification picture attached to it – an Indian man in his fifties, with an expressive face and clean-shaven head. He went closer to the man, face-to-face, tapped his own helmet on the side to signify that his comms were non-functional.

Bending forward, he touched his helmet against that of the stranger. The simplest way to communicate in a vacuum or low-pressure environment was by direct vibration. He said, "Greetings! My name is Leonid Volkov, Chief Engineer at Mars Kosmodrom-2. I got lost in yesterday's storm, and my power supply is critically low, and..."

Before he could babble any more, the man raised a hand, silencing him. "Welcome home, Leonid."

Stricken by a sweeping wave of love, Leonid stood back. When the stranger lifted the reflective filter screen of his faceplate, he saw the sun in the man's eyes. A tsunami of unwavering certitude flooded his silenced mind in a single crushing moment. He knew at once that his oldest questions would be answered; that a new cycle of life had begun for him. He knew too that once safely back in the habitat at MK-2, when he would remove his own bright orange pressure suit, like a butterfly emerging from its crackled chrysalis, he would at last recognise himself as one of the sun-eyed children – just born.

Leonid looked around and marvelled, filled with ineffable bliss. Beyond the eastern, mountainous rim of Jezero Crater, the golden sun was rising on the far-off plains of Isidis Planitia. Mars threw its splendid orange light in the most magnificent dawn he had ever seen. The Divine was everywhere around him, and in him. His burning heart was glowing in its image.

He knew it would never leave him.

In that moment, 180 million kilometres away, the subtle body of Planet Earth quivered, like a forgotten Garden of Eden, swept by an infinitesimal ripple of bliss.

Every star
Every being
Every speck of interstellar dust
The entire Universe
Is one single body

Invocation, 21 February 2021

GLOSSARY

Acid – slang for LSD

Alm – the high altitude Swiss grazing grounds

Ashram – spiritually oriented community

Ashramite – dweller in an ashram

Atta – wheat flour

Banian – vest

Bastille – small fort

Beedies – hand-rolled cigarettes in tobacco leaf; a poor man's cigarette in India

Bhagavad Gita excerpts protagonists –

Krishna: King and divine incarnation (avatar). Also known as: Hari, Keshava, Vasudeva, Narayana

Arjuna: leader of the Pandava army. Also known as: Partha, Kiriti

Sanjaya : the narrator

CBI – Central Bureau of Investigation (the Indian FBI)

Chai – name for tea from the Bosphorus to East Asia; varying in preparation with the local culture

Chasseur Alpin – French Alpine commando

Chetty – large metallic pan, about 2 feet in diameter, used to move sand, bricks or cement; often carried on the head

Charas – hashish, compacted cannabis resin

Charpoy – light cot made of a wooden frame netted with woven coir (coconut fibre) rope

Chillum – conical clay or stone pipe used by sadhus to smoke charas

Clochard – French tramp

Col - French for mountain 'pass' (Col de la Pucelle)

Concreting – the act of filling the moulds (or shuttering) of a RC (Reinforced Concrete) structure

Dacoit – brigand, bandit

Darian calendar – a system of time-keeping designed to serve possible future human settlers on planet Mars

Delhi belly – commonly used to signify food poisoning

Dhaba – roadside tea-shop/basic eatery usually patronised by truckers

Dahi – curd, yoghurt

EVP – Extra Vehicular Activity

Firangi – foreigner

Gurdwara – Sikh place of worship usually having a resthouse for pilgrims

Gurkha – Nepali warrior tribe

Guru – teacher

HUD – Head Up Display

Jaja – French slang for cheap red wine

Jawan – Indian rank and file soldier

Jehanne, la Pucelle – inappropriately mentioned in history books as Jeanne d'Arc or Joan of Arc; names not in use during her lifetime

Jelebi – Indian sweet

Keet – woven palm leaves used to make waterproof hut roofs

Képi – a rigid cap, part of the French police uniform

Kukri – a deadly crescent-shaped Gurkha dagger

Kurta – long shirt

Lakh – Indian unit = 100,000

League – archaic unit of distance, approximately 4-5 kms.

Lederhosen – traditional leather pants (usually short) worn in the Swiss countryside

Maestri – a skilled craftsman, such as a master carpenter

Maya – the illusion of the reality of sensory experience and experienced qualities and attributes of oneself

Mandir – a Hindu temple; can be as simple as an elementary place of worship materialised by a tiny building or awning, containing images of a deity; usually adorned with orange flags

Muruku – crispy spiral shaped Indian snack

Naan - flat, elongated bread made in a tandoor oven

Nana - Automatic rifle AA-52, the 'chick'

Neem - a tree with medicinal properties

Noël! – used in the 15th Century as an exclamation of joyful celebration, not necessarily related to Christmas

Paan – chopped areca nuts and condiments folded in a betel leaf; chewed as a stimulant; popular across India

Pakol – traditional Afghan head gear

Perahan tunban – traditional male Afghan dress

Pukka – impeccable

Rājmā – an Indian dish of red kidney-beans in a spicy sauce

Raagi – poor man's cereal

Rasa – the nourishing energy behind food, air, water etc.

Sadhak – one who follows sadhana, a spiritual path

Samadhi – Mahasamadhi refers to a yogi leaving his body in a state of Samadhi; by extension, also the name of the courtyard where Sri Aurobindo's body lies

Samosa – an Indian snack

Sanyasa – renunciation of the world

Sannyasi / sadhu – spiritual mendicant

Sarmatian – a fierce tribe that lived north of the Black Sea during the Roman period

Service tree – the tree that shades Sri Aurobindo's samadhi

Shannai – woodwind instrument of the clarinet family

Shangri-la – a mythical ideal society hidden in the far reaches of the Himalayas, yet to be discovered

Shuttering – a mould in which cement concrete is poured

Sol – a Martian day as per the Darian Mars calendar (24 hours, forty minutes Earth time)

SOP – Standard Operating Procedure

Tandoor - spherical clay oven, wood fired, with a circular opening on top

Tawa – a simple steel plate used to make rotis on the fire

Thali – Indian assortment of dishes served on a large plate (or banana leaf), making up a full meal

Tarte – large black beret worn by Alpine troopers (literally, 'pancake' in French)

Vadai – crispy, spicy South Indian beignet

Varagu – a poor man's cereal

Vibhuti – emanation, partial incarnation, power of the Divine manifested in a human being

AUTHOR NOTES

Chapter 9: The events mentioned took place prior to the initiation of the Samjhauta Express between Lahore and Amritsar, inaugurated in 1976 as a result of the Shimla Agreement of 1972. Initially a daily train, its fate kept changing with the political upheavals affecting both countries. The Samjhauta Express operated on a bi-weekly basis for a long time. As of the date of completing this book, due to renewed political tensions, it has once again been suspended on both sides.

Chapter 16: Orléans was the first of several victorious battles led by the Maid, that took the Dauphin to his coronation at Reims, as the uncontested King of France.

Chapter 17: Ekalavya is a young warrior featured in the Mahābhārata. Droṇācārya, the Master-in-Arms, whom he secretly revered as his guru, claimed Ekalavya's right thumb as *Guru Dakshina* (tuition fee), the ancient practise of repaying a teacher/guru for passing on knowledge.

Chapter 20: For those unfamiliar with the *Bhagavad Gita*:

i. Sanjaya is the narrator

ii. Arjuna is the leader of the Pandavas army; also referred to by the names (relating to specific qualities): Partha, Kiriti, Pandava (family name).

iii. Krishna, avatar of Vishnu, King of Dwarka; also referred to by the names (relating to specific qualites): Hari, Keshava, Vasudeva, Narayana

Chapter 21: Satprem's book *Le Sannyasin* (1973) is translated into English as *By the Body of the Earth* or the *Sannyasi*.

Chapter 22: The Service Tree, centrally located in the main courtyard of the Ashram, gives shade to the simple, white marble tomb where Sri Aurobindo's body lies in *Samadhi*, as per Hindu yogic tradition. By extension, the courtyard of the Ashram is referred to as 'the Samadhi'.

Chapter 28: *Million d'oiseaux d'or*, quoted from the French poet-visionary Arthur Rimbaud; could be translated as 'Myriads of golden birds'.

Chapter 30: There is no known written record surviving today, specific to this rescue operation. However, there are multiple records (through bills of purchase, of horses and other supplies, for instance) of the presence and movements of Dunois, La Hire (Etienne de Vignoles) and De Rais in the immediate vicinity of Rouen, throughout the duration of the Maid's captivity and trial; also the occupation of Louvais, located at a short distance (less than one riding day), from Rouen. Since Rouen was not a strategic place of interest at this stage of the conflict, it seems fair to surmise that the only possible reason for their collective presence in the area was to attempt to save the Maid. The fact that the English had taken such enormous military precautions to guard her, and more so on the day of her execution, speaks for itself. They would not have been so worried by simple threats of uprising from the local populace, already subdued.

It would be unfair to further enforce the myth that she had been completely abandoned to her fate by the French King, her Captains, and the French people. Pronouncing a negative judgement on the unsuccessful outcome of the operation would be to seriously underestimate the complexity of such an undertaking, considering the military and political situation, at a time of primitive transportation and communication, in the middle of a full-fledged war, 250 kilometres deep inside enemy lines. The English had played it safe by taking her far away, even out of Burgundy.

Shortly after the martyrdom of the Maid, Louvais was lost, and in the ensuing strife, La Hire was captured by the English and imprisoned. He ultimately escaped from the Tower of Dourdan, where he was incarcerated, and returned to battle, as one of the most successful military commanders under Charles VII.

Thanks to the unstoppable, nationwide movement of revolt that had been initiated by the Maid's powerful actions, and further compounded by the national outrage at her ignominious execution, France finally rid itself of the English twenty-two years after Jehanne's demise.

Chapter 31: Jean D'Aulon was re-captured near Rouen. He recovered from his wounds and suffered another stint of captivity, in the London Tower this time, in what seems to have been his destiny. He was released later against ransom, in 1432, and returned to serve King Charles VII. He was with the King when Paris was finally reclaimed in 1437, and served as the King's ambassador to several fiefs in the south of France. He was Jehanne's most important witness when he testified in writing at her rehabilitation trial by the Church in 1456. At 68 years of age, in 1458, he died of natural causes.

Chapter 32: During the '60s and '70s, the 'Trail' or the 'Route' referred to the hippie-migration long road from Europe to India, via Eastern Europe, Turkey, Iran, Afghanistan, Pakistan. Hence the term 'routard' later applied to the backpack traveller.

In those days, no self-respecting Indian male urinated standing up since it was considered inappropriate. The same trend governed Afghanistan and Pakistan.

Chapter 33: Basel-Mulhouse Airport has since been renamed EuroAirport Basel-Mulhouse-Freiburg.

Chapter 35: Forty years of hard work and successive waves of Builders were required to complete the construction of Matrimandir.

Epilogue: At the time of this book going to press, the autonomous exploration vehicle *Perseverance* has successfully landed in Jezero Crater and is preparing itself for its "sign of microbial life" search mission, across the ancient delta.

Forthcoming:
THE SUN-EYED CHILDREN
VOLUME II - MARS

ACKNOWLEDGEMENTS

Roger Toll guided me patiently from the point of view of a professional writer and editor.

Miriam John laboured for a sizeable part of the way, editing promptly; never irritated by my occasional obstinacy.

Kalki, my daughter, read the manuscript in its early stage, and summoned great courage to tell her dad that his writing was terrible, with his collection of gallicisms.

Sarah Emmerich, a French author *(La Suivante)*, had the patience to read the book twice and express her views from a different perspective.

Sandrine Denier, gave me the confidence that there would be a passionate audience of seeking souls for such strange story-telling.

Aurovrata Venet, for bringing clarity into the space-time concepts and validating the science.

Suhail Mathur of The Book Bakers, my fearless literary agent, made possible the publication of my first two books.

Wish To Publish With Us?

We are always keen to look at interesting new content across genres. Please mail submissions to:
submissions@leadstartcorp.com

Proposals should include:

1. Synopsis

   A summary of the book in 500 – 1000 words. Please mention the word count of the manuscript.

2. Sample chapters / Poetry

   A couple of chapters from the book; these need not be in order, just send the best two chapters of the book. Or a few poems if the same is a collection of poetry.

3. A Note About The Author

   An interesting note about yourself (about 200 words).

4. Additional Information

   - Target audience
   - Unique selling proposition
   - List of illustrative content (if any)
   - Other comparative titles
   - Your thoughts on marketing the book